WORDS

THAT MAKE

YOU

LAUGH

WORDS THAT MAKE YOU LAUGH

ARTICLES

by

G. W. Abersold, PhD.

Royal Candlelight Christian Publishing Company

"Royalty in the Making"

Those who wish to respond to the contents of this book may

contact the authors by email at billandstella8080@att.net.

Royal Candlelight Christian Publishing

P.O. Box 3021
Fontana, California 92334
www.royalcandlelight.com
info@royalcandlelight.com
Internet TV Website: Ustreamtv.com (Royal Candlelight)

ISBN-10: 0692283250
ISBN-13: 978-0692283257

Printed in the United States of America

WORDS THAT MAKE YOU LAUGH

BY G.W. ABERSOLD, PhD

WORDS OF ACKNOWLEDGEMENT

I have a list of names of the people who sent me many of the jokes in this book; too many to mention. However, there is one person to whom I am especially grateful – Frank Melton.

Our friendship began several years ago while playing golf. We then developed a habit involving humor. I would ask him for a joke on any subject: a dog, a country, etc. He then would ask me for a joke on any subject. Anytime we played golf, we swapped jokes. Then he moved to Utah; however, he still sends me jokes. I never stumped him; but he stumped me numerous times. By the way, Frank is a country/western enthusiast. He has his own band. I call him the "Willie Nelson" of St. George, Utah.

Stella and I play the same game, but not golf...Thanks a million Frank!

I am also grateful to Paul and Lynn Williams and their publishing company, Royal Candlelight Christian Publishing. They have supervised the editing, designing and marketing of my books, "Words to Think About" and now "Words That Make You Laugh."

Above all I appreciate my wife Stella for researching and organizing the book and motivating me to finish it.

Besides Frank Melton, I dedicate this book to the thirty-five contributors of their humor to it. I believe the jokes will add to the fund of gelotology (laughter) in the world.

Contents

ARTICLES

Contents *(Continued)*

Contents *(Continued)*

Contents *(Continued)*

Contents *(Continued)*

INTRODUCTION

GELOTOLOGY IS LAUGHTER

The word "Gelotology" is not well known in academic or medical circles. Words such as Oncology, Cardiology, Hematology; the "ology" means "the study of"' cancer, the heart, blood and laughter. Gelos means laughter in Greek. Several medical schools have departments that are focusing attention on the healing benefits of humor and laughter. Such is the case at Loma Linda. Dr. Lee Berk is one professor involved in the study. A few years ago I interviewed Dr. Berk on the subject of his research. He confirmed his early dependence on the work of Norman Cousins Ph.D.

I was in the class when Dr. Cousins related an outstanding experience. He began by establishing a baseline blood sample. He then went into a self-imposed hypnotic state and then let his mind concentrate on negative things (war, fatalities, anger, jealousy etc.) At his signal another sample of blood was taken. The result between the two samples was startling. The white blood count (immune system) had DROPPED significantly.   He then began the same process of hypnosis but reversed the suggestions (peace, joy, happiness, etc.) An amazing result transpired. The white blood count had increased 95%. In other words, his immune system had doubled.

Dr. Beck copied the same process with different results. He had several young people have blood tests. In the first one, the white blood count went way down. In the second test the white blood count increased 125 percent. Amazing evidence of how the mind affects the body.

All of this information should be viewed in the light of Norman Cousins' previous experience with terminal illness. His collagen illness was diagnosed as terminal. But through laughter and mega-vitamin C, he became well.

Psalm 126:2 states, "Then was my mouth filled with laughter and my tongue with singing." Obviously laughter is not an aberration but indigenous to being alive. It is undoubtedly important.

A study published in Psychology Today said that every day we need at least four hugs and twenty laughs. A baby laughs at least twenty times an hour. The benefits of laughter are magnanimous. It is a trigger; a stimulus in four distinct ways.

FIRST, it triggers the secretion of ENDORPHINS from the brain. They have the same molecular formula as morphine. Both are painkillers.

SECOND, it stimulates white blood cells (as per Cousins and Berk) that increase the potential of the immune system. White blood cells act as Special Forces that attack and destroy the enemies of infection that invade the body, causing sickness. Negative thoughts and emotions weaken the immune system.

THIRD, it stimulates and nourishes the brain's thinking process. Before one laughs, there must be a comprehension of the "punch line." For example, a couple was about to have breakfast, when the wife remembered she needed milk. "Honey, would you go to the store and get us a carton of milk?" She continued, "And if they have eggs, get us six." He returned with six (6) cartons of milk. The amazed wife retorted, "Why six cartons of milk? The husband said, "Because they had eggs." Think about it.

The FOURTH benefit of laughter is that it minimizes stress and alleviates tension in the body. Laughter has been described as giving the organs of the body a massage.

A few years ago I traveled around the world, making a study of humor. Several observations were obvious. Every nationality made fun of another one. I also learned that the Chinese seldom tell a joke, but they love cartoons. In every country I visited I would ask, "What is your favorite joke?" In Paris, a French gal said, "What's the difference between men and mosquitoes?" I didn't know, and she said, "Mosquitoes only bother me in the Summer time."

At each country I tabulated the favorite kinds of humor/jokes. The most favorite was SEXUAL jokes. In Turkey they loved to tell homosexual stories. The double entendre and insinuations were prominent.

The second favorite was jokes about POLITICIANS. Their ignorance and infidelities were favorites. Germany and England in particular told political stories.

The third favorite, believe it or not, was jokes about SENIORS. In Spain, particularly Madrid, there were benches every few feet filled with seniors swapping jokes about themselves. The   fourth favorite was ETHNIC humor. I include blonde jokes in this group. There's no dearth of material for either ethnic or blonde jokes.

The fifth favorite was RELIGION. Ministers, nuns, the Catholic Church, celibacy, pedophiles; nothing seemed sacred. I never told them I was a retired minister.

I'm often asked how I remember jokes and where do I get them. The answers are simple; from friends, TV, reading, other comics. When traveling Stella and I often play a game: "Tell me a joke about . . . ." I also clip jokes or write them and scotch tape them in my date book. I'm always on the look-out for a good joke.

Amen. Selah. So be it.

Any joke or thought that is repeated is either intentional or accidental!
Your choice!

ARTICLES

❖

ADVERSITY and HUMOR

History has shown that adversity often breeds an atmosphere of humor. For example, much of black humor as well as music came out of the years of slavery. The same applies to the Jews and their experience in the Holocaust. Many comics and humorists who write about humor are now saying the same thing about September 11th. The war in Afghanistan is also included, coupled with the anthrax situation. There is plenty of motivation for humor if the premise is true.

Robert Thompson, professor of popular culture at Syracuse University in New York, says, "Humor is a necessary lubricant in any troubling situation." Humor expert Anne Collins Smith puts it this way: "The human mind can 't withstand that much unrelenting sadness. Humor is an outlet where we like to take refuge." Another writer comments that while war is hell, it does provide opportunities for comedy.

Most of us are aware of the mental and physical good from laughter. It releases endorphins from the brain. It gives us hope in what seems like hopeless situations.

I've been an advocate for this approach for several years through these articles. Several years ago while traveling around the world, I made a study of the most popular subjects for humor. The results: sex, politics, seniors, ethnic and religion. Today let's focus on those jokes with a religious flavor.

The Secretary to Pope John Paul announced to him that he had some good news and some bad news. Which did he wish to hear first? The Pope responded, "The good news." "Well," the Secretary said, "We've just received a phone call from Jesus. He is on earth and He's on the phone and wishes to speak to you, Your Holiness." The Pope is excited with that word and then asks about whatever can be bad news. The Secretary says, "He's calling from Salt Lake City, Utah." If you don 't get the implication, you'll never get the humor.

This is not a joke; but it's worth recording. The great comic Red Skelton said, "I live by this credo: "Have a little laugh at life and look around you for happiness instead of sadness. Laughter has always brought me out of unhappy situations. If I can make people laugh, then I have served my purpose for God."

Rev. Warren Keating of Yuma, Arizona said this was the best prayer he ever heard: "Dear God, please help me be the person my dog thinks I am." I've heard several variations of this joke. About 10 o'clock one cold February morning a man was in bed sound asleep. His mother came into the room. "Son, it's time to get up. You gotta get ready for church," she implored.

"I'm too tired. Leave me alone," he said. "Son, you gotta get up and get ready for church." He protested, "I'm not going to church. Give me one good reason why I have to go to church." She says, "I'll give you two good reasons: one, it's Sunday and two, you 're the pastor!"

A missionary heard about a native who had five wives. "You are violating a law of God," he said, "so you must go and tell four of those women they can no longer live here and consider you their husband." The native thought a few moments, then said, "I'll wait here. You tell'em."

I love this short squib. An usher passing a collection plate in a church overheard a small child exclaim: "Daddy, don't pay for me! I'm only four."

A man is stumbling through the woods, totally drunk, when he comes upon a preacher baptizing people in the river. He proceeds to walk into the water and subsequently bumps in to the preacher. The preacher turns around and is almost overcome by the smell of alcohol, where upon he asks the drunk, "Are you ready to find Jesus?" The drunk answers, "Yes, I am."

So, the preacher grabs him and dunks him in the water. He pulls him up and asks the drunk, "Brother, have you found Jesus?" The drunk replies, "No, I haven't found Jesus." The preacher, shocked at the answer, dunks him into the water again for a little longer. He again pulls him out of the water and asks again, "Have you found Jesus my brother?" The drunk again answers, "No, I haven't found Jesus." By this time the preacher is at his wits end and dunks the drunk in the water again—but this time holds him down for about 30 seconds and when he begins kicking his arms and legs he pulls him up. The preacher again asks the drunk, "For the love of God have you found Jesus?" (Are you ready for this????????????) The drunk wipes his eyes and catches his breath and says to the preacher, "Are you sure this is where he fell in?"

Amen. Selah. So be it.

AGING

Aging is an inevitable process. The only criterion is to live longer. The Psalmist David gave the ideal longevity as "three score and ten," or 70 years. The Book of Genesis 6:3, "Man's allotted years are 120."

The passing centuries have not been kind to we humans. Jesus was an old man at age 33. Men and women did not live longer than 45 in the early 1900's. Today the average age to live is in the 80's. By the year 2050, it is estimated humans will live close to 100.

The media and the young set have a tendency to mock anyone 50 or older. My standard remark to anyone challenging my age is, "Remember, you'll be where I am one of these days."

Moses was one of the great heroes in the Bible. He is considered the "father" of Israel. It is recorded that he led them out of slavery at the age of 80. And he was not the last person to be a leader in the 80's.

Benjamin Franklin was a leader in the forming of our nation. He was also a creative inventor. Much of his success came when he was in his 80's.

Mother Teresa worked diligently in the slums of India most of her life. She did extensive service in her 80's. Pope Frances I is 76 and will be 77 in December.

What can be said about Winston Churchill, George Burns,

Mahatma Gandhi, Ronald Reagan and Nelson Mandela? All excelled in their 80's. Just to name a few.

A recent article in a local newspaper has created a storm of interesting insights. David Mintz, CEO of Tofutti in Cranford, NJ stated, "I want employees with energy and enthusiasm, fresh thinking and quickness to catch on, able to work at a frenzied pace, starting the day early and working late." And then he concluded with the words, "and I found them in older workers."

A couple of things are happening in the work force today. More and more seniors are going back to work. Maybe not in their original pre-retirement jobs, but some kind of employment. Why? Because they are dependable, very knowledgeable about things like computers. And they are creative.

I've been especially pleased to see seniors working in fast food venues, driving trucks, selling cars, etc., answering phones and giving lectures.

The second thing I notice is the great number of seniors that are going back to school. The object is to finish their education and getting prepared for new vocations.

Two people I know personally illustrate my point. One is trained as a legal secretary. She is 56 years of age and is taking classes "on line" in preparation to graduate from college for a new career.

The second is a man who retired at age 50; forced to retire. He graduates from Seminary next year and plans to enter the ministry.

By the way, just today I heard on TV that CEO Howard Shultz of Starbucks is hiring more and more seniors .

The role of seniors in our modern world is significant For instance I have a list of the 25 richest people in the world. All of them are seniors. Carlos Slim Helu is worth 73 billion-age 73. Bill Gates is worth 67 billion – age 57. Amancio Ortega is worth 57 billion-age 57. Warren Buffett is worth 57.5 billion-age 82. On and on; all 25 are seniors .

By the way Momma Walton (Wal-Mart) and her four children together are worth 78 billion. Momma is 86 and 4 kids average 56 years. All seniors.

While professional sports cater to the young, the owners are seniors. About 80 percent of individuals that go on cruises are seniors. They buy cars, buy new clothes, invest in the stock market and have bank accounts and are ranking officers in the military. Believe it or not, many box office winners are seniors. Harrison Ford, Mel Gibson, Myrl Streep, Betty White, Alan Alda and Angie Dickenson.

Other professionals are filled with seniors: college professors, politicians, scientists and ministers. Finally, on September 27 I turned 86 years old. I endorse this commercial.

Amen. Selah . So be it.

AGNOSTIC

The word AGNOSTIC is enjoying a revival of usage and understanding. Particularly among the socially elite, the progressive academics and the wealthy. People like Bill Gates, Warren Buffett, Larry King, James Taylor and Alan Dershowitz.

They swear allegiance to the word. In days gone by there were followers like Winston Churchill, Mark Twain, Carl Sagan, Marie Cure and Thomas Huxley.

The latter (Huxley) was the first person to use it in common usage or print in 1869. He used it primarily to oppose the religious view of Gnosticism. The Gnostics were one of the five religions competing for dominance in the first century. The other four were: Christianity, Judaism, Mithraism and Roman Imperialism.

With Constantine's help, Christianity was the winner. However, the Gnostics are also having a revival of interest since 1945 when scores of parchments with their views were discovered in Nag Hammadi, Egypt.

Outside of their original Greek meaning the words "agnostic" and Gnostic" have little in common. The fundamental view of the Gnostic was to view knowledge as the key to salvation rather than faith or works.

Agnosticism is simply the assertion that "I don't know." Webster provides clarity. "A person who holds that the existence of the ultimate cause, as a god or God, and the essential nature of things are unknown and unknowable."

A distinction with "atheism" is important. They are NOT the same. The difference? Atheists, without hesitation, deny any kind of God. "There is no God." While Gnostics affirm, "I don't know."

There is some speculation where Huxley got the source for his inspiration. Some researchers suggest Socrates and his classic reference to "know yourself." Others including myself, suggest the reference to the book of Acts to the "unknown God." (Acts 17:23)

The essence of agnosticism focuses on their doubt of a belief in God and a clarification of His (Her) attributes. In this context such words as Omnipotence , Omniscient and Omnipresent are used.

However, my literary mentor, Leslie Weatherhead, suggests other aspects of deity. Such as beauty over ugliness; harmony rather than discord; values over against unimportant; love versus hatred; logic rather than confusion; tranquility over dissonance, intelligence versus ignorance, creativity, compassion and love. (I John 4:7) "love is of God."

My initial response to the professing agnostic is graphically expressed in Leslie Weatherhead's book, "The Christian Agnostic." He posits the question, "Have you ever experienced a state of mind that brings joy and peace at hearing a bit of harmony; or being transfixed by a radiant sunset or being mesmerized by a logical opinion of a brilliant scholar?"

To Weatherhead these are evidences of a transcendent force; the Ground of Our Being or Intelligent Designer.

The problem that most agnostics have is their tendency to equate Deity with certain age-old attributes, as I've suggested.

Bill Gates obviously has no trouble in accepting the principles of finance. Or Steven Hawking the logic of gravity and entropy. The "Don't know" of agnosticism's never enters their mind. They "know" who developed those theories.

In the New Testament in I John 4:7 are the words, "To know love is to know God. "I ask any professing agnostic," Do you love your wife or your children?" Surely you do. Then how can you be hesitant about the axiom just quoted. Belief in love and belief in God are synonymous.

I have a suggestion for those who profess to be an agnostic. They are similar to the columnist that wrote, in answer to someone that denied any of life's problems, "They are not paying attention."

"Agnostics" here is what Elizabeth Barrett Browning wrote, "Earth's crammed with heaven, and every common bush aflame with God; but only those who see take off their shoes. The rest sit around plucking blackberries."

The implication is clear. Open your eyes. God surrounds you.

Amen Selah. So be it.

ALI

Ali is a friend of mine. A native Pakistani, he and his wife Forzana have lived in Highland for 27 years. Their children went to school here. The daughter and one son are married. Besides being a devout Muslim, he is a successful businessman. His wife is a beautician and an enthusiast for the U.S.A. Ali always has a joke and a bit of philosophy.

The other day he shared this bit of wisdom with me. There are four stages in a man 's life, relating each stage to an animal.

First, as a baby and a child, he is a BIRD. He's trying his wings, flapping his arms, soaring and exploring. Curiosity is his modus operandi.

Then as a young person he is a DOG. Running, sniffing, expressing his dog (human) nature. Adventure is his modus operandi.

Third, as an adult he is a WATER BUFFALO: work, work, work. A pack horse would also be an appropriate figure. He's tied to the grindstone making a living. His modus operandi would be making money for the family.

The fourth stage is the OWL. It is reflective of old age and retirement. He sleeps all day and stays awake all night. His modus operandi is wisdom and good advice.

What does a turkey sound like before Thanksgiving? She gives the answer with a loud gobble, gobble. What does it sound like after Thanksgiving? She gives the answer with lips tightly closed. Silence.

Recently a friend sent me a newspaper article giving examples of humor; "bloopers" in church bulletins: Attend the conference here at the church; you will hear an excellent speaker and have a healthy lunch. The church will host an evening of fine dining, superb entertainment and gracious hostility. The potluck will be held at 5 pm, prayer and medication to follow. This evening at 7 pm. there will be a hymn sing in the park. Bring a blanket and come prepared to sin. At the evening service tonight the sermon topic will be, "What 's Hell?" Come early and listen to our choir practice . Eight new choir robes are currently needed, due to the addition of several new members and to the deterioration of some older ones. No wonder that within a few years the church has grown from six members to 1200 members.

Three astronauts were going to live for two years in outer space. NASA told them they could take with them one thing or person they really loved.

The first decided to take his wife. The second wanted to learn German so he took a German teacher. The third one wanted a two year supply of cigarettes.

After two years they returned to earth and a press conference was held. The husband and wife had a new baby. The second astronaut was speaking fluent German.

The third one was nervous, disheveled and acting crazy.

His first words were: "Does anyone have a match?"

Here are two humorous stories. A man walked by a table in a hotel and noticed three men and a dog playing cards. The dog was playing with extraordinary performance. "This is a very smart dog," the man commented. "Not so smart," said one of the players. "Every time he gets a good hand he wags his tail."

Tom had proposed to young Maureen and was being interviewed by his prospective father-in-law. "Do you think you are earning enough to support a family the older man asked the suitor." "Yes, sir," replied Tom, "I'm sure I am." "Think carefully now," said Maureen's father warningly. "There are twelve of us."

A lady is having a bad day at the roulette tables in Vegas. She's down to her last fifty dollars. Exasperated, she exclaims, "What rotten luck I've had today! What in the world should I do now?" A man standing next to her suggests, "I don't know. Why don't you play your age?" He walks away. Moments later, his attention is grabbed by a great commotion at the roulette table. Maybe she won! He rushes back to the table and pushes his way through the crowd. The lady is lying limp on the floor with the table operator kneeling over her. The man is stunned. He asks, "What happened? Is she all right?" The operator replies, "I don't know. She put all her money on 29 and 36 came up. Then she just fainted."

Amen. Selah. So be it.

ALI AND ALI

Mohammed Ali and Sayed Ali have two things in common. They were and are one of the best in their vocation. Mohammed was a boxer; one of the best and Sayed is owner of the All Star Auto Shop...the best I've met. The second thing they have in common is telling jokes. The boxer is always telling jokes and so is the mechanic. When I need a good mechanic I go to Ali. When I want to hear a good story and laugh I go to Ali.

Here's his latest. A guy named John lived in Mississippi. He was a believer. He believed God would take care of him, no matter what. Well, it started to rain and rain and rain. A Highway Patrolman stopped and told John to come with him, the river was rising. John said, "No God will take care of me."

Pretty soon the yard was overflowing and a boat came by. He told John to get in the boat, the river was rising. John said, "No. God will take care of me." John finally was on the rooftop. A helicopter came by and told John to get in. John said, "No. God will take care of me."

The water rose and John drowned. In heaven he remonstrated with God. "Where were you? You promised to save me." God said, "Listen John. I sent the policeman, a boat and a helicopter and you wouldn't be helped. I did everything possible to help you."

The other day I was the speaker at Ballard's Rehab Center

in West San Bernardino. The audience was made up of therapists , patients and family members. Denis Kaney was heading up the program and had invited me to speak. Following my stand-up his step-son Jeff Oxarat, twelve years old, told me he had a joke. It seems that a Jew, a Chinaman and a blond Pollock worked in construction together.

One day the Jew said, "If l have one more Kosher sandwich for lunch I'm going to jump of these steel girders." The Chinaman said the same thing about his rice. The blonde Polish man said the same thing about his Polish sausage sandwich. The next day when he opened his lunch, the Jew saw it was kosher and he jumped off. The same result for the other two. At their funerals the first wife was crying and said, "If only I had made a different lunch." The second wife, weeping, said she wished she had given her husband a different lunch. The third wife said of her blonde husband, "If only he had not made himself the same sandwich." Some of you must belong to the same humor mill because I received this bit of humor from several of you.

An 8-year-old little girl went to her dad, who was working in the yard. She asked him, "Daddy, what is sex?" The father was surprised that she would ask such a question; but decides that if she is old enough to ask the question, then she is old enough to get a straight answer. He proceeded to tell her all about the "birds and the bees." When he finished explaining, the little girl was looking at him with her mouth hanging open. The father asked her, "Why did you ask this question?" "Mom told me to tell you that dinner would be ready in just a couple of secs. Finally, you have to be a little bit religious to appreciate the following humor. It's titled, "Hymns for the Over 50 Crowd."

1. "Just a 'Slower' Walk With Thee"
2. "It Is Well With My Soul," But My Knees Hurt.
3. "Nobody Knows the Trouble I 'Have Seeing'."
4. "Precious Lord, Take My Hand," and help me up.
5. "Count Your Many 'Birthdays,' Count them One by One."
6. "Go Tell It On the Mountain", But speak up.
7. "Give Me the Old 'Timers' Religion."
8. "Blessed 'Insurance.''
9. "Guide Me O Thou Great Jehovah.''

I've Forgotten Where I've Parked the Car. Do you know the States? ALASKA: One out of every sixty-four people has a pilot's license. ARKANSAS: Has the only active diamond mine in the U.S. CALIFORNIA: Its economy is so large that if it were a country, it would rank seventh in the entire world. DELAWARE: Has more scientists and engineers than any other state. IDAHO: TV was invented in Rigby, Idaho, in 1922. MARYLAND: The Oujia board was created in Baltimore in 1892. MISSOURI: Is the birthplace of ice cream cone. UTAH: The first Kentucky Fried Chicken restaurant opened here in 1952. WYOMING: Was the first state to allow women to vote. *Amen. Selah. So be it.*

ALLEY OOP

I cannot remember a time when humor was not a part of my life. From the time I was able to read, the "funnies" were a weekly experience. My favorites were "Alley Oop," "Lil' Abner" and "Mandrake the Magician." These were followed by jokes told by teenage boys that were seldom funny and always naughty .

Playing tricks on one another was a way of life. Making fun of each other was supposed to be funny but was often hurtful. I first became aware of the benefits of humor when I started speaking in public and studied public speaking. Humor was always used as an icebreaker. It was just a short hop, skip and a jump to studying major comedians like Benny, Hope, Burns and Skelton.

The benefits of humor have shifted drastically in recent years. It is more often viewed now as an aid to optimal wellness. Whatever the usage; humor is good.

A blonde walks into a bank in New York City and asks for the loan officer. She says she's going to Europe on business for two weeks and needs to borrow $5,000. The bank officer says the bank will need some security for the loan, so the blonde hands over the keys to a new Rolls Royce. The car is parked on the street in front of the bank , she has the title and everything checks out. The bank agrees to accept the car as collateral for the loan. The bank's president and officers all enjoy a good laugh at the blonde for using a $250,000 Rolls as collateral against a $5,000 loan. An employee of the bank then proceeds to drive the Rolls into the bank's underground garage and parks it there.

Two weeks later, the blonde returns, repays the $5,000 and the interest, which comes to $15.41. The loan officer says, "Miss, we are very happy to have had your business and this transaction has worked out very nicely; but we are a little puzzled. While you were away, we checked you out and found that you are a multi-millionaire. What puzzles us is why would you bother to borrow $5,000?" The blonde replies…"Where else in New York City can I park my car for two weeks for only $15.41 and expect it to be there when I return?" Pretty smart.

A blonde is driving along in her Porsche convertible when her cell phone rings. It's her husband and he says, "I wanted to call to tell you the TV news says some idiot is driving the wrong way on the freeway, so be careful." The blonde yells back "I know and it isn't just one, there are hundreds of them!"

Jake was dying. His wife, Becky was maintaining candlelight vigil by his side. She held his fragile hand; tears running down her face. Her praying roused him from his slumber. He looked up and his pale lips began to move slightly, "My darling, Becky," he whispered. "Hush, my love," she said. "Rest. Shhh, don't talk." He was insistent. "Becky," he said in his tired voice, "I have something I must confess to you." "There's nothing to confess" replied the weeping Becky. "Everything's all right. Go to sleep." "No, no, I must die in peace Becky. I slept with your sister, your best friend, her best friend, and your mother!" "I know" Becky whispered softly. "That's why I poisoned you."

Perhaps you missed these interesting words of advice to Osama bin Laden. It is called, "Five ways to annoy bin Laden."

5. Ask whether the Taliban get cable because you haven't seen "Sex and the City" for weeks.

4. Refer to him as "Osama same so same banana fana to fana me my mo mama. Osama."

3. Claim you once saw him at a Hooters in Muncie wearing a yarmulke.

2. At dinner say the Northern Alliance has much prettier place settings.

1. Explain that America is a land of freedom and opportunity filled with people of every race, religion and background including millions of women strong enough to kick the al-Qaida out of him.

There was a tradesman, a painter called Wayne, who was very interested in making a penny where he could, so he often would thin down paint to make it go a wee bit further. As it happened, he got away with this for some time; but eventually the Baptist Church decided to do a big restoration job on the painting of one of their biggest buildings. Wayne put in a bid and because his price was so low, he got the job. And so he set to erecting the trestles and setting up the planks and buying the paint and, yes, I am sorry to say, thinning it down with turpentine. Well, Wayne was up on the scaffolding painting away; the job nearly completed when suddenly there was a horrendous clap of thunder and the sky opened, the rain poured down, washing the thinned paint from all over the church and knocking Wayne clear off the scaffold to land on the lawn among the gravestones surrounded by telltale puddles of the thinned and useless paint. Wayne was no fool. He knew this was a judgment from the Almighty, so he got on his knees and cried: "Oh God! Forgive me! What should I do?" And from the thunder, a mighty voice spoke... (you're going to love this)

"Repaint! Repaint! And thin no more!"

Amen. Selah. So be it.

ANALYSIS OF ARTICLES

The other day I read an interesting analysis of several articles. Each article emphasized one of the following.

1. The Pythagoras Theorem consists of 24 words.

2. The Lord's Prayer has 66 words.

3. The Archimedes Principle has 67 words.

4. The Ten Commandments has 179 words.

5. The Gettysburg Address has 386 words.

6. The Declaration of Independence has 1300 words.

7. The U.S. Regulation on the sale of cabbage has 26,911 words.

In contrast, the following bits of wisdom are much shorter than number 7 and much more meaningful. Maria Shriver was asked in a recent interview about the best days in her life; she said, "The day I was born and the day I learned why."

Through the years I've made it a habit to collect bits of humor. They stimulate my mind and add meaning to it.

Albert Schweitzer was asked one time what he did when he was depressed. He was a great philosopher, a great physician and a world class organist. His response was amazing. He said, "I go out and work in my rose garden."

William James is considered by many as the greatest American born psychologist. His advice to himself and to others regarding depression was, "Act the way you want to feel and pretty soon you will be feeling the way you're acting." Amazing therapy. I often find that humor can also provide words of wisdom. A man was walking on the beach and accidently kicked and broke a bottle that released a genii.

For being released, the genii said he would grant him anything he wished. "Well, I've always wanted to go to Hawaii, but I'm afraid to fly and I don't like going on a ship. Could you make a highway from L.A. to Honolulu?" The genii responded, "What is another choice?" The man thought about it and asked, "Could you make it so I will understand women?" The genii responded with these humorous words, "Would you like a two lane or a four lane highway?"

Recently I found a good description of a list of success at various ages. At age four, success is not wetting his pants. At age twelve, success is having friends. At age sixteen, success is getting a driver's license. At age twenty, success is having sex. At age thirty-five, success is having money. At age fifty, success is having more money. At age sixty, success is having sex. At age seventy, success is getting a driver's license. At age seventy-five, success is having friends. At age eighty, success is not wetting your pants.

Several years ago I started collecting sayings or proverbs. I call them "Abersold's Laws" and currently I have fifty-five of them. Here are a few samples. "The one who has the least emotional involvement controls the relationship." Another one: "If you don't profess so much, people will not expect so much."

Another one: "We do not cease to play because we grow old; but we grow old because we cease to play."

Another one: "Lack of planning and preparation on your part does not constitute an emergency for me." A final one: "Each of us is important and has something to give; listen to the music within you and believe in yourself; don't be afraid, and take the risk of living."

One of the best books I've ever read is, "Five Smooth Stones," written by Ann Fairbairn. The basic theme of the book is a Latin proverb, "Life is loaned to man and not given."

When I was in Seminary and taking a class in homiletics (the art of preaching,) the professor challenged us with the words, "Remember to emotionalize the truth." He was saying that as preachers they needed to give a viable illustration to clarify their ideas. Illustrations are usually simple and emotional and seldom philosophical. They illustrate a single truth.

In the 1930's Admiral Richard Byrd was America's leading explorer in the Arctic and Antarctic. On one trip to the Antarctic he made plans to fly several hundred miles deep into Antarctica. He was to stay in a half-submerged cabin for six months.

After a month of monitoring weather conditions and other studies, he decided to go outside. It was dangerous. Blizzards could quickly isolate him from his cabin. That's what happened. However, he didn't lose his cool. He placed his staff in the ice and began to circle it. Never losing sight of his cabin and an eye on his pole; he make it back safely to the cabin. The truth it illustrates should be obvious. A goal will bring its own reward.

Amen. Selah. So be it

ANN LANDERS

As with many of you, I was an avid reader of Ann Landers. Her philosophy, advice and short, pithy answers always caused me to think or laugh. Her recent death reminded me of several favorite articles. Read these and remember.

Everybody who has a dog calls him "Rover" or "Boy." I called mine "Sex." He's a great pal, but he has caused me a great deal of embarrassment. When I went to city hall to renew his dog license, I told the clerk I would like a license for Sex. He said, "I'd like one, too!" Then I said, "But this is a dog." He said he didn't care what she looked like. Then I said, "You don't understand. I've had Sex since I was nine years old." He winked and said, "You must have been quite a kid."

When I married and went on my honeymoon, I took the dog with me. I told the motel clerk that I wanted a room for my wife and me, and a special room for Sex. He said, "You don't need a special room. As long as you pay your bill we don't care what you do." I said, "Look, you don't seem to understand Sex keeps me awake at night." The clerk said, "Funny, I have the same problem." One day I entered Sex in a contest, but before the competition began the dog ran away. Another contestant asked me why I was just standing there looking disappointed. I told him I had planned to have Sex in the contest. He told me I should have sold my own tickets. "But you don't understand I said, "I had hoped to have Sex on TV. He said, "Now that cable is all over the place, it's no big deal anymore."

When my wife and I separated, we went to court to fight for custody of the dog. I said, "Your Honor, I had Sex before I was married." The judge said, "The courtroom isn't a confessional, stick to the case, please! Then, I told him that after I was married, Sex left me. He said, "Me, too."

Last night, Sex ran off again. I spent hours looking all over town for him. A cop came over to me and asked. "What are you doing in this alley at 4 o'clock in the morning?" I told him that I was looking for Sex. My case comes up Friday. She published this one every Thanksgiving for years.

We come to this table today O Lord, humble and thankful and glad. We thank Thee first for the great miracle of life, for the exaltation of being human, for the capacity to love. We thank Thee for joys both great and simple; for wonder, dreams and hope; for the newness of each day; for laughter and song and a merry heart; for compassion waiting within to be kindled; for the forbearance of friends and the smile of a stranger; for the arching of the earth and trees and heavens and the fruit of all three; for the wisdom of the old; for the courage of the young; for the promise of the child; for the strength that comes when needed; for the family united here today. Of those to whom much is given, much is required. May we and our children remember this. Then, she always gave good advice for all of us. Her rules for living have great appeal.

1. Never take a sleeping pill and a laxative on the same night.
2. There can be a fine line between "hobby" and "mental illness."
3. People who want to share their religious views with you almost never want you to share yours with them.
4. You should never confuse your career with your life.
5. No matter what happens in life, somebody will find a way to take it too seriously.
6. Nobody cares if you can't dance well; just get up and dance.
7. Never lick a steak knife.
8. Take out the fortune before you eat the cookie.
9. The most destructive force in the universe is gossip.
10. Nobody can give me a clear and compelling reason why we observe daylight saving time.
11. A person who is nice to you; but rude to the waiter is not a nice person.
12. Your friends love you, no matter what.

Her rules for living have great appeal.
1. If you open it, close it.
2. If you turn it on, turn it off.
3. If you unlock it, lock it up.
4. If you break it, admit it.

5. If you can't fix it, call in someone who can.

6. If you borrow it, return it.

7. If you value it, take care of it.

8. If you make a mess, clean it up.

9. If you move it, put it back.

10. If it belongs to someone else, get permission to use it.

11. If you don't know how to operate it, leave it alone.

12. If it's none of your business, don't ask questions.

We will not soon forget Ann Landers .

Amen. Selah. So be it.

BEST ADVICE GIVEN

A recent article in Fortune Magazine triggered my imagination. It dealt with a unique subject. What is the best advice you've ever received? Famous people like Warren Buffett were asked and they gave their answer. My contention is that we common folks also have answers for the best advice we've received .

Mine came when I was a kid; from my Dad. He only had a sixth grade education; but he was a wise man. He advised me to read. In the process he instilled in me a love for books. Horatio Alger and Zane Grey were favorite authors. The subjects in their books inspired. Moral values and hard work have their rewards.

He opened a bank account for me; ten cents a week. His advice was to save what I could. Along with that he advised me to work hard. I've never forgotten either one.

We never owned a car; but he walked me to church every Sunday. That advice affected me greatly. I follow it every week.

The benefit of education is never lost. Reverend Jones advised me to go to college; which I did. Later on Wilhelmina advised me to go to graduate school; which I did. Learning is habit forming. Discipline and curiosity are by products. Today, I'm always reading at least six books and carry them with me.

Until about thirty years ago my writing consisted mainly of academic dissertations. Marilyn advised me to write like I preached; short, understandable, informational and inspirational. I started writing for newspapers. Since then I have written hundreds of them and two books: Words To Live By and Words To Think About. I've received a great number of "words of wisdom" from what I call my "literary mentors." They were certainly words of advice.

The first one was from Bishop Fulton J. Sheen. It was one of his books entitled, Life Is Worth Living. Personal advice to be sure. Along with it I always quote the words of Henry Ward Beecher; "God asks no one if he will accept life. Our only choice is what we do with what we have."

Don is a good friend of mine. He gave me one of the best words of advice I've ever received. "Bill, never take your friends for granted." Friendship is a relationship. It must be cultivated. Much like a plant, a flower. Nurtured, watered and catered to. Among my friends I have three that are rabid members of the Tea Party. The opposite of me. We can nurture our friendship by getting together often. The conversation is always interesting and stimulating.

Years ago I read everything that James Baldwin wrote. As a gay black man he was years ahead of his time. Again, he was one of my literary mentors. He said, "The challenge of living is to be present in everything that you do, from baking bread to making love." I've changed the last phrase to; from getting up in the morning to going to bed at night.

I've been fired three times in my lifetime. It was never a pleasant experience. Paul gave me good advice that was applicable to each one. "When one door closes, God always opens one or more." It was especially true after the first and third firing. However, following the second one a literary mentor gave one of the best words of advice I've ever received. He said, "Everyone needs to learn how to do more than one thing, in case they lose their job."

I interpreted that as meaning the development of marketable skills. I started a company, Take Charge; earned a Ph.D., became a hypnotist, sold insurance, became a stock broker, and gave over five hundred lectures. I earned money from all of them.

I've asked several friends about the best advice they ever received. Here are a few of their answers:

Bob said, "Do the best you can with what you've got." Warren said, "Stop drinking and trust in God." Jackie stated, "If you need a helping hand, look to the end of your arms." Becky's was, "After every rain cloud, there is always a rainbow." Stella said, "Get over it." John's advice came from his father; "Don't drink or smoke." Beth received this meaningful advice from her mother; "Will this make any difference five years from now?"

The Bible is full of universal advice. One should be sufficient, "Judge not that you be not judged."

Amen. Selah. So be it.

BILL COSBY

Bill Cosby is without a doubt an icon of television; especially in the comedic venue. In a recent newspaper article he is reported as saying, "Like everyone else who makes the mistake of getting older I begin each day with coffee and obituaries." I particularly remember his classic rendition of the story of Noah and the Ark. I like something else he said. "Immortality is a long shot I admit; but somebody has to be first." He becomes very insightful when he says, "There is hope for the future because God has a sense of humor , and we are funny to God."

Cosby is often very serious; especially when he talks about blacks and what they need to do to change their status. He's also serious about the positive affect of humor. "Through humor you can soften some of the worst blows that life delivers. And once you find laughter, no matter how painful your situation might be, you can survive it."

A new Republican Congressman was sitting in his office when a distinguished man was approaching. The Congressman quickly picked up his phone and began talking. "Yes, Mr. President I appreciate your call. I agree with your position. I'll be happy to have lunch with you tomorrow. Goodbye Mr. President."

He turned to the distinguished gentleman and said, "Are you from CNN?" "No!" "Are you from NBC, ABC or CBS?" "No." the man said. "Then who are you?" "I'm the AT&T man. I'm here to connect your phone."

Pete, a guy I met at Bally 's told me this one: A car driven by an eighty year old grandmother with four passengers was going very slow on a freeway. A CHP pulls her over and asks her about her slow speed. She said, "I was going the speed limit, which is fifteen miles per hour. See the sign? I always drive at the speed limit." "No, lady," the officer said, "That's the number of the highway. " He looked in the back seat where three elderly women sat with their hair sprayed out and glazed eyes. He asked about their appearance and the driver said, "We just got off Freeway 210."

Charlie always has a humorous story. Here 's his latest. A couple in their eighties were about to get married. She said, "I want to keep my house. " He said, "That's fine with me." She said, "And I want to keep my Cadillac." He said, "That's fine with me." She said, "And I want to have sex six times a week." He said, "That's fine with me...Put me down for Friday!"

Mike where have you been? As an eighty year old, I like this one. The preacher came to call the other day. He said, "At my age I should be thinking of the hereafter." I told him: "Oh, I do it all the time. No matter where I am in the parlor, upstairs, in the kitchen, or down in the basement, I ask myself: "Now, what am I here after?"

I like holiday jokes. Frank sent me this one. A man in Phoenix calls his son in New York three days before Christmas and says, "I hate to ruin your day, but I have to tell you that your mother and I are divorcing; forty-five years of misery is enough." "Pop, what are you talking about?" the son screams. "We can't stand the sight of each other any longer, "the father says. "We're sick of each other, and I'm sick of talking about this, so you call your sister in Chicago and tell her."

Frantic, the son calls his sister, who explodes on the phone. "Like heck they're getting divorced," she shouts, "I'll take care of this." She calls Phoenix immediately, and screams at her father, "You are NOT getting divorced. Don't do a single thing until I get there. I'm calling my brother back and we'll both be there tomorrow. Until then, don't do a thing, DO YOU HEAR ME?" and she hangs up. The old man hangs up his phone and turns to his wife. "Okay," he says, "they're coming for Christmas and paying their own way."

A guest at a posh hotel ordered breakfast in the dining room. "I'd like one egg that is undercooked, and another that is so overcooked that it is tough and chewy. I'd also like grilled bacon that is mostly fat and served a bit on the cold side, plus burnt toast, butter straight from the freezer so that it's impossible to spread and a cup of very weak, lukewarm coffee."

"That's a complicated order, sir," said the bewildered waiter. "I'll have to check with the chef." The guest replied, "It can't be that difficult. It's exactly what you brought me yesterday."

Amen. Selah. So be it

BIRDS

The American bald eagle was adopted as the official bird emblem of our country m 1782. "It was chosen because of its majestic beauty, great strength, long life and because it was native to North America." It was chosen over Benjamin Franklin's choice; the common native turkey.

It was called the "bald" eagle for its unique white head that appeared as bald. But, in reality the name was "balde" eagle after the British judges that wore a white wig. The wigs were referred to as "balde."

The "e" was dropped so the birds became just the bald eagles. In the wild they often live up to fifty years. Full grown, they have a wing span up to seven feet and can dive at one hundred miles an hour. Bald Eagles feed primarily on fish and carrion.

An important question is causing sincere questions from scientists. Which are the oldest living creatures; dinosaurs or birds?

For many years the answer was definitely in favor of the dinosaurs. Birds, including chickens, were evolved from them. "A new study of ancient fossils suggests that birds are ancient enough that dinosaurs may have evolved from them."

While the argument continues to rage I came down on the side of dinosaurs, like T-Rex and raptors have evolved into modern birds like falcons, vultures, condors, eagles (of all kinds), terns, pigeons, etc. that can fly; and birds like chickens and the ostrich, that cannot fly.

Birds with short or no wings can't fly because of their limited wings and the fact their bones are solid. Those that can fly have hollow bones.

I recently read a novel by Lindsay McKenna," The Defender." The heroine, Katie Bergstrom, operated a raptor rehabilitation facility outside of Jackson Hole, Wyoming. Interestingly, the information regarding raptors in the novel parallels the real Teton Raptor Center in Jackson Hole, Wyoming. Field biologists and environmental educators Roger Smith and Margaret Creel established the center in 1997. Rehabilitating wounded birds and lecturing extensively in various venues are significantly the same.

Dinosaurs became extinct about sixty-five million years ago. They were cold blooded reptiles. They had scales as an outer covering. Birds are warm blooded and have feathers as an outer covering. The change is a result of the evolutionary process.

The world's biggest living bird is the OSTRICH. They are native to Africa but are now farmed throughout the world. They can grow up to nine feet and weigh three hundred pounds. An ostrich egg weighs as much as two dozen chicken's eggs. The ostrich has small wings and can't fly. They have very little fat and several restaurants in Southern California specialize in offering ostrich burgers.

Besides ostriches, penguins, chickens, ducks, geese and

turkeys cannot fly. Consider chickens. They are carnivorous. Their beaks, their talons (only three toes); they eat anything. When one chicken develops blood; he's a goner. They all attack. Rooster fights are legendary. They are raptors.

"The Golden Eagle is one of the largest, fastest, nimblest raptors in North America." Their feathers have a usually bright gleam on the back of their head and neck. They have unusually strong beaks and talons. Rabbits are their favorite food and they often attack small coyotes and bears.

Psychological profiling is often a technique used to identify serial killers. Those individuals that work with and care for the golden eagle that been wounded or sick are called falconers. The eagles are trained to land on their forearms with a leather gauntlet.

In the rehab program the Teton falconers have developed an eagle profile. Since they do not have eyelids to protect their eyes, Golden Eagles do not fly in rain or snow.

One falconer described the raptors as earthly angels. "They come down to improve our lives and make us better human beings."

The eagles always sense a high strung falconer and won 't set on their arms. They also mate for life. Amazingly, they remember faces and seem to memorize everything they see. The moods of falconers always affect them. The considered opinion of many falconers is that "the Golden Eagle is at the top of the raptors food chain.   *Amen. Selah. So be it.*

BOB HOPE

Without a doubt, Bob Hope was one of the greatest comedians ever. He was convinced that laughter had constructive power. A laugh, he said, "can transform almost unbearable tears into something bearable, even hopeful."

Jerry Lewis is also noted as a great humorist. He calls humor a "safety valve." "Those who have the ability to laugh at themselves are those who survive," he claims.

A friend recently sent me a list of suggestions on "How to Stay Young." One, was to throw out nonessential numbers like age, weight and height. I especially liked number two: keep only cheerful friends. Grouches pull you down.

Regarding laughter, "Laugh often, long and loud. Laugh until you gasp for breath and enjoy the simple things." For further thought don 't take guilt trips. Take a trip to the mall, to a foreign country; but NOT to where the guilt is.

I really like this one. "Tell the people you love that you love them at every opportunity. " "Don 't sweat the petty things and don 't pet the sweaty things."

A man recently picked a new primary care physician. After two visits and exhaustive lab tests, he said he was doing fairly well for his age. A little concerned about that comment, the guy couldn't resist asking him, "Do you think I'll live to be eighty?" The doctor asked him, "Well, do you smoke or drink?" "No", was the response . "I've never done either."

Then the doctor asked, "Do you eat rib-eye steaks and barbeque ribs?" The guy said, "No, I heard that all red meat is very unhealthy. " "Do you spend a lot of time in the sun, like playing golf, sailing, ballooning, motorcycling, swimming, or rock climbing?" Finally, he was asked, "Do you gamble, drive fast cars or sexually fool around?" "No," he said "I have never done any of those things." Then the doctor gives the kicker. "Then why do you give a hoot if you live to be eighty?"

A husband was sitting quietly reading his paper when his wife walked up behind him and whacked him on the head with a rolled up magazine . "Ouch!! What was that for?" he asked. "That was for the piece of paper in your pants pocket with the name Mary Lou written on it," she replied. "Two weeks ago when I went to the races, Mary Lou was the name of one of the horses I bet on," he explained.

"Oh honey, I'm so sorry," she said. "I should have known there was a good explanation." Three days later he was watching a ball game on TV when she walked up and hit him in the head again; this time with an iron skillet, which knocked him out cold. When he came too, he asked, "Now what was that for?" She replied, "Your horse called."

The second one is the ultimate response to a Dear John letter. A Marine was deployed to Afghanistan. While he was there he received a letter from his girlfriend. In the letter she explained that she had slept with two guys while he had been gone and she wanted to break up with him. AND, she wanted pictures of herself back. So, the Marine did what any squared-away Marine would do. He went around to his buddies and collected all the unwanted photos of women he could find. He then mailed about 25 pictures of women (with clothes and without) to his girlfriend with the following note: I don't remember which one you are. Please remove your picture and send the rest back."

A pastor, known for his lengthy sermons, noticed a man get up and leave during the middle of his message. The man returned just before the conclusion of the service. Afterward; the pastor asked the man where he had gone. "I went to get a haircut," was the reply . "But," said the pastor, "why didn't you do that before the service?" "Because," the gentleman said, "I didn't need one then."

A minister was seated next to a cowboy on a flight to Texas. After the plane was airborne, drink orders were taken. The cowboy asked for a whiskey and soda, which was brought and placed before him. The flight attendant then asked the minister if he would like a drink. He replied in disgust, "I'd rather be savagely raped by brazen prostitutes than let liquor touch my lips." The cowboy then handed his drink back to the attendant and said, "Me too. I didn't know we had a choice."

For those of you who feel disenfranchised, read this last story carefully. A bus carrying only very ugly people crashes into an oncoming truck and everyone inside dies. They then get to meet their Maker and because of the grief they have experienced the Maker decides to grant them one wish each before they enter paradise. They are all lined up and the Maker asks the first one what the wish is. "I want to be gorgeous," and so the Maker snaps his fingers and it is done. The second one in line hears this and says "I want to be gorgeous too ." Another snap of his fingers and the wish is granted. This goes on for a while, but when the Maker is only halfway down the line, the last guy in the line starts laughing. When there are only about ten people left the guy is rolling on the floor, laughing his head off. Finally, the Maker reaches this guy and asks him what his wish will be. The guy eventually calms down and says. "Make'em all ugly again." So....THE NEXT TIME YOU'RE LAST IN LINE....CONSIDER YOURSELF BLESSED!!!!!!

Amen. Selah. So be it.

BURNOUT

One of the most devastating stressors we face and one of the least talked about in stress management seminars is BURNOUT. The most common usage of the term is in rocketry. "The termination of effective combustion in a rocket engine due to exhaustion of propellant." So says Webster's dictionary. However, the dictionary also gives another definition. "Fatigue, frustration or apathy resulting from prolonged stress, overwork, or intense activity." The term came to prominence in 1980 when Dr. Herbert Freudenberger's book, "Burnout" was published. While there are physical symptoms that seem to accompany burnout, the major indications of it are emotional and mental exhaustion. It is further identified as being a depletion of physical, mental and emotional resources. The individual becomes worn out after striving excessively to reach an unrealistic expectation that was imposed either by self or by the values of others.

Nine of the ten most stressful vocations are in the helping professions. According to research air traffic controllers are number one, secretaries are second, with teachers number three.

In my own study I place mothers with young children at the top of the list. The multiple tasks that are theirs is a burden that is so demanding that burnout is a sure thing.

The fallout from burnout is of epidemic proportion. I call it maladaptive behaviors. Booze, drugs (aspirin and tranquilizers in particular) smoking, eating and weight gain, sexual promiscuity and chronic depression seem to be the primary unacceptable results of bum-out.

However, the more subtle symptoms are: chronic fatigue, reduced production and impaired performance, criticism of family members or work colleagues, insomnia and bodily pain, short tempered reactions to the recipients of their services, responsibility with limited control and a feeling of being trapped.

Further vocations that are prone to burnout are professions like nursing, the clergy, social workers, caretakers, salesmen, waitresses, doctors, newspaper people, police, firemen, military, etc.

Why are these professions vulnerable to burnout? Primarily because there is never an end to their work. Manual labor is forgotten at the end of the day. Not so the work of teachers. Their task in on-going.

Furthermore, all of them have tremendous responsibility, but limited control. Think of the traffic controllers. What a great responsibility; but they have limited control over the pilots. And of course, those working in the helping professions usually have a limited pay scale and are plagued with a feeling of being trapped. Promotions are limited. This is a common complaint of young mothers with all they have to do; often without any help from the spouse.

I advocate three basic solutions to the burnout syndrome.

First, limit the demands made upon time and energy by simplifying your life. Cut down on the nonessential activities or solicit help from family members.

Second, modify your life style by changing expectations. Those in the helping professions are often very idealistic which creates excessive demands. And third, perhaps the most important, reclassify or compartmentalize your life. Find quality meaning in options. If work is the major cause of burnout, find meaning i:n an avocation. If it's health, focus more on the family. If it's your marriage that is contributing to burnout, develop more meaningful friendships.

Here are a few practical ways of managing burnout. Practice diaphragmatic: breathing, get a body massage, practice Jacobsen's progressive muscle relaxation, take catnaps, relax to music, engage in meditation, sit in a Jacuzzi, roll you shoulders forward; then backward, a program of exercising, practice telling jokes, play one hour a day, take a warm bath, think positive thoughts, take mini-vacations (hours or days), dancing, hobbies and socialize with those whom you do NOT work with. Relaxing is always an individual decision. Make it fun.

Amen. Selah. So be it.

CARL HURLEY COMIC

Carl Hurley, stand-up comic, is nationally known. He begins his show with a question: "Are you happy?" If you answer, yes, he says, "You better let your face know."

For several hours the other Saturday I was unhappy and disgusted. I had gone to a hurricane fund raiser to do a magic gig. It was at a Senior Center-not Highland. The act before mine had a would-be joke teller. He read them. His jokes were vulgar and without good taste. They were filthy. He concluded with the comment, "If you didn't laugh at these you don't have a sense of humor."

There is a type of humor when the double entendre is acceptable; but never explicit dirty humor where the human genitalia is emphasized.

I like the humor of Jack Benny, Red Skelton, George Burns, Steve Martin or Robin Williams. Chris Rock and his ilk don't do much for me. That's why I usually include information about the benefits of laughter along with humorous stories.

Carl Hurley, the above mentioned clean comic, also stresses the positive benefits of laughter. He says, "Laughter is good for you. It makes you feel better physically. You'll feel better mentally and emotionally. Laughter is good for everyone."

Here's what I mean. Very appropriate for the football season. Football FINALLY makes sense...A guy took his blonde girlfriend to her first football game. They had great seats right behind their teams bench. After the game, he asked her how she liked the experience. "Oh, I really liked it," she replied, "especially the tight pants and all the big muscles, but I just couldn't understand why they were killing each other over twenty-five cents. "Dumbfounded, her date asked, "What do you mean?" "Well, they flipped a coin, one team got it and then for the rest of the game, all they kept screaming was: 'Get the quarterback! Get the quarterback!' I'm like…Hellooooooo? It's only 25 cents!!!!!!!"

I love these "laws of the natural universe." Law of Mechanical Repair: After your hands become coated with grease, your nose will begin to itch. Law of the Workshop: Any tool, when dropped, will roll to the least accessible corner. Law of the Telephone: When you dial a wrong number, you never get a busy signal. Law of the Alibi: If you tell the boss you were late for work because you had a flat tire, the very next morning you will have a flat tire. Variation Law: If you change lines (or traffic lanes), the one you were in will start to move faster than the one you are in now (works every time.) Bath Theorem: When the body is fully immersed in water, the telephone rings. Law of Close Encounters: The probability of meeting someone you know increases when you are with someone you don't want to be seen with. Law of the Result: When you try to prove to someone that a machine won't work, it will.

Love means When my grandmother got arthritis, she

couldn't bend over and paint her toenails anymore. So my grandfather does it for her all the time; even when his hands got arthritis, too…That's love.

When someone loves you, the way they say your name is different. You just know that your name is safe in their mouth. Love is when a girl puts on perfume and a boy puts on shaving cologne and they go out and smell each other. Love is when you go out to eat and give somebody most of your French fries without making them give you any of theirs. Love is what makes you smile when you're tired. Love is when my mommy makes coffee for my daddy and she takes a sip before giving it to him, to make sure the taste is ok.

Often I receive jokes from friends. Here are two of them. A lady was picking through the frozen turkeys at the grocery store, but she couldn't find one big enough for her family. She asked a stock boy, "Do these turkeys get any bigger?" The stock boy replied, "No ma'am, they're dead."

The cop got out of his car and the kid who was stopped for speeding rolled down his window. "I've been waiting for you all day," the cop said. The kid replied, "Yeah, well I got here as fast as I could." When the cop finally stopped laughing, he sent the kid on his way without a ticket.

Amen. Selah. So be it.

CHARLIE PROSE

The other day I went with a group of seniors from Highland to Laughlin. The purpose was to visit my previously lost money, to eat good food and to hear Charlie Prose. He's one of the best clean comics I know about. A regular-one month a year-he has been performing at the Riverside Casino for fifteen years. I've heard him at least five times.

A jovial, stocky Italian from the Atlantic City area, he is multiple talented. He's a comedian, he sings, he prances, he's an MC and he plays the piano. Prose also has an outstanding back-up group. His director plays the keyboard. There is a drummer and a guitarist. Two young women sing support parts.

David Grayson has traveled with him the last several years. His style parallels Frank Sinatra and Tony Bennett. He is always a part of the show.

Charlie's videos are usually a part of all bus groups into Atlantic City. He is a favorite of seniors. The only part of his family he talks about are his father and two daughters. The girls are often used as foils for his jokes. In addition to the entertainment, Charlie Prose has two special features. First, he works the crowd. By that I mean he moves into the audience. Teasing them and talking with them.

Prose is patriotic. Make no mistake about it. He waves the flag. Every show is closed with a patriotic rendition. The closest he gets to a suggestive joke is a double entendre. He must love this story because he told it every one of the five times I've heard him. A father is giving his son the typical father-son talk. "Son, remember if you touch yourself you're going to go blind." The son says, "Dad, Dad, I'm over here."

Charlie loves to make fun of the Catholic Church, while letting his devotion to it shine through. He will use the sing-song singing of the priest with make believe words.

He's an advocate of the use of Latin in the Mass. He says, "Now that we use English, the Protestants know what we're doing. When we used Latin, they always lost at Bingo."

He'll spice his jokes with pithy comments like: "You better laugh because science has proven that people who don't laugh have a tendency to pass gas." Or, "Remember that it is a fact that one out of three people is not very smart. In fact, they are dumb. Now, look at the person on either side of you. One of the three is dumb."

It seems that every time I hear Charlie Prose he has a new stuttering joke. He's good at it. As a former stutterer I can appreciate how good he does it. Imagine the stuttering. A guy goes into a bar and asks for a whiskey. Another guy tells him he used to stutter but his wife cured him. How? With mad, passionate love making. He tells the first guy he ought to try it. A few days later he meets the same fellow in the bar and asks if he's been cured. "No," he says. "But you sure have a nice house."

Prose now has two grandchildren whom he dearly loves. He says, "Grandchildren are the reward we have for not killing our kids." He tells the kids that he and they have a common enemy, their mother. Then he will laugh and in a conspiratorial tone give the advice his "Poppa" gave him, "Never eat yellow snow." Don't forget that in between jokes he will sing and/or play the piano always verbally involving the members of his group.

Another favorite theme involves cruise ships. The statements that dumb people make: "Do members of the crew live aboard the ship?" "What time is the midnight buffet?" "What do they do with the ice shavings?" "Is there a buffet on the life boats?"

I love this one. A young boy asks his mother how old she is. She informs him that he should never ask a lady her age. When he informs a friend about this, the friend says he can have all the answers by looking at her driver's license. Upon getting it, he informs his mother that he knows she is thirty-one years old. Also she weighs one hundred twenty pounds. She's five feet six inches tall and has black hair. Then comes the kicker. "Also, I know why Dad left. You got an F in sex."

The main thing about Charlie Prose is his presentation. He's amiable and he projects warmth. His major theme throughout is, "We've got to laugh more. What our world needs is laughter." If you get a chance, try to hear Charlie Prose.

Amen. Selah. So be it.

CHILDREN

I recently read an item in a national church magazine. It had to do with the use of humor in the church. Sixty eight percent of the responders said it had a very great place. Thirty-two per cent said that sometimes there was a place.

Zero percent said rarely and zero said no place at all. The question then was asked, "Does humor make sermons more memorable?" Forty-three percent said they strongly agreed. Sixteen percent were neutral in their opinions and zero disagreed with the premise.

Joel Osteen, pastor of the largest Protestant church in the U.S. always begins his sermon with a joke. A recent story was about a pastor at the gate of heaven. He was given a plain cotton robe. Another man came up and was given a bright silken robe. When the pastor asked St. Peter why the disparity, he was told, "When you preached, people slept. But when that taxi driver drove, everyone prayed."

Many of the churches in the Inland Empire have an annual evening of Christian comedy. In La Mirada there is an agency called, Clean Comics of America. They book comics for churches. One sure evidence of the increase of humor in churches is the plethora in the last few years of books of clean jokes. Many of the books are directed to pastors.

The following items can be told in church. Many readers

have sent me prayers by kids. Dear God, Please put another holiday between Christmas and Easter. There is nothing good in there now. – Amanda

Dear God, I read the Bible. What does beget mean? Nobody will tell me. – Love, Alison

Dear God, I like the story about Noah the best of all of them. You really made up some good ones. I like walking on water, too. – Glenn.

Be careful about this one. This may come as a surprise to those of you not living in Las Vegas, but there are more Catholic churches there than casinos. Not surprisingly, some worshipers at Sunday services will give casino chips, rather than cash, when the basket is passed. Since they get chips from so many different casinos, the churches have devised a method to collect the offerings. The churches send all their collected chips to a nearby Franciscan Monastery for sorting and then the chips are taken to the casinos of origin and cashed in. Of course, this is done by a chip monk.

"Continuing education" squibs. Here are ten items.

1. Cats have over one hundred vocal sounds. Dogs only have about ten.
2. "Dreamt" is the only English word that ends in the letters "mt."
3. It's impossible to sneeze with your eyes open.
4. Leonard Da Vinci invented the scissors.

5. Maine is the only state whose name is just one syllable.
6. Peanuts are one of the ingredients of dynamite.
7. Rubber bands last longer when refrigerated.
8. The sentence: "The quick brown fox jumps over the lazy dog" uses every letter of the alphabet.
9. The words 'racecar,' kayak' and level' are the same whether they are read left to right or right to left (palindromes).
10. There are more chickens than people in the world.

Can blonde jokes be told in church? They can if an apology is offered first. Two blondes living in Oklahoma were sitting on a bench talking…one blonde says to the other: "Which do you think is farther away; Florida or the moon?" The other blonde turns and says, "Helloooooooo, can you see Florida?"

A police officer stops a blonde for speeding and asks her very nicely could he see her license. She replied in a huff, "I wish you guys would get your act together. Just yesterday you take away my license and then today you expect me to show it to you!"

But my favorite is a correspondence between George Bernard Shaw and Winston Churchill. George Bernard Shaw sent Winston Churchill a note inviting him to the first night performance of Saint Joan. He enclosed two tickets, "one for you and one for a friend if you have one." Expressing his regret at being unable to attend, Churchill replied, asking if it would be possible to have tickets for the second night…"if there is one."

Amen. Selah. So be it.

CHIMPANZEES

Many scientists, including neurobiologists and psychologists, believe that, "during the first years of life, the more than 100 billion neurons in our brains develop elaborate networks of connection with each other across junctions known as synapses."

The billions and billions of synapses are impossible to calculate. No wonder that the Psalmist (David) said, "We are fearfully and wonderfully made." Psalm 139:14.

Another translation states, "I will praise you, oh God, for I am awesomely made and wonderfully complex, with many parts, ideas, desires and beliefs."

Most humans, regardless of ethnic diversity, have the same physical characteristics. Which we may differ in moral values, social and cultural practices, all humans have them.

The best way to evaluate our complexities is to compare us with our closest living relations-chimpanzees. "The brain of a chimpanzee has a volume of 370ML on average." In contrast we humans, on average, have a brain average of 1350ML. Quite a difference. Brain size doesn't indicate much. Two other factors must be considered. First, our brains have a significantly higher brain surface. They are much more wrinkled. Second, humans have a much larger frontal lobe. This is where abstract and logical thought happens to be. Chimpanzees are not even close.

Chimpanzees are often confused with monkeys. They are NOT in the same family. They are in the great ape family, like orangutans and gorillas. There is only one species of human homo sapiens...you and me.

Among chimpanzees there are two species; the commonly known ones and the BONOBOS. "These two types of chimpanzees are completely different from each other." The bonobo is the more intelligent of the two. There are a number of characteristics that are different. It has been reputably reported that they have all but .025 percent DNA as humans.

It is unrealistic to use DNA analysis to prove similarities between two diverse objects. For example, "We have about half the same DNA as a banana, and yet people do not use this to emphasize how similar bananas are to us."

Studies have shown the high number of parallel activities each species has in common. Bonobos spend a great deal of time socializing. Much of it is grooming. Juvenile and adolescent chimps will often play by chasing and tickling each other.

Shows of affection are also common. Hugging and kissing is normal. Bonobos are especially frisky. Their mates are chosen and last a lifetime. Statistics also show a difference between two bonobos and humans above the number of close friends each has. Humans have between one hundred fifty and two hundred while bonobos have about fifty.

Interestingly, communication skills among chimpanzees

are complex. "They communicate verbally by using a variety of hoots, grunts, screams, pants, and other vocalizations." However, as with humans, their communications consist mainly of gesture and facial expressions. "Many of their facial expressions-surprise, grinning, pleading, and comforting are the same as those of humans."

Perhaps the most obvious similarity between bonobos and humans is the fact that both bipedal (they walk on two legs.) Also, the bonobos are long legged.

In following up on my initial belief about humans that God has made us "wonderfully complex," the meaning is that we are unique, different, diverse and special. Nowhere in recorded history is our nature and other complexities better described than in the Bible. In Genesis 1:27 it states that we "are created in the image of God." Then in the Book of Psalms, chapter 8:5; the writer tells us that, "we are created a little lower than the angels."

Then, in Romans 8:17, the Apostle Paul states, "we are the children of God." This is followed up with the words, "then heirs of God and joint-heirs with Christ." I can think of no other higher evaluation of who and what we are. No chimpanzee or bonobo is even close. We all are special in God's sight.

Amen. Selah. So be it.

CHRISTMAS TRADITIONS

I love the Christmas season. Mainly because I understand "the reason for the season" the birth of Jesus. It creates a different mood in the environment: excitement, happiness, joy, friendship, and celebration; all of them. Also it engenders a bit of humor and stimulating a lot of traditions.

Humor centers around children. A few years ago there was a large manger in the town square of a mid-western city: angels, shepherds, wise men, Mary, Joseph and the baby Jesus. Two days before Christmas the baby Jesus disappeared. Kidnapped.

On Christmas morning a six year old red haired boy was seen pulling a red wagon with baby Jesus in it. When asked "why", he said, "I promised Him that if I got a red wagon for Christmas I'd give Him a ride in it." The scene is a children's program with recitations. One four year old kid had a one liner. "He (Jesus) is the light of the world." He forgot it and his mother was seated in the first row. She whispered, "I am the light of the world." The little boy responded loudly, "My MOTHER is the light of the world."

Traditions come and go. But most Christmas traditions seemingly last forever. For instance, the importance of music; Christmas carols and cards. Many of them national or ethnic in origin. Handel's "Messiah" and "Joy to the World" from England. "Away in a Manger" by Martin Luther from Germany; "Silent

Night" and "O Come Let Us Adore Him" from Italy; "Hark! The Herald Angels Sing" by Charles Wesley from England. "O Little Town of Bethlehem" and "White Christmas" from the United States.

Santa Claus and gifts originated from St. Nicholas in Turkey and from Holland. Christmas trees started in Germany. The origin of names of the wise men, Caspar, Melchior and Balthazar, is unknown. From the White House Christmas Tree to community decorations and parades, traditions abound. In Redlands we have "The Feast of Lights" and a parade. Lights are everywhere.

Many churches present Handel's "Messiah" and others have Christmas Cantatas and programs. The Salvation Army always has the bell ringers and malls usually have a Santa Clause.

For years a friend of mine serves three kinds of soup- oyster, clam chowder and chili-to friends and neighbors on Christmas Eve. Stella and I always drive around to see the decorations on homes.

Just as all politics is local, so Christmas traditions. As a minister of a local church for twenty-two years, Christmas was always a high point. A Santa for the children to a manger scene, lights in the bay trees, votive lights along the sidewalks, and the sanctuary with poinsettias and trees. On Christmas Eve we had three services: 7:00 PM for the children's program, 9: 00 PM for the Chancel Choir, and 11:00 PM for worship and Holy Communion. Stella and I have our own traditions. Our home   is decorated the last of October to the 6th of January. We have a lighted tree, several nativity figures, door decoration and other Christmas items. This year we added a train set (to grant my wishes) in front of the TV. Stella has created a village inside the train tracks. For sixteen years we have had from 6-8 single seniors for Christmas Day dinner. I read the Christmas Bible story and we sing carols. Our family from thirty-five to forty-five gather on the Sunday before Christmas for dinner and gift exchanges.

Other traditions are a part of many families. Fruit Cake and eggnog is a must as well as watching Jimmy Stewart in "It's A Wonderful Life."

The big day for many Mexicans is "the day of the Kings", or January 6th . This is when gifts are given. It is celebrating the arrival of the wise men to visit the Christ child. The display of Christmas cards is also a very popular tradition. Christmas is also celebrated by watching Charles Dickens' "The Christmas Carol" featuring Scrooge.

A unique feature of most families, no matter how small the gift, is the giving gifts. When I was very young, my Dad opened a Christmas savings account for me of ten cents a week. At Christmas time I had $5.20 to buy gifts for family members. It became traditional.

I am a firm believer that each family should establish its own holiday traditions.   *Amen. Selah. So be it.*

CLEAN COMICS OF AMERICA

There is a national organization called, "Clean Comics of America." It is headquartered in La Mirada, California. Participants often have gigs at nightclubs on Saturday night and a church gig on Sunday. Their performance is the same...clean. Such an emphasis is not unusual considering the Bible's emphasis on humor, laughter and Joy.

Solomon, the writer of the Book of Proverbs, states, "A merry heart does good like a medicine; but a broken spirit dries the bones." (Proverbs 17:22) Again he says, "A merry heart makes a happy countenance." (Proverbs 15:13)

I love this phrase; "He that is of a happy heart has a continued feast." (Proverbs 15:15) Jesus himself said, "Be of good cheer. I have overcome the world." (John 16:33)

Here's a good story. Several elderly church members were being asked the secret of their longevity. "And why do you think God has permitted you to reach the age of ninety-two?" Without hesitation one sweet lady responded, "To test the patience of my relatives."

For those of us getting hard of hearing, consider this one. Three retirees, each with a hearing loss, were taking a walk one fine March day. One remarked to the other, "Windy, ain't it?" "No," the second man replied, "It's Thursday." And the third man chimed in, "So am I, let's have a Coke."

Time has a way of changing our perspectives. A pilot always looked down intently on a certain valley in the Appalachians. "What's so interesting about that spot?" asked a fellow pilot. "See that stream? Well, when I was a kid, I used to sit down there on a log, fishing. Every time an airplane flew over, I would look up and wish I were flying. Now I look down and wish I were fishing."

Since Stella and I spend considerable time on cruises (I'm a lecturer), I particularly liked this story. When a sudden storm blew up at sea, a young woman leaning against the ship's rail, lost her balance and was thrown overboard. Immediately another figure plunged into the waves beside her and held her up until a lifeboat rescued them. To everyone's astonishment the hero was the oldest man on the voyage-an octogenarian. That evening he was given a party in honor of his bravery. "Speech! Speech!" the other passengers cried. The old gentleman rose slowly and looked around at the enthusiastic gathering. "There's just one thing I'd like to know," he said testily. "Who pushed me?"

For those of you who are knowledgeable about Bible history you'll appreciate this one. A keen lover of rare books met an unbookish guy who had just thrown away an old Bible (packed away for generations in the attic of his ancestral home). "Somebody named Guten-something had printed it," he added. "Not Gutenberg!" gasped the book lover. "You've thrown away one of the very first books ever printed. One copy sold at auction recently for over $400,000." The other man, still unmoved, said, "Oh, my copy wouldn't have brought a dime-some fellow named Martin and Luther had scribbled notes all over it."

The afore mentioned comedian told this one the other night. A father calls home and gets the voice-softly-of his daughter. "Sally," he says, "Let me talk to your mother." She whispers back, "I can't." He hears noise in the background and asks who it is. "It's a policeman." He says, "Get him on the phone." "I can't," says Sally. The same thing happens with a fireman. Finally the father asks where she is. She informs him that she is in the closet. In response to his question of why she is there, she whispers the punch line. "They are looking for me."

An atheist professor was teaching a college class and he told the class that he was going to prove that there is no God. He said, "God, if you are real, then I want you to knock me of f this platform. I'll give you 15 minutes!" Ten minutes went by. He kept taunting God, saying, "Here I am, God. I'm still waiting." He got down to the last couple of minutes and a Marine just released from active duty, and newly registered in the class, walked up to the professor, hit him full force in the face, and sent him flying from his platform. The professor struggled up, obviously shaken and yelled, "What's the matter with you? Why did you do that?" The Marine replied, "God was busy; He sent me."

An elderly man was stopped by the police around

2a.m. and was asked by the officer where he was going at that time of night. The man replied, "Well, I'm on my way to a lecture about alcohol abuse and the effects it has on the human body; as well as smoking, and staying out late.

The officer then asked, "Really? And, who's giving that lecture at this time of night? The man replied, "That would be my wife."

Amen. Selah. So be it.

EXITING A GREAT PERFORMANCE

COMMUNICATE WITH HUMOR

One of the most effective methods of communication in conversation or public speaking is the use of humor. It can be used as an icebreaker in both. It can also be used as a vehicle for conveying ideas.

Occasionally I get a joke from the newspapers, magazines or television. However, the best source of humor is from other people. Many of my friends keep me well supplied. You need a minimal amount of Bible knowledge to understand the complete bit of humor.

An elderly lady was returning from an evening out and was distressed to see a burglar in her home. She yelled to him: "Acts 2:38."; the burglar froze. The lady dialed 911. When the burglar was taken away, the officer said to him, "I can't believe you let a little old lady stop you with a Bible verse. The burglar replied, "A Bible verse? I thought she had an axe and two 38 guns." Acts 2:38: "..Repent, in the name of Jesus Christ for the forgiveness of your sins;..."

Morris Schwartz is dying and is on his deathbed. He is with his nurse, his wife, his daughter and 2 sons, and knows the end is near. So he says to them: "Bernie, I want you to take the Beverly Hills houses." "Sybil, take the apartments over in Los Angeles Plaza." "Hymie, I want you to take the offices over in City Center." "Sarah, my dear wife, please take all the residential buildings downtown."

The nurse is just blown away by all this and as Morris slips away, she says to the wife, "Mrs. Schwartz, your husband must have been such a hardworking man to have accumulated so much property." Sarah replies, "Property shmoperty…the schmuck had a newspaper route."

One day a little girl was sitting and watching her mother do the dishes at the kitchen sink. She suddenly noticed that her mother had several strands of white hair sticking out in contrast on her brunette head. She looked at her mother and inquisitively asked, "Why are some of your hairs white, Mom?" Her mother replied "Well, every time that you do something wrong and make me cry or unhappy, one of my hairs turns white." The little girl thought about this revelation for a while and then said, "Mommy, how come ALL of grandma's hairs are white?"

Know it all teacher. The little girl was talking to her teacher about whales. The teacher said it was physically impossible for a whale to swallow a human because even though it was a very large mammal its throat was very small. The little girl stated that Jonah was swallowed by a whale. Irritated, the teacher reiterated that a whale could not swallow a human; it was physically impossible. The little girl said, "When I get to heaven I will ask Jonah." The teacher asked, "What if Jonah went to hell?" The little girl replied, "Then you can ask him."

I forget where and when I first heard the following joke,

but I laugh every time I think of it. The difference between the words "completed" and "finished" have been debated endlessly.

But at a recent conference in London, attended by some of the leading linguists in the world, Samsundar Balgobin, a Guyanese, came up with a winning solution. "When you marry the right woman; you are completed. But, when you marry the wrong woman; you are finished. And when the right one catches you with the wrong one, you are completely finished." His answer earned a standing ovation lasting more than five minutes.

One of my favorite jokes that I've told scores of times is about two sixty year olds; married for thirty years. They are walking together at the beach. Probably Huntington Beach. Accidently the husband kicks a bottle; it breaks and out pops a genii. He says, "I've been incarcerated in that bottle for four hundred years; you've set me free. I'm going to grant each of you one wish. Whatever you want." He turns to the sixty year old woman, married for thirty years. She says, "I've always wanted to be rich." The genii grants her a million dollars. He then turns to the sixty year old man, married thirty years, and asks what he wants. He replies, "I've always wanted to be married to a woman thirty years younger than myself." IMMEDIATELY, he was turned into a NINETY year old man.

Amen. Selah. So be it.

CONTENTION IS HUMOR FOUND

My contention is that humor is where you find it. The other night Larry King on CNN replayed an interview with Tip O'Neal, former Speaker of the House of Representatives.

He died in 1994 but left a legacy of Irish humor. A story about Henry Ford was one of his favorite stories. Ford was visiting a small town in Ireland and was approached by a committee requesting a donation. He wrote a check for $5,000.00. The next day the local newspaper came out with a huge headline: "Henry Ford donates $50,000.00 to our city."

The committee immediately went to Ford to apologize. Henry Ford asked for his check back and said, "How much would it take to build a hospital here?" The answer was, $50,000.00. His answer was, "I'll give you $50,000.00 if you honor one request." They agreed. His request was that above the door leading into the hospital would be the words, "I came among you and you took me in!" They had suckered him. They had conned him.

Most everyone interested in sports has heard of Bobby Knight. He's volatile, cantankerous and a great coach. He also holds grudges. His wife, Karen, has a favorite phrase that Bobby says she tells him. It is both humorous and meaningful. She says, "Bobby, the horse is dead, it's time to get off."

Many thanks to e-mail for this gem from Frank Melton. A married man left work early on Friday afternoon. Instead of going home, he spent his check on carousing at the local bar.

When he finally got home he was confronted by his angry wife. After a couple hours haggling she says, "How would you like it if you didn't see me for a couple of days?" He said, "That would suit me just fine." The next day came and went. He didn't see his wife. Another day passed with the same result. Then another day. Then the next day the swelling went down a bit and he could see her a little, just out of the corner of his left eye.

While visiting England George W. Bush was invited to tea with Queen Elizabeth. He's concerned about her leadership philosophy. She says it is to surround herself with intelligent people. He asks how she knows they are intelligent. "I do so by asking them the right question," says the Queen. She illustrates this theory by calling Tony Blair.

"Mr. Prime Minister, please answer this question: Your mother has a child and your father has a child, and this child is not your brother or sister. Who is it?" Tony Blair responds immediately "It's me, ma'am." "Correct. Thank you and good-bye sir," says the Queen. She hangs up and says, "Did you get that, Mr. Bush?" "Yes, your majesty. Thanks a lot. I'll definitely be using that technique."

Upon returning to Washington, President Bush presents the question to Jesse Helms. He stammers and asks for time to study. Finally after researching it without success, he asks Colin Powell. Powell immediately says, "It's me you dumb cracker."

Helms runs to the White House and triumphantly says, "Mr. President, I know the answer. It is Colin Powell." Bush looks at Helms and gives him that famous smart-ass disgusted grin and replies, "Wrong you dumb idiot, it's Tony Blair." Dumb blonde jokes are back in vogue again.

A blind man with his dog enter a bar and he sits on a stool. After sitting there for awhile, he asks if anyone would like to hear a dumb blonde joke. The bar becomes deathly quiet. In a husky voice, the woman next to him says: "Before you tell that joke, you should know something. The bartender is blonde, the bouncer is blonde and I'm a 6 foot tall, 200 pound blonde with a black belt in karate. What's more the woman sitting next to me is blonde and she's a weight lifter. The lady to your right is a blonde and she's a pro wrestler. Think about it seriously, Mister. You still wanna tell that joke?" The blind guy says, "Nah, not if I'm gonna have to explain it five times." Hooray for the prolific presence of humor.

Amen. Selah. So be it.

CREATION HUMOR

I've been writing the Laugh a Little, Live a Lot, column for about seven years. In that time one thing stands out. On the first day, God created the dog. God said, "Sit all day at the door of your house and bark at anyone who comes in or walks past. I will give you a lifespan of twenty years." The dog said, "That's too long to be barking. Give me ten years and I'll give you back the other ten." So God agreed.

On the second day, God created the monkey. God said, "Entertain people. Do monkey tricks and make them laugh. I'll give you a lifespan of twenty years." The monkey said, "How boring. Monkey tricks for twenty years? I don't think so. Dog gave you back ten; so that's what I'll do, too. OK?" And God agreed.

On the third day, God created the cow. God said, "You must go to the field with the farmer all day long and suffer under the sun, have calves and give milk to support the farmer. I will give you a lifespan sixty years." The cow said, "That's a tough life you want me to live for sixty years. Let me have twenty, and I'll give back the other forty and God agreed again. On the fourth day, God created man. God said, "Eat, sleep, play, many and enjoy your life. I'll give you twenty years."

Man said, "Only twenty years? Tell you what. I'll take my twenty as well as the forty the cow gave back, the ten the monkey gave back and the ten the dog gave back. That makes eighty."

"OK," God said. "You've got a deal."

That's why the first twenty years we eat, sleep, play and enjoy ourselves. For the next forty years we slave in the sun to support our family. Then, for the next ten years, we do monkey tricks to entertain the grandchildren. Our last ten years, we sit on the front porch and bark at everyone.

With millions of readers, I daily follow the humor of Dennis the Menace. I kept the squib from a week ago. Dennis is telling his father that his mother has given a demand. "Dad, mom wants to know about dinner. Thaw out, Take out or Go out?"

They are the five first place winners in the international Pun Contest. 1. A vulture boards an airplane, carrying two dead raccoons. The stewardess looks at him and says, "I'm sorry sir, only one carry on allowed per passenger." 2. Two fish swim into a concrete wall. The one turns to the other and says, "Dam." 3. Two Eskimos sitting in a kayak were chilly, so they let a fire in the craft. Unsurprisingly it sank, proving once again that you can't have your kayak and heat it too. 4. Two hydrogen atoms meet. One says "I've lost my electron." The other says "Are you sure?" The first replies "Yes, I'm positive." 5. Did you hear about the Buddhist who refused Novocain during a root canal? His goal; transcend dental medication.

Senior citizens are the nation's leading carriers of aids: HEARING aids, BAND aids, ROL aides, WALKING aids, MEDICAL aids, GOVERNMENT aids, and most of all

MONETARY aid to their kids.

A woman and her husband are in bed. She bemoans her physical appearance. "I'm getting old. My body is sagging. I have winkles. I'm overweight; and she moans on and on. Finally, she says, "Do you have a good word?" "Yes," he says. "You have 20/20 vision."

A drunken man, who smelled like beer, sat down on a subway seat next to a priest. The man's tie was stained, his face was plastered with red lipstick, and a half empty bottle of gin was sticking out of his torn coat pocket. He opened his newspaper and began reading. After a few minutes, the man turned to the priest and asked, "Say, Father, what causes arthritis?" The priest replied, "My son, it's caused by loose living; being with cheap, wicked women; too much alcohol; contempt for your fellow man; sleeping around with prostitutes; and lack of bathing." The drunk muttered in response, "Well, I'll be darned," then returned to his paper.

The priest, thinking about what he had said, nudged the man and apologized. "I'm very sorry. I didn't mean to come on so strong. How long have you had arthritis?' The drunk answered, "I don't have it, Father. I was just reading here that the Cardinal Mahoney has arthritis."

A young man wanted to get his beautiful blonde wife something nice for their first wedding anniversary. So he decides to buy her a cell phone. She is all excited, she loves her phone. He shows her and explains to her all the features on the phone.

The next day the blonde goes shopping. Her phone rings and it's her husband, "Hi hun," he says "how do you like your new phone?" She replies "I just love it, it's so small and your voice is as clear as a bell but there's one thing I don't understand though." "What's that, baby?" asks the husband. "How did you know I was at Wal-Mart?"

Amen. Selah. So be it.

CURTAIN RODS

Humor has many venues. It can be appreciated by way of cartoons, or puns, or one liners, or comedy sketches, or pantomimes, or a myriad of other ways. Shaggy dog stories are a favorite of mine. They just go on and on. I particularly like humorous stories with a concluding punch line.

This is the story of an ex-wife and her unfaithful husband. She sat down for the last time at their beautiful dining room table by candlelight, put on some soft background music, and feasted on a pound of shrimp, a jar of caviar, and a bottle of Chardonnay.

WHEN SHE HAD FINISHED, SHE WENT INTO EACH AND EVERY ROOM AND DEPOSITED A FEW HALF-EATEN SHRIMP SHELLS DIPPED IN CAVIAR, INTO THE HOLLOW OF THE CURTAIN RODS.

She then cleaned up the kitchen and left. When the husband returned with his new girlfriend, all was bliss for the first days. Then slowly, the house began to smell. They tried everything, cleaning, mopping and airing the place out. Vents were checked for dead rodents and carpets where steam cleaned. Air fresheners were hung everywhere.

Exterminators were brought in to set off gas canisters, during which they had to move out for a few days, and in the end they even paid to replace the expensive wool carpeting. Nothing worked. People stopped coming over to visit. Repairmen refused to work in the house. The maid quit. Finally, they could not take the stench any longer and decided to move. A month later even though they had cut their price in half, they could not find a buyer for their stinky house. Word got out, and eventually, even the local realtors refused to return their calls. Finally, they had to borrow a huge sum of money from the bank to purchase a new place.

The ex-wife called her ex-husband and asked how things were going. He told her the saga of the rotting house. She listened politely, and saw that she missed her old home terribly, and would be willing to reduce her divorce settlement in exchange for getting the house back.

Knowing his ex-wife had no idea how bad the smell was, he agreed on a price that was about one-tenth of what the house had been worth, but only if she were to sign the papers that very day. She agreed, and within the hour his lawyers delivered the paperwork.

A week later the man and his girlfriend stood smiling as they watched the moving company pack everything to take to their new home, INCLUDING THE CURTAIN RODS. I LOVE A HAPPY ENDING, DON'T YOU?

Since I do a lot of cruising as a lecturer I thoroughly enjoyed this one about a different kind of a retirement plan. About two years ago on a cruise through the western Mediterranean aboard a Princess liner, at dinner we noticed an elderly lady sitting alone along the rail of the grand stairway in the main dining room. I also noticed that all the staff, ships officers, waiters, busboys, etc., all seemed very familiar with this lady. I asked our waiter who the lady was expecting to be told she owned the line; but he said he only knew she had been on board for the last four cruises, back to back.

As we left the dining room one evening I caught her eye and stopped to say hello. We chatted and I said, "I understand you've been on this ship for the last four cruises." She replied, "Yes, that's true." I stated, "I don't understand?" She replied without a pause "It's cheaper than a nursing home."

Here's the proof- when I get old and feeble, I am going to get on a Princess Cruise Ship. The average cost for a nursing home is two hundred per day. I have checked on reservations at Princess and I can get a long term discount and senior discount price of one hundred thirty-five per day. That leaves sixty-five dollars a day for: 1. Gratuities which will only be ten dollars a per day. 2. I will have as many as ten meals a day if I can waddle to the restaurant, or I can have room service (which means I can have breakfast in bed every day of the week.) 3. Princess has as many as three swimming pools, a workout room, free washers and dryers, and shows every night. 4. They have free toothpaste and razors, and free soap and shampoo. 5. They will even treat you like a customer, not a patient. An extra five dollars worth of tips will have the entire staff scrambling to help you. 6. I will get to meet new people every seven or fourteen days. 7. TV broken? Light bulb need changing? Need to have the mattress replaced? No problem! They will fix everything and apologize for your inconvenience. 8, Clean sheets and towels every day, and you don't even have to ask for them. 9. If you fall in the nursing home and break a hip you are on Medicare. If you fall and break a hip on the Princess ship they will upgrade you to a suite for the rest of your life.

Now hold for the best! Do you want to see South America, the Panama Canal, Tahiti, Australia, New Zealand, Asia, or name where you want to go? Princess will have a ship ready to go. So don't look for me in a nursing home, just call shore to ship. P.S. And don't forget, when you die, they just dump you over the side at no charge.

Amen. Selah. So be it.

DEATH OF A JOKE

A recent newspaper article lamented the death of a humor staple. The death of the joke. Warren St. John, columnist, said, "The joke died recently after a long illness of thirty years. Its passing was barely noticed." There is little consensus among comics as to the cause of its death. Penn Jillette of Penn and Teller, world class magicians and comics in Las Vegas, attributes the death to political correctness.

Telling a joke is risky. Unless the applause is immediate, the comic is dead in the water. Short attention spans and our changing society has contributed to the death. One liners are the vogue. Along with observational humor. Comics like Steve Martin, Johnny Carson, Jon Stewart, Bill Mayer, Chris Rock and Robin Williams along with Jerry Seinfeld, all focused on observational and situational comedy.

Going back to the politically correct syndrome, no longer is it acceptable to tell ethnic jokes or sexually disparaging jokes. So much of the joke telling is off limits. Thus, its slow and insidious demise. I guess I'm a throwback to pre-historic days. I believe humorous jokes are still acceptable. Without using dirty words and sexually explicit punch lines.

Jeff Foxworthy is a well know humorist. From the South, he glibly defines what a Redneck is. You are one if: Your good deed for the month was hiding your brother for a few days. You've ever been accused of lying through your tooth. On stag night, you take a real deer. There is more oil in your baseball cap than in your car. You think a hot tub is a stolen bathroom fixture. Truckers tell your wife to watch her language. You have to take the entire day off work to get your teeth cleaned. You've ever been arrested for relieving yourself in an ice machine. You have lots of hubcaps in your house but none on your car.

Recently a friend shared this joke with me. An elderly man was sitting on a park bench. Across from him sat a young man, obviously the hippy type. Patched and ragged clothes. Tattoos and earrings in abundance. Above all a multi-colored hair do. It was predominantly purple and spiked. The old man was intensely gazing at the young man. Nervously he says, "What are you looking at, old man?" He replies, "Well, many years ago I made love to a peacock and I thought you might be my son."

I heard this one on TV the other day. An oldie but goodie. A couple had been married for sixty years. When the man was asked the key to his harmonious marriage he told this story. "After the ceremony we left in a horse drawn carriage. The horse balked. She got out and shook her finger at the horse and said, 'That's one. ' This happened two more times. Then she took a gun and shot the horse and killed it. I remonstrated with her as to why she did it. She then turned to me and said, 'That's one. ' We never had another argument."

Exercise is in. It is the most popular sport in the USA.

This is my favorite story. I just came across this exercise suggested for seniors, to build muscle strength in the arms and shoulders. It seems so easy, so I thought I'd pass it on to some of my friends. The article suggested doing it three days a week. Just don't overdo it.

Begin by standing on a comfortable surface, where you have plenty of room at each side. With a five pound potato sack in each hand, extend your arms straight out from your sides, and hold them there as long as you can. Try to reach a full minute, then relax. Each day, you'll find that you can hold this position for just a bit longer.

After a couple of weeks, move up to ten pound potato sacks. Then fifty pound potato sacks. And eventually try to get to where you can lift a hundred pound potato sack in each hand and hold your arms straight for more than a full minute.

After you feel confident at that level, put a potato in each of the sacks. If you don't get and appreciate the following story, check your I.Q. An elderly couple were celebrating their sixtieth anniversary. The couple had married as childhood sweethearts and had moved back to their old neighborhood after they retired. Holding hands they walked back to their old school. It was not locked, so they entered,. And found the old desk they'd shared, where Andy had carved "I love you, Sally."

On their way back home, a bag of money fell out of an armored car, practically landing at their feet. Andy quickly picked it up, but not sure what to do with it, they took it home. There, he counted the money- fifty thousand dollars. Sally said, "We've got to give it back." Andy said, "Finders keepers." He put the money back in the bag and hid it in their attic.

The next day, two FBI men were canvassing the neighborhood looking for the money, and knocked on the door. "Pardon me, but did either of you find a bag that fell out of an armored car yesterday?" Andy said, "No." Sally said, "He's lying. He hid it up in the attic." Andy said, "Don't believe her she's getting senile." The agents turn to Sally and began to question her. One says, "Tell us the story from the beginning." Sally said, "Well, Andy and I were walking home from school yesterday ... "The first FBI guy turns to his partner and says, "We're outta here."

Amen. Selah. So be it.

DEPRESSION

Some years ago I read an account from Dallas, Texas. A multi-millionaire had hired the research firm of Funk and Gipson to investigate the cases of emotionally and mentally ill patients. They were to search for a common denominator in the attitudes of the patients. After months of study they came up with a conclusion. The vast majority of the mentally and emotionally ill patients had attitudes of RESENTMENT or UNFORGIVENESS. It is common knowledge among therapists that depression is the main presenting problem by prospective clients. It is also the condition that prompts psychiatrists to provide prescription drugs.

The obvious conclusion is that there is a relationship between clinical depression and resentment and an attitude of unforgiveness. Depression destroys happiness and optimal living. It corrodes the soul. It affects the health of the body. This truth was realized as the result of the conflict of the views between Rene Decartes and Hans Selye, M.D.1907-1982

Descartes 1596 - 1650, the father of the Cartesian Philosophy, lived many years before Selye. In fact 257 years. The Cartesian view was that there was no connection between the mind and the body. In other words, depression had no effect on the physical organism. On the other hand, Selye proved that worry/depression affects the endocrine system, which in turn causes ulcers.

Modern medicine was the by-product of Decartes' view until Hans Selye came along. Our modern doctors have finally learned. There is a connection between the mind and the body. Through the years as a minister and a therapist I've known several people whose lives were dominated by the negative emotions of resentment and unforgiveness. Usually they were vindictive and motivated for revenge. The consequences were inevitably detrimental to the person.

Aaron Burr was born in 1756 and died in 1836 at age eighty. Full of promise, he became Vice-President with Thomas Jefferson When he killed Alexander Hamilton in a duel, his fortunes went downhill. His bitterness and failures followed him to the grave.

Jesus was tortured and suffered. He was hanged on the cross; an innocent. Yet, He said, "Father forgive them." He refused to be controlled by bitterness.

Depression has been defined as "internalized anger." The same definition can be applied to bitterness, only it is more obvious in its anger.

The book "Unbroken" is the story about Louie Zamperini. Shot down by the Japanese in World War II, he was captured and tortured for over two years. After his return to the U.S. he became a Christian. Shortly thereafter, he contacted his previous captors and went to Japan and, believe it or not, told them he forgave them for what they did to him. He currently is ninety-six years old.

Previously he was severely depressed, but no more. No anger or vindictiveness. An unbroken man.

The story of Mary Decker Slaney is remarkable. For many years she was a world class runner. In fact, today at age fifty-five she still holds three major distance records-the mile, the 1.500 meters and the 3000 meters races. She was tripped in the 1984 Olympics in L.A. and was unable to compete. Depressed, angry and she was mocked and ridiculed. But a major change, probably religious turned her around. Today she is a mother, a wife, a farmer and happy.

Thomas Edison is known for his many successes, mainly the light bulb. Prior to that he failed a thousand times. His failures did not stop him. Neither did his dyslexia. He refused to succumb to depression and bitterness.

Oprah Winfrey is one of the richest women in the world. In the beginning she was often fired and was told she was not fit for TV. But it did not stop her. She never gave into bitterness or depression and went on to prove her critics were wrong.

There is a basic answer to depression and negative thoughts. NEVER Quit.

Amen. Selah. So be it.

DIFFERENCES

Literature is filled with human conflicts and in particular, differences of opinions. Sometimes they end in violent disagreements. The Bible tells of Cain and Abel. Their differences ended with Cain killing Abel.

Julius Caesar and Brutus disagreed and Brutus stabbed Caesar. Political differences often end in violence. Abraham Lincoln and John F. Kennedy are tragic examples.

The high number of homicides annually in San Bernardino verifies the truth of this observation. Child abuse and spousal abuse are usually preceded by differences of opinion.

Several years ago I wrote a poem I called, "La Differencia."

> I heard a phrase the other day
> That speaks to me so plainly.
> "Neither am I right nor are you wrong,
> It's simply this, we're different."
> How easy it is for me to say,
> That what I do is right.
> Or what you say is always wrong.
> No matter what I think.
> You live slowly, I live fast, I like this and
> you like that.
> Neither am I right nor are you wrong.

It's simply this, we're different.

More years than I would like to think about, a history professor in graduate school made a comment I've never forgotten. He said, "More wars have been fought, more men and women have been killed, more devastation has been resulted from RELIGION than any other reason. Unfortunately religion is the cause for more disagreements between people; more differences among groups, more couples breaking up than for any other reason. Religion.

The issues are clear cut. Consider the hundreds of religions in the world today. The thousands of denominations in existence. The millions of independent members with different opinions Agreement on anything would be near to impossible.

I heard a Bible scholar the other day discussing the greatest miracles in the Bible. His conclusion was recorded in the Book of Acts when it says there were 120 believes in one place, ALL IN ONE ACCORD. A famous Jewish one liner is that whenever two Jews get together, there are always at least 3-5 opinions.

I've been teaching a class on the history of the Bible for thirty-eight years. In the last fifty years great strides have been made in the field. For example the discovery of the Nag Hammadi Scrolls (1945) in Egypt and the Dead Sea Scrolls (1947) in Israel have brought significant information about the history of the Bible.

Archaeology and Science have also added much information to the Biblical translations. Just within the last twenty-five years a plethora of credible scholars have written valuable books. Scholars like Elaine Pagels, James Robinson, Dominic Crossan, Bart Ehrman, Marcus Borg and Bishop John Shelby Spong to name a few.

Two good examples. Recently the dissertation of Dr. Gordon Hynes (Ph.D.) professor at Redlands University for many years was brought to light. In it he catalogued over two hundred examples that the Apostle Paul took from Greek philosophers and poets in his writings. They are either exact words or paraphrased.

The second discovery concerns Universalism, meaning that every person will be saved. The early Patristic Fathers like Origen and Ireneas believed it. It wasn't until the advent of Augustine that the concept of "hell" was introduced. Most of the writings of the Fathers are now available. Both subjects are subject to strong disagreements. I have three basic principles that 1 try to live by. First, as much as possible to "agree to disagree." This is based on respect for the other person. Stella and I have ten very, very good friends with whom we could not disagree with more. Yet, we have lunch with them regularly. We do respect them and their opinion. If the discussion is controversial my second rule is: "Others are entitled to their opinions, but NOT to their own set of facts." Neither am I.

Years ago when I was doing graduate work for my Ph.D. in Humanistic Psychology, a professor gave the class some good advice. He said that when counseling someone: 1) Never tell them what to believe; 2) Never tell them who to vote for, 3) Never tell them how to make love, 4) Never tell anyone how to play golf. Generally I've been successful in three of these. I've miserably failed with one.

Amen. Selah. So be it.

TWO COMICS SWAP JOKES

DR. DEWEY JACOBS

Dr. Dewey Jacobs, Ph.D. psychologist is one of the leading researchers in the USA on the causes and cures for addictions-all kind. He lectures throughout the country and writes extensively on his studies. For many years he directed the Psychology Department at the VA hospital in Loma Linda.

He told me the other day of a program he and his staff initiated there a few years ago. Its focus was those suffering from chronic pain. Veterans of all gender and races were there. The preferred method of treatment was shots and alternative drugs.

His staff developed what is called " psychological intervention." The regular interns with their "shots" were prohibited from entering the chronic pain ward. The process included information about pain and ploys or ruses to get the minds of the patients away from their pain. After a few weeks the results were amazing. Recidivism was negligible.

This is the same process with a major difference that was advocated by Norman Cousins years ago. The intervention used by him and Drs. Han and Berk at Loma Linda, NOW, is humor.

Laughter stimulates the secretion of endorphins from the brain. They have the same molecular arrangement as morphine; a pain killer. Laughter is intervention. The purpose of this article and others like it is to LAUGH A LITTLE AND LIVE A LOT.

Blondes are still in. Two blondes were walking to work.

One looks down and sees a compact. She opens it and explains to her fellow blonde, as she looks at the mirror, "My, this person sure looks familiar." Her friend takes the compact and says, "Certainly, you silly blonde. It's me." Laugh a little.

A young redhead goes into the doctor's office and says that her body hurts wherever she touches it. "That's strange," says the doctor. "Show me." She takes her finger and pushes her elbow and screams in agony. She pushes her knee and screams, then pushes her ankle and screams. Everywhere she touches makes her scream. The doctor then asks, "You're not really a redhead, are you? "No," she says, "I'm actually a blonde." "I thought so," the doctor says. "Your finger is broken." Laugh a little bit more. Fifteen minutes into the flight from Kansas City to Toronto, the captain announced,

"Ladies and gentlemen, one of our engines has failed. There is nothing to worry about. Our flight will take an hour longer than scheduled, but we still have three engines left." Thirty minutes later the captain announced, "One more engine has failed and the flight will take an additional two hours. But don't worry, we can fly just fine on two engines." An hour later the captain announced, "One more engine has failed and our arrival will be delayed another three hours. But don't worry, we still have one engine left." A young blonde passenger turned to the man in the next seat and remarked, "If we lose one more engine, we'll be up here all day! "

A woman, calling a local hospital, said, "Hello, I'd like to talk with the person who gives the information regarding your patients. I'd like to find out if the patient is getting better, or doing as expected, or is getting worse." The voice on the other end of the line said, "What is the patient's name and room number?" She said, "Sarah Finkel, in Room 302." "I will connect you with the nursing station." "3-A Nursing Station. How can I help you?" "I would like to know the condition of Sarah Finkel in Room 302." "Just a moment. Let me look at her records. Oh, yes. Mrs. Finkel is doing very well. In fact, she's had two full meals, her blood pressure is fine, her blood work just came back as normal, she's going to be taken off the heart monitor in a couple of hours and if she continues this improvement, Dr. Cohen is going to send her home Tuesday at twelve o'clock. " The woman said, "Thank God! That's wonderful! Oh! That's fantastic ... that's wonderful news!"" The nurse said, "From your enthusiasm, I take it you must be a close family member or a very close friend!" "Not exactly, I'm Sarah Finkel in 302! Nobody here tells me anything."

A priest and a rabbi were sitting next to each other on an airplane. After a while, the priest turned to the rabbi and asked, "Is it still a requirement of your faith that you not eat pork?"" The rabbi responded, "Yes, that is still one of our laws." The priest then asked, "Have you ever eaten pork?" The rabbi replied, "Yes, on one occasion I did succumb to temptation and tasted a ham sandwich." The priest nodded in understanding and went on with his reading. A while later, the rabbi spoke up and asked the priest, "Father, is it still a requirement of your church that you remain celibate?" The priest replied, "Yes, that is still very much a part of our Faith." The rabbi then asked him if he had ever fallen to the temptations of the flesh. The priest replied, "Yes rabbi, on one occasion." The rabbi nodded understandingly and remained silent for about five minutes. Finally, the rabbi said: "Beats the heck out of a ham sandwich, doesn't it?"

Amen. Selah. So be it.

DR. LEE BERK

A few years ago I had the opportunity to interview Dr. Lee Berk, M.D. in the department of Psychoneuroimmunology at Loma Linda Medical School. They were researching Gel otology- the study of laughter. Along with several other universities in the USA, the study is focusing on strengthening the immune system through humor and laughter.

Several people participated in the research. First of all a blood baseline was established indicating the number of white blood cells, which determines the strength of immunity.

After a relaxation process and directed hypnosis with words and films, the participants' blood samples were taken. The first sample was taken after negative pictures of crime, death and trauma were shown. The result was startling. The white blood cells had a decided DECREASE. This was followed with the opposite. Positive, humorous events and upbeat words and films were shown. The results were significant. In each case the white blood count was INCREASED. The study, beyond doubt, proves the healthy benefits of laughter. Humor, dating back to Hippocrates, has been an essential ingredient for better and longer living.

Here are two from a friend in Arizona. This has to be one of the best singles ads ever printed It is reported to have been listed in The Atlanta Journal. SINGLE BLACK FEMALE seeks male companionship, ethnicity unimportant. I'm a very good looking girl who LOVES to play. I love long walks in the woods, riding in your pickup truck, hunting, camping, and fishing trips, cozy winter nights lying by the fire. Candlelight dinners will have me eating out of your hand. I'll be at the front door when you get home from work; wearing only what nature gave me. Call (404) 875-6420 and ask for Daisy, I'll be waiting ...Over fifteen thousand men found themselves talking to the Atlanta Humane Society about an 8-week-old black Labrador retriever.

A blonde calls Delta Airlines and asks, "Can you tell me how long will it take to fly from San Francisco to New York City?" The agent replies, "Just a minute..." "Thank you," the blonde says, and hangs up.

Blonde stories are still popular. A blonde was seen by her neighbor going out to her mailbox repeatedly during the day. Curiosity finally got the best of her. She asked the blonde why the strange behavior. Her answer is classic blonde: "I keep reading on my computer that I've got mail."

Thanks to Loretta for this blonde story. A blonde who suspects her boyfriend of cheating on her goes out and buys a gun. She goes to his apartment unexpectedly, opens the door, and, sure enough, finds him naked in the arms of a redhead. Well, now she's angry. She opens her purse and takes out the gun. But as she does so, she is overcome with grief and points the gun at her own head. The boyfriend yells, "No, honey, don't do it." "Shut up," she says. "You're next."

Joel Osteen, pastor of America's largest evangelical church begins each sermon with a humorous event. The other week he told this one. A preacher takes a Sunday off to go bear hunting. After several hours of futile hunting he sits down exhausted. Suddenly a bear appears and starts chasing him. Almost exhausted he begins praying. "Oh, God, please convert that bear before it catches me and I'm gone." The bear stops short and begins to pray. "Oh, God, I thank you for this food I'm about to eat."

In the past I've repeated several jokes about President Clinton. Here's one about President George Bush. It seems Mr. Rumsfeld came rushing into a Cabinet meeting and said, "Mr. President, word has been received that three Brazilians were killed." The President lets out a groan, bows his head, obviously in remorse, and prays. Following this episode he hesitantly asks Mr. Rumsfeld, "How many is a bazillion?"

Here's one from a friend. The minister was passing a group of young teens sitting on the church lawn and stopped to ask what they were doing. "Nothing much, Pastor," replied one boy. "We were just seeing who can tell the biggest lie about their sex life." "Boys, boys, and boys!" he scolded. "I'm shocked. When I was your age, I never even thought about sex." In unison they all replied, " "YOU WIN!"

Amen. Selah. So be it.

EARLY CHURCH

Those of you who have some kind of Christian background will be interested in this article. Recently I was doing some research on the Early Church.

In particular the time between 100 A.D. and the Council of Nicea in 325 A.D. I was struck with the pattern of worship by the early Christians. They worshiped the first day of the week, which was Sunday. They did not use the cross as a symbol of any kind, It was viewed as an instrument of death. Psalms were sung, the Sacrament of Communion was observed and the Lord's Prayer was recited.

Now get this. These were followed with eating of food. Somewhat like the old fashioned Southern "dinner on the grounds." Then the group of Christians would engage in dancing. I kid you not about what they did next. The group would engage in telling jokes. That's right. Sharing humorous stories.

A theological rationale for this was viewing the resurrection as a joke on Satan. He thought everything ended with Good Friday. The joke was on the Devil. Since then we've strayed a long way. Humor in the Church is often frowned upon. Jokes and laughter are often viewed as worldly or sinful. I'm not talking about dirty or suggestive stories, but good wholesome jokes.

Here's a good one. Mary was married to a male chauvinist. They both worked full time, but he never did anything around the house. He declared housework was for women. But one evening she came home and the children were bathed, dinner was fixed and the house was clean with flowers on the table. It turned out Charley had read a magazine article that suggested wives would be more romantically inclined if they weren't so tired from having to do all the housework. The next day she couldn't wait to tell her girlfriends at the office. "How did it work out?" they asked. "Well, Charley cleaned up, helped the kids with their homework and folded the laundry." They wanted to know about the romance. "It didn't work out," Mary said. "Charley was so tired he went to sleep before I could get to bed."

I love this blonde joke. It seems a blonde stopped at a gas station to fill her car with gas. Unfortunately she locked her keys in the ignition. Getting a coat hanger from the attendant she worked diligently to hook the door handle and open the door. Her efforts were futile. Finally, another blonde inside the car yelled, "Move the hanger a little more to the right."

If you don't laugh at this one, check your laugh meter—it's broken. Many thanks to Frank. A mother was packing desperately to leave on vacation. Her three year-old daughter was playing on the bed. At one point she said, "Mommy look at this," and stuck out two of her fingers. Her mother reached out and stuck her fingers in her mouth and said, "Mommy's gonna eat your fingers! " and pretended to eat them. She ran outside again and when she returned, her daughter was standing on the bed staring at her fingers with a devastated look on her face. "What's wrong, honey?" She replied, ' ""What happened to my booger?"

I love this bit of basic philosophy. Read it slowly. When white man found this land, Indians were running it.

No taxes . ... .

No debt .... .

Plenty buffalo ... .

Plenty beaver ... .

Women did most of the work ....

Medicine man free ... .

Indian men hunted and fished all the time .. .. .

White man dumb enough to think he could improve system like that.

I heard this one so many years ago it has been recycled. A women checks with the local newspaper about an obituary notice for her recently deceased husband. She is informed that the cost would be 50 cents a word. She thinks about it and says, "Let it read, Fred Brown died." Amused at the women's thought, the editor tells her that there is a seven word minimum for all obituaries. She thinks about it and quickly says "O.K. in that case, let it read, "Fred Brown died; golf clubs for sale."

Amen. Selah. So be it.

EDMUND BURKE

Edmund Burke (1729-1797) supported the American Revolution and was against the French Revolution. A native of Ireland, he early on moved to England where he served in Parliament and was a member of the Whigs political party. He is often referred to as the father of conservatism. Burke is most noted for his statement: "All that is necessary for the triumph of evil is that good men do nothing." While his words are fraught with great danger and suspicion, they are also words to inspire and motivate both men and women into action.

The option to the Edmund Burke view of doing nothing is so common place, it hardly merits mentioning. However, I will. It is the position of pacification or compromise by placating. An example. A few years ago I represented a group before the Board of an important organization. The group was being assessed an additional fee for an unfair charge. Seniors are often taken advantage of. I lost the case. As I walked out of the meeting, the Board Chairman caustically said to me, "The Board does exactly what I tell them to do." I was offended, not by the statement, but by the indifferent attitude of the Board members.

Burke would be appalled today by the indifference of the media: TV, radio or newspapers to many issues. For example our economy is in bad shape. It really is a trickle down economy. And, little attention is given to it. It has been five years since many workers received a pay increase. And yet, a city in the Inland Empire had a City Council vote themselves a 5% pay raise and the city employees a 2% raise. Again, little attention by the media.

Not a word of protest that I know of. The injustice is apparent. A recent study has revealed that there are many rich politicians in all levels of government. I first met an Inland Empire man thirty-five years ago. He had a small business with a small income. Recently he retired from Congress as a millionaire. In Congress, according to recent survey, there are 299 Representatives and 49 Senators that are multi-millionaires. Oh, where are you Edmund Burke?

Our government in Washington, D.C. goes by a misnomer …A Democracy. We are not. We are a Republic. There is a huge difference. Both are governments by the people. But in reality in a Democracy fifty-one percent of the people can put forty nine percent to death. In a Republic, the major concern is for the minorities. The handicapped, gays, blacks, Hispanics, elderly, children, poor, sick (ill), etc.

I'm an admirer of Pope Francis. His emphasis is to implement concerns for the disenfranchised. It is reported that when his best friend in Argentina greeted the Pope, he whispered into his ear, "Don't forget the poor."

In responding to Burke's insight it is important to evaluate the source and the determination of political decisions. The fourth ESTATE IS OFTEN BLAMED FOR MOST ACTIONS. What is it? The press or the media. What are the other three?

France is given credit for the original description. Namely: First is Clergy; Second is Nobility; Third is Commoners and Fourth the Press. However, recently the categories have changed. First is RELIGION; Second is WALL STREET; Third is LOBBYISTS and Fourth is the MEDIA, TV, RADIO, INTERNET and NEWSPAPERS.

Have any of these "estates" influenced the government nationally or even locally? Absolutely. Let's take them from the beginning. Number one; Harriet Beecher Stowe" s book (Uncle Tom's Cabin) provoked the Civil War. Both Jews and Christians (Martin Luther King, Jr.) were at the heart of the Civil Rights movement. Number two; Wall Street and deregulation is directly influencing Congress. Significantly influencing the economy. Number three is in the hundreds. Three of the leading ones are the NRA (guns), AARP (seniors) and the Israelis. All three are extremely powerful and spending huge amounts of money to influence legislation. Number four is not as subtle as the previous three. Talk radio, columnists and Cable TV are geared to influence all elected officials. Rush Limbaugh, Bill O'Reilly, Chris Matthews, Rev. Al Sharpton, Rachael Maddow, to name a few. Newspaper columnists are too many to mention outside of George Will.

Each of us must decide how we will respond to Edmund Burke's statement. *Amen. Selah. So be it.*

ENJOY SIT-DOWN COMEDY

I enjoy doing sit-down comedy. In fact, I've been doing it for about ten years. During the first few minutes I usually relate the results of a research group.

To maintain optimal health and a strong mental and emotional attitude, we need two things. First, each of us needs four hugs per day. This creates warmth, identity and a sense of belonging. Second, each of us needs to have fifteen laughs per day. This should not be so difficult. Studies have shown the average child of two or three years old laughs at least fifteen times each waking hour.

A few weeks ago Stella and I went on a two week bus trip to the National Parks of the west. Fifty percent of the bus was made up of travelers from England. They exhibited their usual stoical attitude and lack of a sense of humor. Believe me, I tried to get them to laugh. Their ho-hum response was certainly discouraging. Obviously this limited my source for fifteen laughs per day. This absence for two weeks contributed to my subsequent illness. I'm better now. I've been laughing more. Louise contributed to this by mailing me ten things to think about. CHILDREN:

1. You spend the first two years of their lives teaching them to walk and talk. Then you spend the next sixteen telling them to sit down and

shut-up.

2. Grandchildren are God's reward for not killing your children.

3. Cleaning your house while your kids are still growing is like cleaning the driveway before it has stopped snowing.

4. There is only one pretty child in the world and every mother has it.

5. Mothers of teens know why animals eat their young.

6. I asked mom if I was a gifted child .... She said they certainly wouldn't have paid for me.

7. Children are natural mimics, who act like their parents despite every effort to teach them good manners.

8. Children seldom misquote you. In fact, they usually repeat word for word what you shouldn't have said.

9. The main purpose of holding children's parties is to remind yourself that there are children more awful than your own.

10. We child proofed our home three years ago and they' re still getting in. Thank you, Louise.

Four year old Joey was eating a hot dog when he dropped it on the floor. He quickly picked it up and was about to take another bite when his mom said, "No, Joey, you can't eat that now, it has germs." Joey pondered the thought a moment and replied, "Jesus, germs and Santa Claus-that's all I ever hear and I haven't seen one of them yet."

"The Joys of Womanhood." One of life's mysteries is how a two pound box of candy can make a woman gain five pounds. The best way to forget all your troubles is to wear tight shoes. Amazing! You hang something in your closet for a while and it shrinks two sizes.

I gave up jogging for my health when my thighs kept rubbing together and setting my pantyhose on fire. Just when I was getting used to yesterday, along came today.

Where have all the good roadside signs gone? Remember these Burma Shave ones? The midnight ride of Paul for beer led to a warmer Hemisphere. Around the curve lickety-split, It's a beautiful car Wasn't it? Passing a school zone, Take it slow let our little Shavers grow. Don't lose your head To gain a minute. You need your head your brains are in it.

Here are a few Murphy's laws:

1. Light travels faster than sound. This is why some people appear bright until you hear them speak. 2. Change is inevitable, except from a vending machine. 3. Those who live by the sword get shot by those who don't. 4. Nothing is foolproof to a sufficiently talented fool. 5. The 50-50-90 rule: Anything you have is a 50-50 chance of getting something right, there's 90%

probability you'll get it wrong. 6. If you lined up all the cars in the world end to end, someone would be stupid enough to try to pass them, five or six at a time, on a hill, in the fog. 7. The things that come to those who wait will be the scraggly junk left by those who got there first. 8. The shinbone is a device for finding furniture in a dark room. 9. A fine is a tax for doing wrong. A tax is a fine for doing well. 10 When you go into court, you are putting yourself into the hands of twelve people who weren't smart enough to get out of jury duty.

Amen. Selah. So be it.

EUGENICS

Eugenics is a very strange word. It came into prominence several years ago and then faded away. However, it has achieved recent prominence because of a paper written by a Harvard University scholar. His basic theory is that blacks, Hispanics and other minorities are mentally inferior to Caucasians-whites.

Martin Kramer is Senior Fellow at the Salem Center in Jerusalem and a faculty member at Harvard University. His basic proposal was to limit the births of "superfluous young men" among Palestinians in Gaza. Palestinians called his proposal "an incitement for genocide." Students at Harvard have argued that "such racist ideas had no place at their University." U.S. national television had a field day with Kramer's' viewpoints for several weeks. The subject of eugenics is a popular source of discussion in Israel. In general it relates to Arabs and Palestinians in particular.

Hitler was blamed for establishing human breeding farms for "Aryans." "In the 1930's and 1940' s, the Nazis developed large scale sterilization and euthanasia programs for the mentally and physically disabled." Death camps for races they believed were "genetically inferior" were sent to the death camps. Over nine million Jews, Gypsies, Masonic Lodge members, were among those killed.

It was in the 1920's that America experimented with

genetics as a "tool" for social change. The United States became the world center of eugenic study and social policy. Amazingly, "from 1907-1960 more than 100,000 innocent Americans were sterilized in more than thirty states."

After World War II, the eugenic movement fell into disfavor. However, a few splinter groups like neo-Nazis, KKK and a few religious radicals continued spreading the eugenic philosophy. A key spokesman was Stanford University physicist William Shockley. He suggested offering cash incentives to people with low IQ scores who would agree to sterilization. Professor Shockley was a Noble Laureate and an acknowledged racist. In spite of this he was responsible for the resurrection of the new eugenics movement.

On September 21 , 1975 the New York Times Magazine reported an amazing account. They reported that doctors in major cities "were routinely performing hysterectomies" on mostly black welfare recipients as a form of sterilization." These operations were referred to as "Mississippi Appendectomies." There is another word that is close to eugenics-genocide.

When Hitler and his Nazis committed genocide, Stalin was a close second. He slaughtered millions of Jews, Germans, Polish and dissident Russians.

Historical anthropologists say that in the early 1500's there were twenty-two million Indians in Mexico. By 1600 there were only two million. Some were victims of venereal disease spread by Cortez and his men. Others were slaughtered by his soldiers. Eugenics under the guise of religion.

Recently a Bible scholar calculated the number of people killed by the Jews after their slavery in Egypt. His number was ten million. All supposedly under the command of Jehovah.

One of the worst eugenic/genocidal atrocities was Armenian victims by the Turks from 1915-1923. One and a half million Armenians were killed in concentration camps out of a total of two and a half million Armenians in the Ottoman Empire. THESE FEW EXAMPLES ARE ONLY A DROP IN THE BUCKET. THERE ARE HUNDREDS THAT HAVE OCCURRED IN THE LAST TWO CENTURIES.

Martin Kramer is a blight on the ethical values of our nation. But he is not alone. A few years ago there was a talk show host on KFI in LA who advocated that whenever any man or woman reached the age of sixty-five, they should be euthanized.

Well bodied as well as the sick, disabled, blind, deaf and crippled. Eugenics and genocide are both evils that need to be expunged from all societies.

Amen. Selah. So be it.

FAMOUS JOKERS

H. L. Mencken, one of the best newspaper columnist's whoever wrote, said, "The Puritans were deathly afraid that there might be a Christian somewhere who was happy. He is also credited with saying that most Christians acted as of they were suffering from hemorrhoids or ulcers.

E. Stanley Jones, the great Methodist missionary to India described Christians as either looking like they had swallowed a rain cloud or a rainbow.

Nietzsche, the philosopher and Christian critic said of Jesus, "Would that Jesus had learned to live and to love the earth- and laughter too."

In 1964 Elton Trueblood noted professor at Elmhurst College and prolific writer, published a most unusual book, "The Humor of Christ." In his preface he bemoans the absence of Bible scholars who avoid a happy or laughing Jesus. A basic reason is probably that Jesus was dealing with serious subjects and the crisis of His crucifixion. He is concerned about "freeing the Gospel from the excessive sobriety that is often emphasized by believers." For him, Jesus was not always engaged in pious talk.

Jesus "use of irony and sarcasm and prolific use of paradox should awaken us to His use of humor." In *Matthew 6:16* we are told, "Do not look dismal." A strong argument that Trueblood uses is about Jesus and children. They surrounded Him and He challenged the disciples to "forbid them not (to come to Him) for of such was the Kingdom of heaven."

A recent study in Psychology Today states that children laugh on the average of 15-20 times an hour. Obviously children would not have been attracted to Jesus if He was always solemn and frowning.

Timothy Freke and Peter Gandy recently wrote a book, "The Laughing Jesus." The reference is taken from the Gospel of Thomas in the Nag Hammadi scrolls.

Jesus did more than hob-nob with sinners; He laughed with them also. This story is one that Jesus would have roared at. One winter morning a couple was listening to the radio over breakfast. They hear the announcer say, "We are going to have 8 to 10 inches of snow today. You must park your car on the even-numbered side of the street, so the snowplows can get through." Norman's wife goes out and moves her car.

A week later while they are eating breakfast again, the radio announcer says, "We are expecting ten to twelve inches of snow today. You must park your car on the odd numbered side of the street, so the snowplows can get through." Norman's wife goes out and moves her car again. The next week they are again having breakfast, when the radio announcer says, "We are expecting twelve to fourteen inches of snow today. You must park... " Then the power goes out. Norman's wife is very upset, and with a worried look on her face she says, "Honey, I don't know what to do. Which side of the street do I need to park on so the snowplows can get through?" With the love and understanding in his voice that all men who are married to blondes exhibit, Norman says "Why don't you just leave it in the garage this time?"

It was mealtime during a flight on Hooters Airline. "Would you like dinner?" the flight attendant asked John, seated in front. "What are my choices?" John asked. "Yes or no," she replied.

The cop got out of his car and the kid who was stopped for speeding rolled down his window. "I've been waiting for you all day," the cop said. The kid replied, "Ye all, well I got here as fast as I could." When the cop finally stopped laughing, he sent the kid on his way without a ticket.

Amen. Selah. So be it.

FINDING HUMOR

Humor is often where you find it. So say I. With about a million other stand-up comics. The other day a friend of mine, Dr. Kendall Baker, sent me a delightful squib from a newspaper. The cartoon is called, "Non Sequitar," by Wiley. The caption on the right says, "God Does the Talk Show Circuit." He is depicted as a congenial fellow with a flowing beard; sitting in a comfortable chair in front of the host who has a resemblance to Jay Leno.

The humor has a bite to it. God is saying, "I think my best creation was the sense of humor. The irony of course, is that the people who claim to believe in me the most are the ones least likely to have one."

Several people have e-mailed a delightful rendition of lessons learned from Noah's Ark. The caption is suggestive: Everything I need to know about life, I learned from Noah's ark. There are eleven of them. 1. Don't miss the boat. 2. Remember we're all in the same boat. 3. Plan ahead. It wasn't raining when Noah built the ark. 4. Stay fit. When you're 600 years old, someone may ask you to do something really big. 5. Don't listen to critics; just get on with the job that needs to be done. 6. Build your future on high ground. 7. For safety's sake, travel in pairs. 8. Speed isn't always an advantage. The snails were on board with the cheetahs. 9. When you're stressed, float awhile. 10. Remember the ark was built by amateurs; the Titanic by professionals. 11. No matter the storm, when you're with God, there's always a rainbow waiting.

Both of the following contributions to our "laugh bank" came to me by way of e-mail. Invariably different names were used. The first one concerns a gentleman and his new suit. The second is a football joke. Mr. Jones has a medical problem. He has constant ringing in his ears and bulging eyes. He finally found a surgeon who said a delicate operation would cost $200,000. Mr. Jones left to consult with Mrs. Jones. They mortgaged their house again and cashed in savings. The day after Mr. Jones felt so great he sent for a tailor. Ordered a new suit, he started to give the tailor his sizes. The tailor said, "You don't have to tell me that. You're forty-six regular jacket with thirty-three inch sleeves, forty inch waist on your trousers with a thirty-two inch inseam, wear a sixteen inch neck shirt with thirty-four inch sleeves and forty inch shorts." Mr. Jones said, "Amazing, except I wear thirty-eight inch shorts." "No, no," the tailor said. "I can see that you're a forty." They bickered until the tailor said, "You're a forty. If you wear thirty-eight, your ears will ring and your eyes will bulge."

The questions subsided. After the game, the host was asking her, "How did you like the game? Aren't you glad our team won? Want to come to next week's game?" His guest had one more of her own, going back to the very start of the game. "Why would they want to kill people just to get that quarter back?"

This one comes from several sources. Ladies, read and weep. A husband and wife are getting ready for bed. The wife is standing in front of a full length mirror taking a hard look at herself. "You know love" she says, "I look in the mirror and I see an old woman. My face is all wrinkled, my breasts are barely above my waist, and my behind is hanging out a mile. I've got fat legs and my arms are all flabby." She turns to her husband and says, "Tell me something positive to make me feel better about myself." He thinks about it for a bit and then says "well there's nothing wrong with your eyesight."

Mike sent me this one. It is long, but well worth reading. A farmer named Clyde had a car accident. In court, the trucking company's fancy lawyer was questioning Clyde. "Didn't you say, at the scene of the accident, 'I'm fine!?" asked the lawyer. Clyde responded, "Well, I'll tell you what happened. I had just loaded my favorite mule, Bessie, into the..." "I didn't ask for any details," the lawyer interrupted. "Just answer the question. Did you not say, at the scene of the accident, 'I'm fine!?" Clyde said, "Well, I had just got Bessie into the trailer and I was driving down the road... "

The lawyer interrupted again and said, "Judge, I am trying to establish the fact that, at the scene of the accident, this man told the Highway Patrolman on the scene that he was just fine. Now several weeks after the accident he is trying to sue my client. I believe he is a fraud. Please tell him to simply answer the question." By this time, the Judge was fairly interested in Clyde's answer and said to the lawyer, "I'd like to hear what he has to say about his favorite mule, Bessie."

Clyde thanked the Judge and proceeded, "Well as I was saying, I had just loaded Bessie, my favorite mule, into the trailer and was driving her down the highway when this huge semi-truck and trailer ran a stop sign and smacked my truck right in the side. I was thrown into one ditch and Bessie was thrown into the other. I was hurting real bad and didn't want to move. However, I could hear ol' Bessie moaning and groaning. I knew she was in terrible shape just by her groans. Shortly after the accident a Highway Patrolman came on the scene. He could hear Bessie moaning and groaning so he went over to her. After he looked at her, he took out his gun and shot her between the eyes. Then, the Patrolman came across the road, gun in hand, looked at me and said "How are you feeling?" Now what would you say?"

Amen. Selah. So be it.

FRED ALLEN

Fred Allen, the old-time comedian said, "It is bad to suppress laughter. It goes back down and spreads your hips." Phyllis Diller said, "A smile is a curve that sets everything straight." Charley Prose, a contemporary comedian that frequents Laughlin, Nevada says, "The person who refuses to laugh has a tendency to pass gas."

A recent article in Psychology Today states that adults need at least fifteen laughs a day for optimal wellness. Two and three year olds laugh an average of twenty times an hour. Let's start the day with these bits of humor. What would the Christmas story be like if there were three wise women instead of Three Wise Men?

First, they would have asked for directions instead of following a star. Second, instead of worshiping, they would have cleaned the manger and helped Mary with the baby. Third, instead of gold, frankincense and myrrh, they would have brought pampers, pabulum and other baby necessities. Fourth, they would have had a baby shower for mother and baby. Fifth, when the Baby cried, they would have taken turns to lovingly hold, sing and talk to the baby Jesus.

As a retired pastor, I thoroughly enjoyed this joke. A pastor comes up to a very stubborn deacon and says, "There is a dead mule outside the church!" The deacon thinks a minute and says, "Well, I don't know what you want me to do about it; you are in the business of dealing with the dead." The pastor bows his head and says, "You're right and one of my sad duties is to notify the next of kin."

I imagine many of you are like me; rather ignorant when it comes to computers. A friend sent me this one. I was having trouble with my computer. So I called Harold the computer guy, to come over. Harold clicked a couple of buttons and solved the problem. He gave me a bill for a minimum service call. As he was walking away, I called after him, "So, what was wrong?" He replied, "It was an ID ten T error." I didn't want to appear stupid, but nonetheless inquired, "An, ID ten T error? What's that, in case I need to fix it again?" The computer guy grinned, "Haven't you ever heard of an ID ten T error before?" "No," I replied. "Write it down," he said, "and I think you'll figure it out." So I wrote out. I D 1 0 T. I used to like Harold.

The following were in church bulletins. 1. Bertha Belch, a missionary from Africa, will be speaking tonight at Calvary Methodist. Come hear Bertha Belch all the way from Africa. 2. Announcement in a church bulletin for a national PRAYER & FASTING conference: "The cost for attending the Fasting and Prayer conference includes meals." 3. "Ladies, don't forget the rummage sale. It' s a chance to get rid of those things not worth keeping around the house. Don't forget your husbands." 4. The peacemaking meeting scheduled for today has been canceled due to a conflict. 5. Remember in prayer the many who are sick of our community. 6 Don't let worry kill you off-let the Church help. 7. Miss Charlene Mason sang "I will not pass this way again," giving obvious pleasure to the congregation.

Many thanks to Louise for this one. A man appears before the Pearly Gates. "Have you ever done anything of particular merit?" St. Peter asks. "Well, I can think of one thing, "the man offers. "Once I came upon a gang of bikers who were threatening a young woman. I told them to leave her alone, but they wouldn't listen. So I approached the largest and most heavily tattooed biker. I smacked him on the head, kicked his bike over, ripped out his nose ring and threw it on the ground. Then I told him, 'Leave her alone or you'll answer to me." St. Peter was impressed. "When did this happen?" "A couple of minutes ago."

Finally, Steve sent these bits of humor. We were celebrating the 100th anniversary of our church, and several former pastors and the bishop were in attendance. At one point, our minister had the children gather at the altar for a talk about the importance of the day. He began by asking, "Does anyone know what the bishop does?" There was silence. Finally, one little boy answered gravely, "He's the one you can move diagonally." (Referring to chess)

A gentleman had been trying for years to meet the Pope. Finally, his wish was granted. When the gentleman approached the Pope he said, "Your Eminence, I am so happy to be given this chance to speak with you and I would like to tell you a joke before I start." The Pope replied, "Of course my son. Go ahead and tell your joke." The gentleman continued, "There were these two Pollacks and... " The Pope interrupted, "My son, do you realize that I am Polish?" "I'm sorry, your Eminence, I'll speak slower ... "

Amen. Selah. Amen.

ABORIGINAL SIT-DOWN COMIC

FUNNIES- COMICS

I cannot remember a time when I was not addicted to the "funnies" or the "comics" as they are called today. Television was unheard of and radios were scarce. The characters in the "funnies" were better than "picture shows." The "funnies" were not always "funny" but they were always informative. Often values such as thrift, courage, perseverance, grit, determination, evil, etc. were stressed. They were popular long before Peanuts, Dennis the Menace, Garfield, Hagar the Horrible and others.

If you can remember these "funnies" you've got some great memories: Alley Oop and his pre-historic battles, Mandrake the Magician, Maggie and Jigs with his gout, the Katzenjammer Kids, Andy Gump, Popeye the Sailor, Dick Tracy, Joe Palooka, Flash Gordon, and of course, my favorite of all time, Li 'l Abner.

The array of characters always fascinated me: the voluptuous Daisy Mae, Mammy and Pappy Yokum, Dogpatch itself, Hairless Joe, Lonesome Polecat, and the Shmoo. The Shmoo provided all the culinary desires one could wish for and with delight. My two favorites of all, beside Daisy Mae, were Joe Splotch and General Bullmoose. They reflected many people I know. Bullmoose believed that what was good enough for him was good enough for everyone. And Joe. He always went around with a cloud over his head-constantly depressed. If you get the opportunity, read up on one answer to the Depression Days-

Dogpatch.

Now for a change of pace. The following stories really triggered my laugh meter. This one has several sources. A man, whose level of drunkenness was bordering on the absurd, stood up to leave a bar and fell flat on his face. "Maybe all I need is some fresh air," thought the man as he crawled outside. He tried to stand up again, but fell face first into the mud. "The heck with it," he thought. I'll just crawl home." The next morning, his wife found him on the doorstep asleep. "You went out drinking last night, didn't you?" she said. "Uh, yes, "he said sheepishly. "How did you know?" "You left your wheelchair at the bar again."

Three elderly ladies are excited about their first Yankees Baseball game. They smuggled a bottle of Jack Daniels into the game. The game is real exciting and they are enjoying themselves drinking Jack Daniels mixed with soft drinks. Soon they realize that the bottle of Jack Daniels is almost gone and the game has a lot of innings to go. Using the clues given, what inning is the game in and what is the status of the game? And the answer is: It's the bottom of the fifth and the bags are loaded!

In a recent Harris online poll 38,562 men across the US were asked to identify woman's ultimate fantasy. 97.8% of the respondents said that a woman's ultimate fantasy is to have two men at once. While this has been verified by a recent sociological study, it appears that most men do not realize that, in this fantasy, one man is cooking and the other is cleaning.

It's amazing how many twists I've heard on this story. You've probably got one of your own. An old man lived alone in Minnesota. He wanted to spade his potato garden but it was very hard work. His only son, who would have helped him, was in Prison. The old man wrote a letter to his son and mentioned his predicament. Shortly, he received this reply, For HEAVEN'S SAKE, Dad, don't dig up that garden, that's where I buried the GUNS!" At 4 A.M. the next morning, a dozen police showed up and dug up the entire garden, without finding any guns. Confused, the old man wrote another note to his son telling him what happened, and asking him what to do next . His son's reply was: "Now plant your potatoes, Dad. It's the best I could do at this time."

A human female's perspective on her next life...if there was one! If you're a bear. You get to hibernate. You do nothing but sleep for six months. I could deal with that. Before you hibernate, you're supposed to eat yourself stupid. I could deal with that, too. If you're a bear, you birth your children (who are the size of walnuts) while you're sleeping and wake to partially grown, cute, cuddly cubs. I could definitely deal with that. If you're a mama bear, everyone knows you mean business. You swat anyone who bothers your cubs. If your cubs get out of line, you swat them, too. I could deal with that. If you're a bear, your mate EXPECTS you to wake up growling. He EXPECTS that you will have hairy legs and excess body fat. Yup ... .l wannabe a bear.

This story came from someplace by someone. I don't know from whom or from where. An elderly Italian man asked the local priest to hear his confession. "Father, during WW-2 a beautiful woman knocked on my door and asked me to hide her from the Germans. I hid her in my attic." The priest replied, "That was a wonderful thing you did and you have no need to confess." "It's worse, Father. I was weak and told her she must repay me with her sexual favors." "You were both in great danger and would have suffered terribly if the Germans had found her. God, in his wisdom and mercy will balance the good and the evil and judge you kindly. You are forgiven." "Thank you, Father. That's a great load off my mind. Ah, I have one more question." "And what is that," asked the priest. The old man replied, "Should I tell her the war is over?"

Amen. Selah. So be it.

GOD HAS A SENSE OF HUMOR

Martin Luther, the primary motivator for the Protestant Reformation, is reported as saying that if God doesn't have a sense of humor, he didn't want to go to heaven.

Abraham Lincoln has been described as America's greatest President. True or not, he certainly was a great humorist. He is reported as saying that God had to have a sense of humor because He made so many funny looking people.

As a life-long public speaker and communicator, I was early on given humorous advice about what to do when nervous. Speakers were advised to imagine the audience as being totally naked. That would certainly cure something. When my spirits are flagging and I'm somewhat depressed I try to be creative. While sitting in an audience before a service (church) I compare other attendees with certain animals. Some preen like peacocks. Others float like gazelles. Some cuddle like a couple of affectionate polar bears. Others snap like poodles. Overweight men (like me) and women waddle like gorillas.

Many people send me tidbits of humor. Don sent this one. "A man was being very closely tailgated by a woman. Suddenly the light turned yellow, just in front of him. She opened her window, stuck her hand out and made that familiar gesture, all the while screaming in frustration as she missed her chance to get through the intersection. As she was still in mid-rant, she heard a tapping sound on her window and looked up into the face of a very serious Police Officer. He ordered her to exit her car with her hands up. He took her to the Police station where she was searched, fingerprinted, photographed, and placed in a cell.

After a couple of hours, another Policeman approached the cell and opened the door. The arresting Officer was waiting with all her personal effects. He said, "I'm very sorry for the mistake. You see, I pulled up behind your car while you were blowing your horn, flipping the guy off in front of you, and cussing a blue streak at him. I also noticed the license plate holder, the 'Honk if you love Jesus' bumper sticker, the 'Follow Me to SUNDAY SCHOOL' BUMPER STICKER. NATURALLY, I ASSUMED YOU HAD STOLEN the car."

I love this bit of humor from the good clergyman. A man suffered a serious heart attack and had open heart bypass surgery. He awakened from the surgery to find himself in the care of nuns at a Catholic Hospital. As he was recovering, a nun asked him questions regarding how he was going to pay for his treatment. She asked if he had health insurance. He replied, in a raspy voice, "No health insurance." The nun asked if he had money in the bank. He replied, "No money in the bank." The nun asked, "Do you have a relative who could help you?" He said, "I only have a spinster sister, who is a nun." The nun became agitated and announced loudly, "Nuns are not spinsters! Nuns are married to God." The patient replied, "Send the bill to my brother-in-law."

Charles is not a minister, but has the instincts for a good one. Here are TV's examples. A father was approached by his small son who told him proudly, "I know what the Bible means!" His father smiled and replied, "What do you mean, you know what the Bible means. The son replied, "I do know!" "Okay" said his father. "What does the Bible mean?" "That's easy, Daddy" the young boy replied excitedly. "It stands for Basic Information Before Leaving Earth."

The minister was preoccupied with thoughts of how he was going to ask the congregation to come up with more money than they were expecting, for repairs to the church building. Therefore, he was annoyed to find that the regular organist was sick and a substitute had been brought in at the last minute.

The substitute wanted to know what to play. "Here's a copy of the service," he said impatiently. "But you'll have to think of something to play after I make the announcement about the finances." During the service, the minister paused and said, "Brothers and Sisters, we are in great difficulty; the roof repairs cost twice as much as we expected and we need $4,000.00 more. Any of you who can pledge $100.00 or more, please stand up." AT THAT MOMENT, THE SUBSTITUTE ORGANIST PLAYED THE STAR SPANGLED BANNER. AND THAT IS HOW THE SUBSTITUTE BECAME THE REGULAR ORGANIST!

Amen. Selah. So be it.

GREAT TIME OF TRAUMA

The 60's and 70's were a time of great trauma and upheaval for our country. We were mired in a senseless war in Vietnam that cost us over 50,000 lives and finally escaped with a modicum of self-respect. We saw three terrible assassinations of JFK, Martin Luther King and Robert Kennedy. The time also saw the resignation of a President as the aftermath of the Watergate folly.

In spite of the despair that plagued our society, those times also witnessed great and wonderful successes. Who can forget the excitement that we felt when Neal Armstrong and others walked on the moon. Those times also brought the onslaught against the Cartesian philosophy that characterized western medicine for hundreds of years. That is: there is no connection between the mind and the body. That view is considered foolishness today, but not back then. This battle was fought by the re-discovery of the work of Hans Selye, M.D. who introduced to us the word "stress" and its affect on the body—psychosomatic illness.

Also, for my study and work there was Dr. Norman Cousins PhD a member of the UCLA Medical School and editor of the National Review of Literature. After recovering from a terminal illness, he gave credit to positive thoughts and laughter. He introduced to us the word "endorphins." Plain, old, ordinary jokes bring mental, physical and spiritual health. That's why I write the articles, Laugh a Little Live a Lot.

Bob, a seventy year old, extremely wealthy widower, shows up at the Country Club with a breathtakingly beautiful and very sexy twenty year old blonde who knocks everyone's socks off with her youthful sex appeal and charm. She hangs onto Bob's arm and listens intently to his every word. His buddies at the club are all aghast. At the very first chance, they corner him and ask, "Bob, how did you get the trophy girlfriend?" Bob replies, "Girlfriend? She's my wife!" They're amazed, but continue to ask. "So, how did you persuade her to marry you?" "I lied about my age," Bob replies. "What, did you tell her you were only 50?" Bob smiles and says, "No, I told her I was 90. " Remember Anna Nicole Smith.

I particularly like jokes that have a punch line that creeps up on me. A rancher died and his widow was left to run the ranch. She advertised for help and a gay man and a drunk applied. She chose the gay man. After a couple of months, the ranch was running smoothly and she suggested he go to town on Saturday and kick up his heels. At 2:30 AM she was waiting up for him, drinking a glass of wine. She said to him, "Take off my blouse." He complied. Then she said, "Take off my shoes." He complied. She said, "Take off my skirt." He complied. Finally, "Take off my bra." He complied and dropped it to the floor. Then she looked at him and said, "If you ever wear my clothes into town again, you're fired."

Since we're in a happy mode, this bit of humor is relevant. She married and had thirteen children. Her husband died. She soon married again and had seven more children. Again, her husband died. But she remarried and this time had five more children. Alas, she finally died. Standing before her coffin, the preacher prayed to the Lord above, thanking Him for this loving woman who fulfilled his commandment to "Go forth and multiply." In his eulogy, the preacher said, "Lord, they're finally together." Leaning over to a neighbor, one mourner quietly asked, "Is he referring to her first, second or third husband?

I really love this quickie. Get ready to laugh. The woman's husband had been slipping in and out of a coma for several months, yet she had stayed by his bedside every single day. One day, when he came to, he motioned for her to come nearer. As she sat by him, he whispered, eyes full of tears, "You know what? You have been with me all through the bad times. When I got fired, you were there to support me. When my business failed, you were there. When I got shot, you were by my side. When we lost the house, you stayed right here. When my health started failing, you were still by my side. You know what?" "What dear?" she gently asked, smiling as her heart began to fill with warmth. "I think you're bad luck."

Amen. Selah. So be it.

GREATEST COMIC

Victor Borge was one of the greatest of all comics. His situation humor always brought the crowd screaming for more. His use of the piano was basic to his slapstick comedy. His purposeful mistakes could be counted on. However, he was an outstanding pianist.

Dave shared with me a statement attributed to Borge. "Humor is something that thrives between man's aspirations and his limitations. There is more logic in humor than in anything else. Because, you see, humor is truth." Not only can real humor reveal truth, it also stimulates the mind. The brain is stimulated when grasping and understanding the nuances of a joke.

Norman Cousins often called laughter "inner jogging." A laugh jiggles the organs of the abdomen, which helps the health process. Think about it. Most comics live to a ripe old age.

Stimulation of your mind and getting a session of inner exercise are two good reasons for reading the rest of this article. The following are actual writings from hospital charts. 1. The patient refused autopsy. 2. The patient has no previous history of suicides. 3. She has no rigors or shaking chills, but her husband states she was very hot in bed last night. 4. Patient has chest pain if she lies on her left side for over a year. 5. On the second day the knee was better and on the third day it disappeared. 6. The patient is tearful and crying constantly. She also appears to be depressed.

7. Discharge status: Alive but without permission. 8. Healthy appearing decrepit sixty-nine year old male, mentally alert but forgetful.

A new pastor was visiting in the homes of his parishioners. At one house it seemed obvious that someone was at home. But no answer came to his repeated knocks at the door. Therefore, he took out a business card and wrote "Revelation 3:20" on the back of it and stuck it in the door. When the offering was processed the following Sunday, he found that his card had been returned. Added to it was this cryptic message. "Genesis 3:10." Reaching for his Bible to check out the citation, he broke out in gales of laughter. Revelation 3:20 begins. "Behold, I stand at the door and knock." Genesis 3:10 reads, "I heard your voice in the garden and I was afraid for I was naked."

Idle thoughts of a retiree's wondering mind. I planted some bird seed. A bird came up. Now I don't know what to feed it. 2) Protons have mass? I didn't even know they were Catholic. 3) All I ask is a chance to prove that money can't make me happy. 4) If the world were a logical place, men would be the ones who ride horses sidesaddle. 5) They told me I was gullible and I believed them. 6) Experience is the thing you have left when everything else is gone. One nice thing about egotists: they don't talk about other people. 7) I used to be indecisive. Now I'm not sure. 8) Show me a man with both feet firmly on the ground, and I'll show you a man who can't get his pants off. 9) Is it me- -or do buffalo wings taste like chicken?

Here are four religious truths. It is important for those of all faiths to recognize them. 1. Muslims do not recognize Jews as God's chosen people. 2. Jews do not recognize Jesus as the Messiah. 3. Protestants do not recognize the Pope as the leader of the Christian world. 4. Baptists do not recognize each other at Hooters.

How true this one is. Thank you, Louise. "I know my older sister loves me because she gives me all her old clothes and has to go out and buy new ones." Lauren age four. "I let my big sister pick on me because my Mom says she only picks on me because she loves me. So I pick on my baby sister because I love her." Bethany, age four. "When you love somebody, your eyelashes go up and down and little stars come out of you."Karen, age seven. "You really shouldn't say 'I love you' unless you mean it. But if you mean it, you should say it a lot. People forget." Jessica, age eight.

A man has six children and is very proud of his achievement. He is so proud of himself, that he starts calling his wife, "Mother of Six" in spite of her objections. One night, they go to a party. The man decides that it's time to go home and wants to find out if his wife is ready to leave as well. He shouts at the top of his voice, "Shall we go home' Mother of six?" His wife, irritated by her husband's lack of discretion shouts right back, "Anytime you're ready, Father of Four." *Amen. Selah. So be it.*

HISTORY OF CREATION

In many respects Genesis 1:1 is the most provocative verse in the Bible. It encompasses the entire history of creation. "In the beginning God created the heavens and the earth." It includes the entire universe. From the beginning with the Big Bang to its continuing expansion. Our earth with its evolution is also included. Call it what you will. Intelligent Design, Random Design or Theistic Design. The verse provides an answer to the question that science asks but does not have an answer. Their best guess is that the Big Bang just happened. Nothing caused it. It spontaneously occurred. The law of gravity just appeared fourteen to fifteen billion years ago. All of the laws that keep the universe operating have neither rhyme nor reason.

It seems to me that it takes a lot of faith to accept that view. I personally prefer to accept the Genesis account with one reservation. It did not originate in the Hebrew or Christian Bible. The earliest recorded evidence points to the Sumerian culture. The Epic of Gilgamesh, composed hundreds of years prior to the Hebrew Bible, contains stories about creation: Noah and the flood, Job and other similar accounts. Only the names of those involved are different.

William Paley (1743-1805) was a minister/scientist in England. Two books, "The Attributes of Deity" and "Natural Theology" give credence to this concept of Intelligent Design.

Paraphrasing his words, he says a rock can be assumed to have been around forever. However, a watch is something else. Someone designed its works. The parts did not accidently fly to the exact order. The inner works did not automatically assemble. In the same way he declares the universe, with its order and predictability, must have an intelligence involved in its creation. He names that Intelligence GOD. If the sun were a "smidgen" closer to earth, we would all be on fire. It the sun was a "smidgen" farther away, we all would freeze.

A recent article in This Week begins with the statement, "Astronomers have calculated that there are eleven billion possible inhabitable planets in our galaxy providing compelling new grounds to believe we're not alone in the universe." The same astronomers say that tens of billions are water-laden planets that are the size of Earth. Logic says that surely some of these have the ingredients necessary for life.

Astronomer Geoffrey Marcy gives further light to our place in our galaxy. He says there are two hundred billion stars plus in our Milky Way galaxy. And the Milky Way is just one of billions of galaxies. The number is increasing as I write this article. His concluding statement, "So if you consider the entire universe, the possibility of intelligent life seems quite high."

Geologists believe that our earth is about four to five billion years old. That staggers our imagination. To help us grasp this truth consider that one million minutes ago, the year was 102

A.D. and Christianity was just getting started. Four and one-half billion minutes ago the date was 6560 B.C.E., several thousand years before the Sumerians developed written pictographs. If our earth's entire history of four to five billion years was condensed into one calendar year the last 2000 years would take place in the final sixteen seconds of December 31st. My eighty-six years, extending backward from the present would take place in the final six-tenths of a second of the year.

Paleontologists and Geologists have agreed on the chronology of life on earth. Approximately 3.6 billion years ago, simple cells appeared on earth. Two billion years ago complex cells developed.

One billion years ago there was multi-cellular life on earth. Five hundred million years ago there were fish, followed by plants. Insects and seeds, about 400 million years. Reptiles invaded our earth 300 million years ago. The first primate came into being 60 million years ago. And 200,000 years ago saw the advent of Homo Sapiens (you and me). The migration from: Africa about fifty thousand years ago. It is the opinion of most Anthropologists that the Aboriginals in Australia and the Pygmies of Africa are the only survivors of the earliest Homo Sapiens. We are either going backward or forward. President John F. Kennedy had the answer over fifty years ago when he said, "The problems of modern men are MAN made. They will only be solved by MAN."

Amen. Selah. So be it.

HOUSE OF LAUGHTER

I have visited Israel on seven different occasions. Each time I made a special effort to visit the house designated as the home of Martha and Mary; friends of Jesus.

Just up the hill is the place where Lazarus, their brother, was buried and Jesus subsequently raised him from the dead. An old Eastern Church tradition says that Lazarus laughed heartedly for years after being raised by Jesus. That is why Lazarus' home in Bethany is called "The House of Laughter." In preparation for this article on humor I share with you a squib given to me by a friend. He has been a regular supplier of mine for good jokes for several years. "Yesterday's the past, tomorrow's the future, but today is a gift. That's why it's called the present. '

Did you know that in Nigeria, the name of God is "Father of Laughter?" The Anglicans are always a source for good humor. An Anglican priest invited his bishop to stay overnight at his home after a confirmation. Before supper the bishop was walking down a dimly lit corridor in the priest's home. The priest's wife, coming up from behind, mistook the bishop for her husband and gave him a clout over the ear. "That'll teach you to ask the bishop to stay when we've got nothing in the house," she snapped. I remember this one from the dim past. A Cardinal was approached one day in the Cathedral by a very excited young priest. "Your Eminence," the priest cried, "There's a Holy man at the door who says He is

Jesus. What should I do?" The Cardinal says, "Look busy. Look busy." This was heard at the door of the church after the service, "Reverend, you don't know how much your sermons have meant to my husband since he lost his mind."

I love this one. Please use your imagination. The most Rev. Robert Nuncie, retired Archbishop of Canterbury, wrote in his book, Seasons of the Spirit, that he once got on a train in England and discovered that all of the other passengers in the car were patients at a mental institution on an excursion. An attendant was counting the patients to be sure they were all there: "one, two, three, four, five..." When he came to Nuncie, he said, "Who are you?" I am the Archbishop of Canterbury," Nuncie replied. The attendant smiled and, pointing at him, continued counting," ...six, seven, eight... "

In all my years of study, I've never read this statement attributed to Martin Luther. "If you're not allowed to laugh in heaven, I don't want to go there."

The following bit of humor is one of my favorites. Particularly because I'm involved in two of the three professions mentioned. It seems that a psychologist, and engineer, and a theologian were on a hunting trip. Seeking shelter, they knocked on the door of a small, isolated cabin. No one was home, but the front door was unlocked, and they entered. They saw something strange. A large, pot-bellied, cast-iron stove was suspended in midair by wires attached to the ceiling beams. Why would a stove be elevated from the floor? The psychologist concluded: "It is obvious that this lonely trapper, isolated from humanity, has elevated his stove so that he can curl up under it and vicariously experience a return to his mother's womb."

The engineer theorized: "The man is practicing laws of thermodynamics. By elevating his stove, he has discovered a way to distribute heat more evenly throughout the cabin." The theologian speculated: "I'm sure that hanging his stove from the ceiling has religious meaning. Fire lifted up has been a religious symbol for centuries. While they were debating the matter, the trapper returned. They immediately asked him why he had hung his pot-bellied stove by wires from the ceiling. The trapper said, "Had plenty of wire, not much stovepipe."

An elderly man in Phoenix calls his son in New York and says, "I hate to ruin your day, but I have to tell you that your mother and I are divorcing: forty five years of misery is enough." "'Pop, what are you talking about?" the son screams. "We can't stand the sight of each other any longer," the old man says. "We're sick of each other, and I'm sick of talking about this, so call your sister in Chicago and tell her," and he hangs up. Frantic, the son calls his sister, who explodes on the phone, "Like heck they're getting divorced. I'll take care of this." She calls Phoenix immediately, and screams at the old man, "Don't do a thing until my brother and I get there. We'll both be there tomorrow. Until then don't do a thing. Do you hear me?" and hangs up. The old man hangs. up his phone and turns to his wife. "Okay," he says. "They're coming for Thanksgiving and paying their own fares… now what do we tell them for Christmas?"

Amen. Selah. So be it.

HUMOR AFFECTS

PEOPLE DIFFERENTLY

Humor affects people differently. It takes imagination to appreciate a joke. There are some people who never get it. They may grin, but it's obvious the point went over their heads. It seems that the laughter gene was left out of their makeup. I know a guy who collects cartoons. He has books of them, but never laughs. Does he keep it inside? I doubt it. He just doesn't get the point.

Others I know have a low threshold for laughter. They laugh at the slightest hint of a joke. Sometimes they laugh before the punch line has been delivered.

Whenever I do sit-down comedy I have several "hooks." Those are stories or one-liners that I use to "grab" the attention of the listeners. If they get it by laughing, I know I've got a good crowd. If not, I'm in trouble. My favorite line goes like this. "Let me tell you a little something about me. My father died two years before I was born." If you don't get it, stop reading now. The rest of the article will be meaningless.

A friend is a laughter. She is a master of Internet humor. She receives them and passes them on. Many of her jokes have a twinge of ornery inference. Consider this one. One night a guy takes his girlfriend home. As they are about to kiss each other goodnight at the front door, the guy starts feeling a little horny.

With an air of confidence, he leans with his hand against the wall and smiling, he says to her, "Honey, would you have sex with me?" Horrified, she replies, "Are you mad? My parents will see us!" "Oh, come on! Who's gonna see us at this hour?" he asks, grinning at her. "No, please. Can you imagine if we get caught?" "Oh, come on! There' nobody around, they're all sleeping!" "No way. It's just too risky!" "Oh, please, please, I love you so much!" "No, no, and no. I love you too, but I just can't." "Oh, yes you can. Please?" "No, no. I just can't." "I'm begging you..." Out of the blue, the light on the stairs goes on, and the girl's older sister shows up in her pajamas, hair disheveled, and in a sleepy voice, she says: "Dad says to go ahead and have sex with him, or I can do it; or if need be, mom says she can come down herself and do it. But for God's sake, tell him to take his hand off the intercom!" Al's laugh is hearty and he has a plethora of jokes. His working years were in the business end of education, but his retirement years are in humor.

I love these. A pompous minister was seated next to a Texan on a flight to Dallas. After the plane was airborne, drink orders were taken. The Texan asked for a whiskey and soda, which was brought and placed before him. The flight attendant then asked the minister if he would like a drink. He replied in disgust, "I'd rather be savagely raped by brazen whores than let liquor touch my lips." The Texan looked at the minister, then handed his drink back to the attendant and said, "I didn't know we had a choice."

The female skier Picabo Street (pronounced Peek-A-Boo). The famous Olympic skier. Picabo Street is not just an athlete, she is a nurse. She currently works at the Intensive Care Unit of a large metropolitan hospital. She is not permitted to answer the telephone, however. It caused simply too much confusion when she would answer the phone and say, Picabo, ICU. A good clean joke is hard to find these days-pass it on!

You've got to meet Ali. He's the owner of All Stars Auto Garage. He's Pakistani and has more jokes than Saudi Arabia has sand. I regularly stop by his place to hear a story. Not only was his joke funny, but it also revealed a basic truth to me. Humor transcends boundaries, language and time. The first time I heard his story was in Jamaica. It was calypso sung to a reggae beat. I heard it later in Aruba and Dominica.

He said he had translated it from Pakistani when he was in Saudi. It goes like this. There is a family with a Mamma and a Pappa. Three daughters and a son. The son meets a girl, falls in love and asks his father if he can marry her. The Pappa says, "No. The girl is your sister, but your Mamma don't know." The scenario repeats several times.

Finally, the son gives up on his Pappa and the punch line follows. His Mamma says, "Marry her, my son, for your Pappa's not your Pappa, but your Pappa don't know." As I said, it's a song in Jamaica.

Amen. Selah. So be it.

HUMOR AND YOUR

IMMUNE SYSTEM

How important is our immune system? It is absolutely vital for health. It is normally so strong that a transplant of any kind is impossible unless it is neutralized.

Cancer runs wild when it is weakened. AIDS is caused by immune deficiency. Wellness is impossible without its strength. That is why so much time and money is being spent on research to find out ways to build it up. Anyway this can be done is good. A small but important way is through laughter. It doesn't cost anything and a prescription is not necessary.

The other day I heard a statement by Dr. Lorraine Day M.D. She is a nationally known orthopedic surgeon from San Francisco and a cancer survivor. She said: "One minute of laughter will strengthen the immune system for twenty-four hours. Conversely, one minute of anger will stymie it for the same amount of time."

Pamela sent me a list of suggestions on: How to Keep a Healthy Level of Insanity.

1. At lunch time, sit in your parked car with sunglasses on and point a hair dryer at passing cars. See if they slow down.

2. Page yourself over the intercom. Don't disguise your voice.

3. Every time someone asks to do something, ask if they want fries with that.

3. In the memo line of all your checks, write "for sexual favors."

5. Don't use any punctuation

6. As often as possible, skip rather than walk.

7. Tell your boss, "It's not the voices in my head that bother me, it's the voices in your head that do."

Political jokes seem to go on forever and ever. How long will Clinton jokes continue? Here's one sent to me from St. George, Utah.

Dear Abby got a letter from Frustrated. Her husband is a cheat and lies about it though professing his love. He has many friends and they know he cheats and lies. He's a hard worker but denies his cheating. Then he admits his cheating and begs for forgiveness. It has been going on so long everyone knows about him. Frustrated ends it with, "I don't know what to do." Dear Abby's answer is short and to the point. "You should dump him:

Now that you are a New York Senator, you don't need him anymore."

Kathy sends a very humorous senior citizen story. Two of them lived in a Mobil home park. He was a widower, she a widow. They had known each other for several years and one night at a potluck dinner he says, "Will you marry me?" After six seconds of careful consideration she says, "Yes. Yes I will." The next morning he's troubled. He can't remember whether she said Yes or No. He goes to the phone and calls her. "When I asked you to marry me, did you say Yes or No?" Her answer thrilled him. "I said yes, yes I will and I meant it with all my heart." Then she continued. "I'm so glad you called, because I couldn't remember who had asked me."

The last two bits of humor have a bit of a twist. Tragically, three friends die in a car crash and they find themselves at the gates of heaven. Before entering they are each asked a question by St. Peter. "When you are in your casket and friends and family are morning upon you, what would you like to hear them say about you?" asks St. Peter. The first guy says, "I would like to hear them say that I was a great doctor of my time and a great family man." The second guy says, "I would like to hear that I was a wonderful husband and school teacher who make a huge difference in our children of tomorrow." The last guy replies, "I would like to hear them say, "LOOK HE'S MOVING!"

A heartwarming story of the advances of women in

achieving equality throughout the world. Barbara Walters of 60 Minutes did a story on gender roles in Kabul several years before the Afghan conflict. She noted that women customarily walked about ten paces behind their husbands. She returned to Kabul recently and observed that the men now walked several paces behind their wives. Ms. Walters approached one of the Afghani women and said, "This is marvelous. Can you tell the free world just what enabled women to achieve this reversal of roles?" "Land mines," said the woman.

Amen, Selah. So be it.

HUMOR: THE BEST MEDICINE

Humor is the international language. Coupled with laughter, they bridge barrier s of language and ethnic alienation.

While hyenas may imitate the sound of laughter, only humans can rationally describe a scene or sequence of words and respond with appropriate laughter. The connection between laughter and mental and physical health is a fairly recent observation. Hippocrates, the father of medicine, advocated two healing procedures: the use of massage and laughter. Since then there have been many attempts to stimulate laughter like court jesters and the theater, but it wasn't until the advent of Norman Cousins in the 1960's and 70's that laughter and healing were connected.

The reason for this lack of connection was the control of the Cartesian philosophy had over medicine. Descartes advocated the total separation of mind and body. According to him, they did not affect each other at all. Western medicine was devoted to this view until more recent years. The movie "Patch Adams" with Robin Williams deals with just this dilemma.

Laughter brings healing to the mind and body. This was the initial conclusion of Norman Cousins. Suffering from a collagen illness, which is a breakdown of the connective tissue of the body, he was in excruciating pain. One evening a friend told him a joke and when Norman laughed, he immediately sensed a lessening of pain. He sent for several Marx brothers' movies and several copies of Allen Punt's "Candid Camera." Amazingly he went from being terminally ill to complete health.

This phenomenon started a research for Cousins at UCLA. The result was the discovery of endorphins that are secreted by the brain into the body when stimulated by laughter. Further study brought more insight by recognizing the similar molecule tie with morphine-both being pain killers-and endorphins are able to strengthen the immune system. The work of Drs. Carl Simonton, Bernie Seigel, Herbert Benson and others has established the Behavioral Medicine discipline.

Currently, Lorna Linda University is leading further studies on the healing properties of laughter and recent articles have told of their progress. Mike Utley, former football player for the Detroit Lions, has given testimony to the importance of humor in their healing process. Several cancer groups in Southern California never begin a meeting without sharing funny stories.

A zoo curator told his assistant to go to the train station and pick up twelve penguins and take them to the zoo. That evening the curator saw his assistant walking downtown with the 12 penguins behind him. He stopped and said, "I thought I told you to take them to the zoo?" The assistant responded by saying, "I did and we had such a good time I decided to take them to the movies." The humor is obvious and usually elicits a laugh. Remember, a little laughter adds a lot to living.

The judge had just awarded a divorce to a lady who had charged nonsupport. He said "to her husband, "I have decided to give your wife $400 a month for support." "Well, that's fine, Judge," he smiled. "And once in a while I'll try to chip in a few bucks, myself."

The Sunday School teacher was describing how Lot's wife looked back and turned into a pillar of salt—when little Jason interrupted, "My Mommy looked back once, while she was driving," he announced, "and she turned into a telephone pole."

A Sunday school teacher was telling her class the story of the Good Samaritan, in which a man was beaten, robbed and left for dead. She described the situation in vivid detail, so her students would catch the drama. Then, she asked the class, "If you saw a person lying on the roadside, all wounded and bleeding, what would you do?" A thoughtful little girl broke the hushed silence, "I think I'd throw up."

A grizzled old man was eating in a truck stop when six members of an outlaw motorcycle gang walked in. Two of them elbowed the old man as they walked by. The third knocked the old man's hat off. The fourth pushed his cigarette into the old man's pie, and the fifth knocked over his glass of milk. The sixth challenged the old man: "You're sitting in my seat." Without a word of protest, the old man quietly left the diner. Shortly thereafter, one of the bikers said to the waitress, "Ha! Not much of a man, was he?" The waitress replied, "Not much of a truck driver, either. He just backed his rig over six motorcycles."

Amen. Selah. So be it.

HUMOR CAN BE DANGEROUS

Unfortunately joking and humor can be dangerous. A number of young people in Santee say that the boy who killed two and wounded thirteen others heard him say something about taking a gun to school. When they questioned him he said, "Oh, I was just joking." In fact, he had a reputation as a prankster. But the tragedy is apparent. Often times passing off bad behavior as a joke is too common.

Humor can also be used as a "put down." Don Rickles has made a career out of this kind of joking. Supposedly his humor is an art. But others use it as way of disparaging another. Caustic comments are too easily minimized by, "I was just kidding."

Psychologists for years have affirmed that humor is often used as a cover-up; usually for a sense of inferiority. The jokester is also wanting attention. When comedians are interviewed by the media they are often asked, "When you were in school, were you the class clown?"

Our approach to humor has gone beyond this. Hopefully we recognize today the essential benefits of humor and laughter. It should be a part of normal and natural behavior. A major source for humor these days is the Internet. I thoroughly enjoyed this bit of advice for someone who is caught napping on the job. The best 10 answers are:

10. They told me at the blood bank this might

happen.

9. This is just a fifteen minute power nap like they raved about in that time management course you sent me to.

8. Whew! Guess I left the top off the White Out. You probably got here just in time.

7. I wasn't sleeping. I was meditating on the mission statement and envisioning a new paradigm.

6. I was testing my keyboard for drool resistance.

5. I was doing a highly specific yoga exercise to relieve work-related stress. Are you discriminatory toward people who practice yoga?

4. Why did you interrupt me? I had almost figured out a solution to our biggest problem.

3. The coffee machine is broken.

2. Someone must've put decaf in the wrong pot. And the No. 1 best thing to say if you get caught sleeping at your desk:

1. ' .... in Jesus' name. Amen.'

The last couple of years have brought the democratic process close to all of us. We are more acquainted with members of Congress than ever before. All members of the legislature, judicial and executive branches of government are in our living rooms by way of television.

I cannot vouch for the veracity of the following, but it does sound very possible. It is pretty scary. Can you imagine working for a company that has a little more than 500 employees and has the following statistics:

29 have been accused of spousal abuse

7 have been arrested for fraud

19 have been accused of writing bad checks

117 have directly or indirectly bankrupted at least 2 businesses

3 have done time for assault

71 cannot get a credit card due to bad credit

14 have been arrested on drug-related charges

8 have been arrested for shoplifting

21 are currently defendants in lawsuits

84 have been arrested for drunk driving in the last Year.

Can you guess which organization this is? Give up yet? It's the 535 members of the United States Congress; the same group of idiots that crank out hundreds of new laws each year designed to keep the rest of us in line.

Mrs. Bartholomew had been in the doctor's office for only a few minutes when suddenly she burst from the room and ran screaming down the hall. Another doctor stopped her and asked what the problem was. She told him what had happened. The second doctor turned on his heels and marched up the hall and accosted the first doctor, who was busy writing on his clipboard. "What on earth is the matter with you?" the second doctor said. "Mrs. Bartholomew is seventy-one years old. She has four grown children and seven grandchildren. And you told her she's PREGNANT?" The first doctor continued writing. Without looking up, he asked, "Does she still have the hiccups?"

Amen. Selah. So be it.

HUMOR COMES IN PACKAGES

Humor comes to us in various packages. A very common form is what is called sit-comedy humor. This would include "Frazier," "Everybody Loves Raymond," and "Lucy." Then, of course, there is stand-up comedy. This package can be divided further. There are those who capitalize on dirty, suggestive humor. Filth would be an appropriate word.

Traditional stand-ups like Jack Benny, Red Skelton and George Burns have brought laughter to most of us. There is also another type of humor that appeals to me. The sarcasm, satire and caustic bite of men like Art Buchwald, Don Rickles, Mort Sahl and others of their ilk stimulates the humor within.

The truculence of Don Rickles can be a little difficult to handle. But the political satire of Mort Sahl really pleases me. He is one of a kind. I've listened to him since his early days at the "Hungry I" in San Francisco. His red sweater and newspaper are memorable. He made a statement that I've never forgotten: "I wish I had a cause; I've got so much enthusiasm."

Appreciation for humor is very individual. The appreciation for different kinds of art is in the eye of the beholder. For humor it is in the mind of the listener. The kind of jokes someone likes says an awful lot about them. My assessment of the contributors to this column is clear. By-and-large they are sensitive to the subtleties of humor. They appreciate humor both intellectually and emotionally.

On a bag of Fritos: You could be a winner! No purchase necessary. Details inside. On a bar of Dial soap: Directions. Use like regular soap. On Nytol sleep aid: Warning. May cause drowsiness. On Sainsbury Peanuts: Warning contains nuts. On a Swedish chainsaw: Do not attempt to stop chain with your hands or genitals.

When I discovered my first gray hair I immediately wrote to my parents "Dear Dad and Mom. You saw my first steps. You might want to experience this with me too." I taped the offending hair to the paper and mailed it. My father's response, titled "Sonnet to a Hair," began: "It's a trustworthy observation. That nothing can compare...In the process of aging...With finding the first gray hair...He signed off with this observation: "That gray hair you sent us is not the first one you gave us!"

A little girl was talking to her teacher about whales. The teacher said it was physically impossible for a whale to swallow a human because even though it was a very large mammal, its throat was very small. The little girl stated that Jonah was swallowed by a whale. Irritated, the teacher reiterated that a whale could not swallow a human; it was physically impossible. The little girl said, "When I get to Heaven I will ask Jonah." The teachers asked, "What if Jonah went to hell?" The little girl replied, "Then you ask him."

This is being written around Easter, Passover and April

Fool's Day. It is a bit of apropos humor. In Florida, an atheist became incensed over the preparation for Easter and Passover holidays and decided to contact the local ACLU about the constant celebrations afforded to Christians and Jews with all their holidays while the atheists had no holiday to celebrate. The ACLU jumped on the opportunity to once again pick up the cause of the godless and assigned their sharpest attorneys to the case. The case was brought before a wise judge who after listening to the long, passionate presentation of the ACLU lawyers, promptly banged his gavel and declared, "Case Dismissed!"

The lead ACLU lawyer immediately stood and objected to the ruling and said, 'Your honor, how can you possibly dismiss this case? Surely the Christians have Christmas, Easter and many other observances. And the Jews; why in addition to Passover they have Yom Kippur and Hanukkah…and yet my client and all other atheists have no such holiday!" The judge leaned forward in his chair and simply said, "Obviously your client is too confused to know about, or for that matter, even celebrate the atheists' holiday!" The ACLU lawyer pompously said, "We are aware of no such holiday for atheists, just when might that be you honor?" The judge said, "Well it comes every year on exactly the same date, April 1st."

Amen. Selah. So be it.

HUMOR JOKES

Adversity breeds humor. I like the phrase. I'm not sure If I heard it or read it. It's doubtful if I originated it. My skills are more in the line of paraphrasing, plagiarism or synthesizing. I like the idea and have used various interpretations of it in the past. Humor has often been tied to the travails of various ethnic groups: Irish, Jews and blacks to name a few.

Those of my generation are well aware of the comedians who honed their skills in the midst of the Great Depression: George Burns, Red Skelton, Jack Benny, Lucille Ball and a plethora of others. Most stand-up comics today have had a rough row to hoe. It's been trial and error. Steve Martin, Eddie Murphy, Seinfeld and others have had a long apprenticeship on the road.

While I entertain through comedy, my approach is different. I combine information on humor-with actual jokes. Also, these articles alone provide plenty of jokes from you readers. Also, again, I'm always asking people I meet about their favorite joke. Yesterday, I asked a sales gal about her favorite. Here it is. A plane was flying over the city and the pilot announced they were too heavy and everyone had to throw something out. One guy threw out an apple; another a rock and the third threw out a bomb. When they landed they saw a gal crying. "Why are you crying?" they asked. "I don't know how, but an apple hit me on the head." Another gal was crying and her answer was, "A brick hit me on the head." The third gal was laughing like mad. When asked "why?" She said, "Well, when I sneezed, my house blew up."

I really laughed when I received this one. The Lady and the Dentist. While waiting for her first appointment in the reception room of a new dentist a lady noticed his certificate, which bore his full name. Suddenly, she remembered that a tall, handsome boy with the same name had been in her high school class almost fifty years ago. Upon seeing him, however, she quickly discarded any such thought. This balding, gray-haired man with the deeply lined face was too old to have been her classmate. After he had examined her teeth, she asked him if he had attended the local high school. "Yes," he replied. "When did you graduate?" she asked. He answered, "In 1953." "Why, you were in my class!" she exclaimed. Then came the ultimate put-down. He looked at her closely and then asked, "What did you teach?"

I was doing sit down for the Joslyn Senior Center the other day, and a friend shared with us this joke. A blonde was driving home and got caught in a really bad hailstorm. Her car was covered with dents, so the next day she took it to the repair shop. The owner saw that she was a blonde, so he decided to have some fun. He told her to just go home and blow into the tailpipe really hard, and all the dents would pop out. So, the blonde went home, got down on her hands and knees and started blowing into her tailpipe. Nothing happened. She blew a little harder, and still nothing happened. Her roommate, another blonde, came home and said "What are you doing?" The first blonde told her how the repairman had instructed her to blow into the tailpipe in order to get all the dents to pop out. The roommate rolled eyes and said, "HEL-LOOOO. You need to roll up the windows first!"

Read and practice the Ten Commandments of Connecting:

1. Slow down frequently, so your soul can catch up with your body!

2. Have a daily conversation with your heart.

3. Your brain and body are the hardware. Your heart is the software that runs it.

4. Intuition is your heart's wisdom. Stay still long enough to hear it.

5. Having angry, hostile feelings in your heart are a strong predictor of a heart attack.

6. To keep your heart healthy, have a sense of purpose or meaning in life, feel happy, and have a sense of belonging.

7. What connection rituals do you have with your children and partner in life?

8. Find something for which to be grateful every morning when you wake up, and every night before you sleep.

9. Sending love to others boosts your immune system, and theirs! It's also called forgiveness.

10. Celebrate life and living and being connected to those you love. The small things, not just mega events!

Chris is a newcomer to this column. He is a heavy equipment operator and a devotee of good humor. I love this, his first contribution. The following ad appeared in a newspaper. SBF Seeks Male companionship, ethnicity unimportant. I'm a svelte, good looking girl who LOVES to play. I love long walks in the woods. Riding in your pickup truck. Hunting, camping. Fishing trips. Cozy winter nights spent lying by the fire. Candlelight dinners will have me eating out of your hand. Rub me the right way and watch me respond. I'll be at the front door when you get home from work, wearing only what nature gave me. Kiss me and I'm yours. Call 555-xxxx and ask for Daisy. The phone number was the Humane Society and Daisy was an eight week old black Labrador Retriever.

Amen. Selah. So be it.

HUMOR MAKES

STRANGE BED FELLOWS

Humor makes strange bed fellows or to change the figure, humor is evident in the most inopportune of times. History gives evidence of humor in the most difficult situations. The pogroms of Russia stimulated the humor of Shalom Alechem: example, Fiddler on the Roof. Slavery in all of its ramifications stimulated both music and humor for blacks. War and national tragedy provides little opportunity or inclination for jokes. However, humor can be an instrument for healing in personal or national grief.

As a therapist I was always astute enough to know that when an individual or couple were able to laugh, then healing and therapy were close at hand. Laughter is good medicine.

Have you heard about the man who was an insomniac, an agnostic and a dyslexic? He stayed awake all night wondering if there really was a dog.

I like the various kinds of lists that make it to my desk. Here are some pithy comments under the heading, Benefits of Getting Older.

- People call at 9:00 PM and ask, "Did I wake you?"
- Things you buy now won't wear out.

- You can eat dinner at 4:30.
- There's nothing left to learn the hard way.
- You can live without sex but not without glasses.
- It's harder and harder for sexual harassment charges to stick.
- In a bank robbery you are likely to be released first.
- Your eyes won't get much worse.
- You sing along with the elevator music.
- Your investment in health insurance is finally beginning to pay off.
- Your secrets are safe with your friends because they can't remember them either.
- Your back goes out more than you do.
- And, your arms are almost too short to read the newspaper.

I really love this one. A teacher is having "show and tell" and asks students to bring a symbol of their faith. The first student says, "I'm a Muslim and I've brought a prayer rug." The next student says, "I'm Jewish and I've brought a Star of David." The third student says, "I'm Catholic and I've brought a Rosary." The last example is applicable to any Protestant denomination. The student says, "I'm (Methodist, Baptist, Presbyterian, etc) and I've brought a casserole dish."

This one is cute. An executive is interviewing a blonde

for a secretarial position. The question. "If you could interview anyone living or dead, who would it be?" The blonde responds, "I would prefer the living one."

A car was pulled over by a CHP officer for speeding. While writing the ticket he noticed several machetes in the car. Upon questioning, he was told the speeder was a juggler and used the machetes in his act. A demonstration was demanded. A dazzling show ensued. Just then, another car passed by. The driver did a double take, and said, "My God. I've got to give up drinking! Look at the test they're giving now."

Have you heard this one? I so, enjoy it again. A drunk stumbled into a Baptismal Service down by a river. He stumbles into the water and the Minister asks him, "Are you ready to find Jesus?" The drunk says, "Yes, I am." Down he goes. When he comes up, the Minister asks, "Did you find Jesus?" The answer, "No, I didn't." Down he goes again with the same result. After two more dips, the Minister holds him down for 30 seconds, brings him up and demands, "Have you found Jesus this time?" The old drunk wipes his eyes and pleads, "Are you sure this is where he fell in?"

I like jokes about seniors, being one myself. A young braggart was poking fun at a male senior. Finally the older man challenged, "I'll bet you a $100.00 that I can load this wheelbarrow with something, take it to that telephone pole, and you can't do it." The braggart said, "Let's make it my week's salary." Satisfied, the old man said to the young guy, "O.K. get in." I love it.

A group of seniors were commiserating with each other. One says, "My arm's so weak I can't lift a cup of coffee." Another one says, "My cataracts are so bad, I can't even see a cup of coffee." Another responds, "My arthritis is so bad, I can't turn my neck at all." The last one says, "My blood pressure is so bad I get dizzy all the time." The consensus comment is memorable. They all agreed. "Well, at least we can all still drive."

Amen. Selah. So be it.

HUMOR TAKES MANY FORMS

Humor takes many forms. I endorse all kinds except filthy language, suggestive types of humor. And certain kinds of ethnic humor. I particularly like ridiculous jokes and jokes that have a twist at the end. Slapstick humor really tickles my funny bone. But of all the myriad types of humor, I particularly enjoy religious and children's jokes.

1. The Fasting & Prayer Conference includes meals.

2. Ladies, don't forget the rummage sale. It' s a chance to get rid of those things not worth keeping around the house. Bring your husbands.

3. Don't let worry kill you off- let the Church help.

4. Miss Charlene Mason sang 'I will not pass this way again', giving obvious pleasure to the congregation.

5. For those of you who have children and don't know it, we have a nursery downstairs.

6. Next Thursday there will be tryouts for the choir. They need all the help they can get.

7. Irving Benson and Jessie Carter were married on October 24 in the church. So ends a friendship that began in their school days.

8. The evening service tonight, the sermon topic will be 'What Is Hell?' Come early and listen to our choir practice.

9. Potluck super Sunday at 5:00PM - prayer and medication to follow.

10. The ladies of the Church have cast off clothing of every kind. They may be seen in the basement on Friday afternoon.

11. Low Self Esteem Support Group will meet Thursday at 7 PM. Please use the back door. Joel Osteen, pastor of a mega-church in Houston, Texas, always begins his sermon with a joke.

A young pilot was flying with his instructor. The teacher was very impressed with his cool and composed student. They came in for a landing, hit the ground hard, bounced fifty feet in the air, came down, and bounced again. They eventually landed with a bang. The instructor was appalled and told his student it was the WORST landing he had ever participated in. The amazed student said, "Me? I thought you were piloting the plane." The Sunday School teacher was describing how Lot's wife looked back and turned into a pillar of salt, when little Jason interrupted, "My Mommy looked back once while she was driving,' he announced triumphantly, "and she turned into a telephone pole!"

A Sunday school teacher was telling her class the story of the Good Samaritan. She asked the class, "If you saw a person lying on the roadside, all wounded and bleeding, what would you do?" A thoughtful little girl broke the hushed silence, "I think I'd throw up."

A Sunday school teacher asked, "Johnny, do you think Noah did a lot of fishing when he was on the Ark?" "No," replied Johnny. "How could he with just two worms?"

A Sunday school teacher said to her children, "We have been learning how powerful kings and queens were in Bible times. But, there is a Higher Power. Can anybody tell me what it is?" One child blurted out, "Aces!'

The Priest said, "Sister, this is a silent monastery. You are welcome here as long as you like, but you may not speak until directed to do so." Sister Mary Katherine lived in the monastery for 5 years before the Priest said to her, "Sister Mary Katherine, you have been here for 5 years. You may speak two words." She said, "Hard bed." "I'm sorry "to hear that," the Priest said, "we will get you a better bed." After another 5 years, Sister Mary Katherine was summoned by the Priest. "You may say another two words, Sister Mary Katherine." "Cold food," said Sister Mary Katherine, and the Priest assured her that the food would be better in the future. On her 15th anniversary at the monastery, the Priest again called Sister Mary Katherine into his office. "You may say two words today." "I quit," said Sister Mary Katherine. "It's probably best," said the Priest, "You've done nothing but complain since you got here."

Amen. Selah. So be it.

HUMOR WHERE YOU FIND IT

Humor is where you find it. Some are from strange places; others from unexpected. Picture this scene. It's Thanksgiving time. Dennis the Menace is sitting with his family at a sumptuous traditional dinner. In a euphoric angelic tone he says, " ...and I'm thankful the Pilgrims didn't have liver an' onions for their Thanksgiving meal."

Did you hear about the little boy and his dog that died? Well, he went to his pastor and shared the news with him. The pastor, wanting to console the boy, said, "Remember, son, he is in heaven with Jesus." The boy responded with the insightful words, "What does Jesus want with a dead dog?"

A man took his talented dog into a bar. Bragging about the dog's talent, he had the dog play the piano and type on the computer. To their surprise, the man said the dog was also bi-lingual. Doubting that, they demanded a demo. The dog immediately said, "Meow, Meow."

I recently returned from a twenty-eight day cruise through the Panama Canal, Caribbean and back. During that time I lectured sixteen times. I began each one with a magic trick and a joke. I used a joke shared with me by a friend. It brought down the house. An elderly widow with meager means put a check for $5,000.00 into the church offering. It surprised and scared the pastor. The next Sunday came the same contribution and so the third Sunday. Finally, he could take it no longer. "Mrs. Jones, how can you afford such giving? I've known you for many years. You're a poor woman. She said, "My son sends me $20,000.00 a month." "What does he do," the pastor asked. "He's a veterinarian," she said. The pastor was even more curious, "What is his specialty." The woman, with measured pride, said, "Well, he has two cat houses in Las Vegas, two in Reno and a very large one in Hollywood."

The following excerpts are from the sayings of Will Rogers. "When I die, I want to die like my grandfather who died peacefully in his sleep. Not screaming like all the passengers in his car." And, "There are two theories to arguing with a woman. Neither one works." Isn't this squib the truth? "Lettin' the cat outta the bag is a whole lot easier than puttin ' it back in." Here's his advice for deflating an ego. "If you get to thinking you're a person of some influence, try ordering somebody else's dog around."

I really like this one. "If you find yourself in a hole, the first thing to do is stop digging." Woe, woe is me. "Never miss a good chance to shut up." After reading a few of these statements, it is not surprising that Will Rogers was considered the greatest humorist of his time. He also said, "Good judgment comes from experience, and a lot of that comes from bad judgment." While I refuse to take this last word personally, I will follow its advice. "After eating an entire bull, a mountain lion felt so good he started roaring. He kept it up until a hunter came along and shot him…

The moral: when you're full of bull, keep your mouth shut." Thank you Will Rogers.

A young couple got married and left on their honeymoon. When they got back, the bride immediately called her mother. "Well," said her mother, "so how was the honeymoon?" "Oh, Mama" she replied, "the honeymoon was wonderful! So romantic ... " Suddenly, she burst out crying. "But, Mama, as soon as we returned, Skip started using the most horrible language. Things I'd never heard before! I mean, all these awful four-letter words! You've got to come get me and take me home. PLEASE, MAMA!" "Sarah, Sarah," her mother said, "calm down! Tell me, what could be so awful; WHAT 4 letter words?" "Please don't make me tell you, Mama," wept the daughter, "I'm so embarrassed. They're just too awful! COME GET ME, PLEASE!!!!" "Darling, baby, you must tell me what has you so upset. Tell your mother these horrible four-letter words!" Still sobbing, the bride said, "Oh, Mama...words like: Dust, Wash, Iron, Cook". "I'll pick you up in ten minutes" said the mother.

Amen. Selah. So be it.

HURLEY AGAIN

Carl Hurley is one of America's best comics. Born in 1941 in a two-room cabin, he hails from a farm in the Appalachian mountains of eastern Kentucky. Today, after many years in education he is known as "America's Funniest Professor."' His funny side began in a one-room country church. It was followed with humor in grade school and then high school.

He graduated from college in 1965. In 1971 he was awarded a doctorate in education from the University of Missouri in Columbia. In 1982, with more than two hundred engagements, he opted for the world of comic entertainment. His appearances range from standup comedy to convention speaking. He is known for his infectious laughter with a wheeze, a twinkling eye and a wide grin. He says, "I try to encourage people to look for humor in life; to take life seriously but not too seriously." He feels strongly that humor brightens life's heavy load and makes life more enjoyable.

Hurley emphasizes laughter as a healing agent for all of life's ills. He always begins his gig with a question, "Are you happy? Well, you better tell your face." Carl's humor is always clean with a decided homespun, country flavor.

Here are a few samples. He tells about Aunt Sadie. To answer his question as to how she feels, she says, "Well, my hearing is bad, my sight is awful and I can't move my legs. My hands are crooked with arthritis. But thank God, I can still drive."

Carl Hurley has a rotund figure. In other words, he's fat. With a hearty laugh he tells of the salesman who tried to sell him a lap-top computer. His retort is hilarious. "Young man it's been years since I had a lap."

He tells about a bus load of seniors who were going on a mystery trip. No one knew where they were going. To make the trip more interesting, the leader took bets about where they were going. The winner would get the money. Again, with a chuckle, Hurley would say, "Every time, the bus driver would win."

He tells about a young fellow who tells him how his mother dislikes every girlfriend he brings home. Hurley's suggestion is that he get a girlfriend just like his mother. The boy says, "I did, but then my Dad didn't like her."

I love this story. The office has a wild party with plenty of drinking. The boss decides he better take his secretary home-she's soused. Nothing happens. The next night he and his wife are going out for dinner. He notices a single shoe on the floor of the car. Thinking it belongs to his secretary and hoping to allay his wife's suspicions, he carefully gets the shoe and at the first opportunity tosses it out of the window. Now the punch line. When they arrive at the restaurant, they start to get out and his wife says. "Where's my shoe? I can't go in with only one shoe." The better part of wisdom was for this husband never to say a word.

Hurley loves to throw out two liners. Two snakes are

talking. One says, "Are we poisonous?" "Why?" says the other snake. "Because I just bit my tongue." Or while waiting for his steak in a restaurant he sees the waiter coming with his thumb on the steak. After setting the steak down, Hurley asks him about his thumb. The waiter says, "To keep it from falling on the floor a second time."

All of his stories are accompanied with his belly laugh and belly giggling with his wheezing. He tells of two good old boys who have stopped at a bar to hoist a few beers. They sit on the end and there is a large mirror at the other end. One guy says, "Look over there. Two guys that look just like us." His partner says, Let's take a couple of beers to them." "No, just wait because they just got up and are coming this way." One more humorous account. A preacher is riding his bike. He's new to the church and needs a lawn mower. Seeing a young boy trying to sell one he offers to trade his bike for the mower. Later the boy rides by and sees the preacher pulling the rope and trying without success to start it.

The kid says, "Preacher you've got to cuss at it. " The preacher responds, "I gave that up years ago. I can't even remember any words." The boy responds, "You keep up pulling the starter and they'll come back to you."

Amen. Selah. So be it.

IMMUNE SYSTEM

One of the most interesting books I have read in recent years was copy righted in 2010. It's called, "The Healing Code"' written by Alexander Loyd, Ph.D. and Ben Johnson, M.D. The primary reason I like it so much, is that it presents several basic views that I researched in my doctoral dissertation (Ph.D.) in 1981. Since then (32 years) I have given over five hundred seminars on these views.

"A major emphasis is to heal the source of your health, sources, or relationship issues. Both men are professing Christian believers so faith in God is a primary source of healing. It is a given in the ultimate goal of healing." However, the human, medical, physical and universal reason for all healings is our IMMUNE SYSTEM. What exactly is it? Webster's Dictionary clarifies it: "The Immune system is a complex network of cells that protect the body from pathogens and destroy the infected malignant cells."

This system is universal in that every person alive has one. It is a "miraculous healing system that can heal any physical or non-physical issue that a person might have." Under the right circumstances any illness can be healed. This includes cancer, arthritis, heart trouble, pneumonias or even Alzheimer. This is the view in the Healing Code. In fact, most doctors affirm that any healing comes about because of the working of the immune system. They can perform surgery and/or offer medication but the healing comes about because of the immune system.

People of faith would equate the system with the work of the Divine. If humans are the product of God's creativity, and if the immune system is the result of the evolutionary process, then God started it. A leading physician states: "This is the only area of health where there has never in history been a validated case of harm." The natural question arises that if this system is within each of us, why is there sickness in the first place? The answer is very simple. The one thing that can turn off or slow down the work of the immune system is STRESS.

In 1998 Dr. Bruce Lipton of the Stanford University Medical School and a highly respected cell biologist stated, "Stress is the cause of at least 95 percent of illness and disease. The remaining 5 percent is genetic or caused by an accident." Stress has been defined as the "non-specific response of the body to any demand made upon it."

Hans Selye, M.D. gave this definition and created the "Fight or Flight" theory. He also revealed the fact that worry caused ulcers, thereby destroying the Cartesian view that there was no connection between the human body and the mind.

The stress movement came into full prominence in the 1960's-1980's. In my 1981 doctoral dissertation I made several observations about it. 1) It is cumulative. Stress mounts up. 2) It affects both genders and all ethnic groups. 3) There is both bad stress (distress) and good stress (eustress.) 4) Developing "maladaptive behaviors" is the main way many people seek to alleviate the affects of stress. Like smoking, drinking (booze), using drugs, eating too much, engaging in sexual affairs and committing criminal acts.

The causes of stress are as unique as there are individuals. However, there are a few obvious causes. Hans Selye's classic illustration depicts the beginning of stress with prehistoric cave man. He goes out hunting for food and confronts a saber tooth tiger. His life is threatened. He's under stress. His eyes dilate; hunger and sex are forgotten; his heart races; adrenal in hits his leg muscles and he runs the first four minute mile back to his cave. After a while, things settle down. His eyes are normal; hunger and sex drives return; adrenaline is gone; his heart and pulse return to normal.

Now think of modern man. There are many stressors that can affect our immune system. Job related (insecurity), family problems, our national economy, the weather, increase in crime, personal hassles, our health, terrorism and war to name a few. All these affect our IMMUNE SYSTEM.

Amen. Selah. So be it.

ISLAMIC WOMAN

Did you hear the Islamic woman on 60 Minutes on May 2nd? A Pakistani, she was born in Birmingham, England. Her parents thought for several years that she was a school teacher. In reality she is a stand-up comedian. A very popular one at that. A devout Muslim, she, non-the-less, is attempting to bring people of all faiths together. She has been threatened and feels her life is often on trial. Dressed in typical Arab clothing, she says, "I want people to laugh. It is often the only way to deal with life." The most difficult time was right after September eleven. She denounces it and contends that the Koran condemns terrorism.

The accolades given President Ronald Reagan would fill several books. The contributions were and are endless. For me, however, his greatest contribution to America was his sense of humor. He always had a joke and he expected one in return. It is truly amazing how humor seems to be stimulated by adversity. Think of the great comedians of the past and present. They are usually Jewish, black or Irish. No ethnic group has suffered more than these three. Yet, severe adversity has been a part of each.

Now for a change in direction. I recently remembered a humorous event. Shortly after Pope Paul was elected a local priest told this story about him. In Rome, a young priest got on an elevator and to his amazement the Pope was on it. Numbness set in. Stuttering set in. To ease his unease he said, "Your Holiness, could I tell you a joke?" The Pope graciously accepted but said, "Remember, I'm Polish." Then the priest committed the unbelievable faux paux. "That's all right. I'll tell it slowly." I'm just repeating what the priest told me.

The recent death and funeral services made all of us appreciate President Ronald Reagan. His sense of humor particularly attracted me. He was quick with short retorts. When asked how his meeting went with Bishop TuTu of South Africa, he responded with the cryptic words, "So So."

Put your mind to this one. "Dear Tide, I am writing to say what an excellent product you have! One evening about a month ago, while at home, I spilled some red wine on my new white blouse. My husband started to berate me about my drinking problem and how expensive the blouse was. Well, one thing leads to another and I ended up with a lot of his blood on my white blouse, as well. I tried to get the stains out using the bargain brand detergent my cheap husband bought, but they just wouldn't come out. I went to a local convenience store and got a bottle of liquid Tide with bleach alternative, and all of the stains came out! They came out so well, in fact, that the forensic DNA tests were all negative! I thank you, once again, for the great product! Well, gotta go, I have to write a letter to the Hefty bag people. Sincerely, Recently Widowed."

Here are ten views on housekeeping. 1. I don't do windows because…I love bird and don't want one to run into them and hurt themselves. 2. I don't wax floors because...I am terrified a guest will slip, hurt themselves, I'll feel terrible and they may sue me. 3. I don't mind the dust bunnies because...they are very good company and I have named most of them, they agree with everything I say. 4. I don't disturb cobwebs because...I want every creature to have a home of their own and grandson loves spiders. 5. I don't Spring Clean because...I love all the seasons and don't want them to get jealous. 6. I don't plant a garden because....I don't want to get in God's way, He is an excellent designer. 7. I don't put things away because...I will never be able to find them again. 8. I don't do gourmet meals when I entertain because...I don't want my guests to stress out over what to make when they invite me over for dinner. 9. I don't iron because...I believe them when they say Permanent Press. 10. I don't stress much on anything because...A Type Personalities die young and I want to stick around and become a wrinkled up crusty old lady!

Ten guidelines for good living: 1. Accept that some days you're the pigeon, and some days you're the statue. 2. If you can't be kind, at least have the decency to be vague. 3. It may be that your sole purpose in life is simply to serve as the warning to others. 4. Never buy a car you can't push. 5. The early worm gets eaten by the bird, so sleep late. 6. When everything's coming your way, you're in the wrong lane. 7. Birthdays are good for you; the more you have, the longer you live. 8. You may be only one person in the world, but you may also be the world to one person. 9. Some mistakes are too much fun to make only once. 10. A truly happy person is one who can enjoy the scenery on a detour.

Amen. Selah. So be it.

JESUS and HUMOR

Many Bible reading believing Christians overlook the humor of Jesus. The Gospels are filled with examples. One of the more common expressions of His humor is the deliberate use of preposterous statements. To get His points across Jesus would often exaggerate or us e ridiculous accounts. This is called the use of hyperbole.

An excellent example is the dictum about the rich man and the needle's eye. "It is easier for a camel to go through the eye of a needle than a rich man to enter the kingdom of God." These words are found in Matthew, Mark and Luke. The exaggeration creates a most humorous idea.

Another illustration that is funny has to do with judging others. Using a play on words to express the hyperbole, Jesus speaks of those who see the "speck" in their brother's eye, but ignore the log in their own eyes. One writer says, "It is an effective way of exposing one absurdity by the use of another."

Jesus would have loved the following humorous stories. Nancy sent me this one. In the hospital the relatives gathered in the waiting room, where their family member lay gravely ill. Finally, the doctor came in looking tired and somber. "I'm afraid I'm the bearer of bad news," he said as he surveyed the worried faces. "The only hope left for your loved one at this time is a brain transplant. It's an experimental procedure, very risky but is the only hope. Insurance will cover the procedure, but you will have to pay for the brain yourselves."

The family members sat silent as they absorbed the news. After a great length of time, someone asked, "Well, how much does a brain cost?" The doctor quickly responded, "$5,000 for a male brain, and $200 for a female brain." The moment turned awkward. Men in the room tried not to smile, avoiding eye contact with the women, but some actually smirked. A man unable to control his curiosity, blurted out the question everyone wanted to ask, "Why is the male brain so much more?" The doctor smiled at the childish innocence and explained to the entire group, "It 's just standard pricing procedure. We have to mark down the price of the female brains, because they've actually been used."

Here is one of the funniest stories I've heard. Several men are in the locker room of a golf club. A cell phone, on a bench, rings and a man engages the hands free speaker function and begins to talk. Everyone else in the room stops to listen. Man: "Hello." Woman: Honey, It's me. Are you at the club?" Man: "Yes." Woman: "I am at the mall now and found this beautiful leather coat. It's only $1,000 is it okay if I buy it?" Man: "Sure, go ahead if you like it that much." Woman: I also stopped by the Mercedes dealership and saw the new 2007 models. I saw one that I really liked." Man: "How much?" Woman: "$90,000." Man: "Okay, but for that price. I want it with all the options." Woman: "Great! Oh, and one more thing. The house I wanted last year is back on the market. They're asking $950,000." Man: "Well, then go ahead and give them an offer of $900,000. They will probably take it. If not, we can go the extra 50 thousand. It's really a pretty good price." Woman: "Okay. I'll see you later! I love you so much!" Man: "Bye! I love you, too." The man hangs up. The other men in the locker room are staring at him in astonishment, mouths agape. He smiles and asks, "Anyone know who this phone belongs to?"

Talk about exaggeration. A woman goes to the doctor for her yearly physical. The nurse starts with certain basic items. "How much do you weigh?" she asks. "115," she says. The nurse puts her on the scale. It turns out her weight is 140. The nurse asks, "Your height?" "5 foot 8," she says. The nurse checks and sees that she only measures 5 foot 5. She then takes her blood pressure and tells the woman it is very high. "Of course it's high!" she screams, "When I came in here I was tall and slender! Now I'm short and fat!" Think about the following. We'll begin with a box, and the plural is boxes, but the plural of ox becomes oxen, not oxes. One fowl is a goose, but two are called geese, yet the plural of moose should never be meese. You may find a lone mouse or a nest full of mice. Yet the plural of house is houses, not hice.

Amen. Selah. So be it.

JESUS' STATUES

Recently while reviewing some of my pictures from Brazil I became interested in the world wide statues of Jesus. The newest statue of Jesus is a bronze 105 feet statue located in a small mountain town in the country of Syria. A Muslim country. It was and is supported by Great Britain and Russia: and also King Assad.

The project took eight years; and then three days to raise it. The question is often asked, "Why put up such a statue in turbulent Syria." The organizer, Samir al-Ghadban quotes a Christian leader who said, "Jesus would have done it." It is very difficult to believe that the project is a success considering the views of King Bashar Assad, and the Muslim Shiites. The words of al-Ghadban will suffice, "it was and is a miracle."

The most visible and well-known statue of Jesus is "Christ the Redeemer" in Rio de Janeiro, Brazil. It is 98 feet tall and has a pedestal of 26 feet, making it 124 feet. Its arms stretch 92 feet and weight 635 tons. It is located at the peak of the Corcovado Mountain, overlooking the city. The statue was constructed between 1922 and 1931. It was dedicated between 1922 and 1931 and was dedicated on October 1931 and consecrated October 12, 2006. On July 7, 2007 it was declared one of the New Seven Wonders of the World.

The idea behind it was first proposed in the 1850's by a Catholic priest. The idea died but was renewed by the Catholic

Church in 1921. The title in Portuguese is "Christo Redentor" and is a symbol of peace. The overall cost in today's economy was $250,000. The statue has been struck by lightning several times and was vandalized with spray paint in 2010. I have personally visited the statue and can affirm its awesomeness.

"For almost all the giant Jesus statues ever made, Jesus is given the same pose: standing tall with arms outstretched-a symbol of peace, protection and blessing." The honor of being the tallest Jesus Statue is argued because of some having a crown, and bases. Counting Rio and Syria, I will list nine others of the tallest.

1. Christ the King in Swiebadziv, Poland. It is 117.8 feet tall with a 108 foot crown and was completed in 2010.

2. Christ of Peace is in Cochabamba, Bolivia. It is 112 feet with a 22 foot base. It was completed in 1994.

3. Cristo del Otero is in Palencia, Spain and was completed in 1931. It is 98.5 feet tall.

4. Cristo Resocitado is in Tlalnepantla de Baz, Mexico. It is also 98.5 feet tall and the date of completion is unknown.

5. Kristus kase Berkat is in Manado, Indonesia. It is also 98.5 feet tall and was completed in 2007.

6. Cristo Rei is in Almada, Portugal. It was completed in 1959 and is 92 feet tall.

7. Christ of Vung Tau is in Vong Tau, Vietnam. It was completed in 1993 and is 92 feet tall.

8. Christ the King of Dill is in Dill, East Timor and was completed in 1996. It is 88.6 feet tall.

9. Cristo Rey de Cali is in Cali, Colombia. It was completed in 1953 and is 85 feet tall.

.

One other statue of Jesus is worthy of mention. It is called "Christ the Redeemer of the Andes. Its importance is not based on its height. It is only forty feet high. Its importance is political and religious. The statue was unveiled on March 13, 1904 as a celebration of the peaceful resolution of the border dispute between Argentina and Chile. It was placed high in the Andes at 12,572 feet. The dispute was over the border between the countries. The figure faces the border with a cross in Jesus' left hand and the right hand extended in blessing.

A plaque is at the base with this inscription (in Spanish) 'Sooner shall these mountain crags crumble to dust than Chile and Argentina shall break this peace which at the feet of Christ the Redeemer they have sworn to maintain."

Amen. Selah. So be it.

JEWISH HUMOR

Have you heard the story of the two elderly women who regularly played cards? In fact, they had played each other for several years. One day one of the ladies said, "You know, we've played cards for many years and I've never known your name. What is your name? The other woman paused and waited thoughtfully for five, ten and finally fifteen minutes. She finally said, "How soon do you need to know?"

Here is a blonde joke that really cracked me up. A blonde was walking along the riverbank. She looked across the river and saw another blonde over there and yelled across to her, "Hey can you tell me how to get to the other side?" The second blonde looked up and down the river, thought for a few minutes, and then yelled back "You are on the other side."

Jews have made unique contributions in the field of humor. Of course the obvious contribution is the great number of comedians past and present who were or are Jews. What's the difference between a Rottweiler and a Jewish mother? Eventually the Rottweiler lets go. What did the waiter ask the group of Jewish mothers? "Is anything all right."

Sam Levy was driving down the road and gets pulled over by a policeman. Walking over to Sam's car, the policeman says. "Your wife fell out of the car 5 miles back." Sam replies "Thank God for that. I'd thought I'd gone deaf."

And now, my favorite one. A man calls his Jewish mother in Palm Beach, Florida. "Mom, how are you?" "Not too good," says the mother. "I've been very weak." The son says, "Why are you so weak?" She says, "Because I haven't eaten in 38 days". The man says, "That's terrible. Why haven't you eaten in 38 days?" The mother answers, "Because I didn't want my mouth to be filled with food if you should call."

This joke really stimulates my laugh meter. A man dashed into a pharmacy and asked the druggist for something to stop hiccups. The druggist filled a glass with water and threw the water into the customer's face. "Why did you do that?" the man shouted, red-faced and drenched. "Well, you don't have the hiccups anymore, do you?" the druggist asked. "No!" the man yelled. "But my wife out in the car still does!"

I heard the following story years ago and for the life of me cannot remember where or from whom. It seems a certain very erudite Rabbi was a very popular lecturer. He had a personal driver who chauffeured him to all his engagements. One day the driver, who was bored, said, "Rabbi, I've heard your lecture so many times, I bet I could give it." "Fine," the Rabbi said. "Let's change clothes and you give the lecture tonight." Everything went fine until the question and answer period. A very complicated question and academic was asked by a member of the audience. The imposter was stumped. However, his creativity came to the front. He said, "That question is so simple even my driver can answer it.

Driver come up here and answer it."

Several friends have shared the following: Diets and Dying: Here's the final word on nutrition and health. It's a relief to know the truth after all those conflicting medical studies . The Japanese eat very little fat and suffer fewer heart attacks than the British or Americans. The French eat a lot of fat and also suffer fewer heart attacks than the British or Americans. The Japanese drink very little red wine and suffer fewer heart attacks than the British or Americans. The Italians drink excessive amounts of red wine and also suffer fewer heart attacks than the British or Americans. Conclusion: Eat and drink what you like. Speaking English is apparently what kills you.

Quotes from great women. Enjoy! Helen Hayes (at 73): The hardest years in life are those between ten and seventy. Bette Davis: Old age ain't no place for sissies. Rhonda Hansome: A man's got to do what a man's got to do. A woman must do what he can't. Caryn Leschen: Thirty-five is when you finally get your head together and your body starts falling apart. Dolly Parton: I'm not offended by all the dumb blonde jokes because I know I'm not dumb; and I'm also not blonde. Eleanor Roosevelt: Nobody can make you feel inferior without your permission.

Amen. Selah. So be it.

JOKE TRIGGERS

If music has charms to sooth the savage beast, then certainly words bring insight to change lives. A sentence or phrase has untold power. Think of Lincoln's Gettysburg Address or the U.S. Constitution. The power in a "no" or a "yes," can create all kinds of possibilities.

I love the phrases that project information. Debra sent the following:

A duck's quack doesn't echo, and no one knows why. In ten minutes, a hurricane releases more energy than all the world's nuclear weapons combined. On average, one hundred people choke to death on ballpoint pens every year. On average people fear spiders more than they do death. Elephants are the only animals that can't jump. Only one person in two billion will live to be one hundred-sixteen or older. It's possible to lead a cow upstairs... but not downstairs.

Women blink nearly twice as much as men. It's physically impossible for you to lick your elbow. A snail can sleep for three years. No word in the English language rhymes with "MONTH." The average life span of a major league baseball: seven pitches. Our eyes are always the same size from birth, but our nose and ears never stop growing-scary!!! The electric chair was invented by a dentist. All polar bears are left handed. An ostrich's eye is bigger than its brain. A crocodile cannot stick its tongue out. Americans on average eat eighteen acres of pizza every day. Almost everyone who reads this article will try to lick their elbow.

A pessimist's blood type will always b-negative. A Freudian slip is when you say one thing but mean your mother. Shotgun wedding: A case of wife or death. I used to work in a blanket factory, but it folded. If electricity comes from electrons, does morality come from morons? Marriage is the mourning after the knot before. A hangover is the wrath of grapes. Sea captains don't like crew cuts. Does the name Pavlov ring a bell? A successful diet is the triumph of mind over platter. Time flies like an arrow. Fruit flies like a banana. A gossip is someone with a sense of rumor. Without geometry, life is pointless. When you dream in color, it' s a pigment of your imagination. Reading whilst sunbathing makes you well-red. When two egotists meet, it's an I for an I.

Read this one and laugh. A blonde called in a repairman to fix her electric clock. He examined it and told her, "There's nothing wrong with the clock. You didn't have it plugged in." She replied, "I don't want to waste electricity, so I only plug it in when I want to know what time it is." "Cash, check or charge?" I asked, after folding items the woman wished to purchase. As she fumbled for her wallet I noticed a remote control for a television set in her purse. "So, do you always carry your TV remote?" I asked. "No," she replied, "but my husband refused to come shopping with me, so I figured this was the most evil thing I could do to him."

Two elderly ladies meet at the launderette after not seeing one another for some time. After inquiring about each other's health one asked how the other's husband was doing. "Oh! Ted died last week. He went out to the garden to dig up a cabbage for dinner, had a heart attack and dropped down dead, right there in the middle of the vegetable patch." "Oh dear! I'm very sorry," replied her friend. "What did you do?" "Opened a can of peas instead!"

"Forgive your Enemies" The preacher, in his Sunday sermon, used "Forgive Your Enemies" as his subject. After a long sermon, he asked how many were willing to forgive their enemies. About half held up their hands. Not satisfied, he harangued for another twenty minutes and repeated his question. This time he received a response of about 80%. Still unsatisfied, he lectured for minutes and repeated his question. With all thought now on Sunday dinner, all responded except one elderly lady in the rear. "Mrs. Jones, that is very unusual. How old are you?" "Ninety-three" was her response. "Mrs. Jones, please come down in front and tell the congregation how a person can live to be ninety-three and not have an enemy in the world." The little sweetheart of a lady tottered down the aisle, very slowly turned around, and said: "It's easy, I just outlived the b ..... s."

A taxi driver picked up a fare in downtown Los Angeles. After a couple of miles the passenger tapped the driver on his shoulder. The driver went crazy. He rammed into two cars, went through a red light and ended up hitting a fire hydrant. The passenger apologized profusely. "It's not your fault," the driver said. "Today is my first day driving a taxi. For twenty years I was driving a hearse for a mortuary."

Amen. Selah. So be it.

JOKES LIKE GOOD MUSIC

One of my contentions about humor is that good jokes are like good music, they bear repeating. I can listen to Placido Domingo again and again. The same thing applies to jokes. Most of us have a tendency to forget jokes, even if we write them down- and always if we don't.

My mind was triggered the other day about a joke that I had not thought about for years. It seems that three men are in the hospital and all three are diagnosed as terminally ill. They all have the same doctor. He sees the first man who is a Catholic. "Mr. Santini, you're going to die. Do you have a last request?" "Yes," he says. "I'd like to see my priest and receive the last rites of the Church." The second man is a Protestant. "Mr. Jones, you're going to die. Do you have a last request?" "Yes, doctor," he says. I would like to see the members of my family." The third man is Jewish. "Mr. Goldberg, you're going to die. Do you have a last request?" "Yes, doctor, I do," he says. "I want to see a different doctor."

I think some jokes get recycled every five years. Here's a long one that is a good example. After being nearly snowbound for two weeks last winter, a Seattle man departed for Miami Beach, where he was to meet his wife the next day at the conclusion of her business trip to Minneapolis. They were looking forward to pleasant weather and a nice time together. Unfortunately there was some sort of mix-up at the boarding gate, and the man was told that he would have to wait for a later flight. He tried to appeal to a supervisor but was told the airline was not responsible for the problem and it would do no good to complain.

Upon the arrival at the hotel the next day, he discovered that Miami Beach was having a heat wave, and its weather was almost as uncomfortably hot as Seattle's was cold. The desk clerk gave him a message that his wife would arrive as planned. He could hardly wait to get to the pool area to cool off, and quickly sent his wife an e-mail message, but due to his haste he made an error in the address. His message therefore arrived at the home of an elderly preacher's wife whose even older husband had died only the day before. When the grieving widow opened her e-mail, she took one look at the monitor, let out an anguished scream, and fell to the floor dead. Her family rushed to her room where they saw this message on the screen: "Dearest Wife: Departed yesterday as you know. Just now got checked in. Some confusion at the gate. Appeal was denied. Received confirmation of your arrival tomorrow. Your loving Husband. P.S. Things are not as we thought. You're going to be surprised how hot it is down here."

I don't think this joke is limited to the Irish. Several copies came by way of e-mail. An Irishman had been drinking at a pub all night. The bartender finally said that the bar was closing. So the Irishman stood up to leave, fell flat on his face. He tried to stand one more time; same result. He figured he'll crawl outside and get some fresh air and maybe that would somber him up. Once outside, he stood up and fell on his face again. So he decided to crawl the four blocks home.

When he arrived at the door he stood up and fell flat on his face. He crawled through the door and into his bedroom. When he reached his bed he tried one more time to stand up. This time he managed to pull himself upright, but he quickly fell right into the bed and was sound asleep as soon as his head hit the pillow. He was awakened the next morning to his wife standing over him, shouting, "SO YOU 'VE BEEN DRINKING AGAIN!" Putting on an innocent look, and intent on bluffing it out he said, "What makes you say that?" "The pub just called; you left your wheelchair there again."

(A) The Japanese eat very little fat and suffer fewer heart attacks than the British or Americans.

(B) On the other hand, the French eat a lot of fat and also suffer fewer heart attacks than the British or Americans.

(C) The Japanese drink very little red wine and suffer fewer heart attacks than the British or Americans.

(D) The Italians drink excessive amounts of red wine and also suffer fewer heart attacks than the British or Americans.

(E) Conclusion: Eat and drink what you like. It's speaking English that kills you.

Amen. Selah. So be it.

LAUGH AND STAY YOUNG

Michael F. Roizen, M.D. and Mehmet C. Oz, M.D. have written a best-selling book entitled, "You: Staying Young." In discussing humor they say: "When we laugh, natural killer cells that destroy tumors and viruses increase, along with gamma interferon (a disease fighting protein) and T cells and B cells (which make disease fighting antibodies).

Laughing lowers blood pressure, increases oxygen in the blood with deeper respiration, and helps address the effect of mental stress on the arteries." They end this paragraph with the words, "And you can't beat the price." They also talk about the mental benefits of humor. Jokes stimulate the brain cells. To grasp the meaning of a humorous story exercises the mind. So, enjoy the following and repeat them to others.

Dear Abby-they left her speechless. Dear Abby: What can I do about all the sex, nudity, language and violence on my VCR? Dear Abby: I have a man I never could trust. He cheats so much I'm not even sure this baby I'm carrying is his. Dear Abby: Our son writes that he is taking Judo. Why would a boy who was raised in a good Christian home turn against his own? Dear Abby: I was married to Bill for three months and I didn't know he drank until one night he came home sober. Dear Abby: you told some woman whose husband had lost all interest in sex to send him to a doctor.

Well, my husband lost all interest in sex years ago and he is a doctor.

"If you don't read the newspaper you are uninformed, if you do read the newspaper you are misinformed." Mark Twain.

"I contend that for a nation to try to tax itself into prosperity is like a man standing in a bucket and trying to lift himself up by the handle." Winston Churchill.

"Government's view of the economy could be summed up in a few short phrases: If it moves, tax it. If it keeps moving regulate it. And if it stops moving subsidize it." Ronald Reagan.

I always enjoy jokes with a religious twist. One Sunday morning, a mother went in to wake her son and tell him it was time to get ready for church, to which he replied, " I'm not going." "Why not?" she asked. "I'll give you two good reasons," he said. "One, they don't like me, and two, I don't like them." His mother replied, "I'll give YOU two good reasons why YOU SHOULD go to church. (1) You're fifty-nine years old, and (2) you're the pastor."

A Jewish Rabbi and a Catholic Priest met at the town's annual 4th of July picnic. Old friends, they began their usual banter. "This baked ham is really delicious," the priest teased the rabbi. "You really ought to try it. I know it's against your religion, but I can't understand why such a wonderful food should be forbidden! You don't know what you're missing. You just haven't lived until you've tried Mrs. Hall's prized Virginia Baked Ham. Tell me,

Rabbi, when are you going to break down and try it?" The rabbi looked at the priest with a big grin and said, "At your wedding."

I received this blonde joke from several people. Read it and laugh. A blonde and her husband are lying in bed listening to the next door neighbor's dog. It has been in the backyard barking for hours and hours. The blonde jumps up out of bed and says, "I've had enough of this." She goes downstairs. The blonde finally comes back up to bed and her husband says, "The dog is still barking, what have you been doing?" The blonde says, "I've put the dog in our backyard, let's see how they like it."

The title for these Q and A questions is enough to make me laugh: Pregnancy, Estrogen and Women. Q: Should I have a baby after thirty-five? A: No, thirty-five children is enough. Q: I'm two months pregnant now. When will my baby move? A: With any luck, right after he finishes college. Q: What is the most reliable method to determine a baby's sex? A: Childbirth. Q: My wife is five months pregnant and so moody that sometimes she's borderline irrational. A: So what's your question? Q: My childbirth instructor says it's not pain I'll feel during labor, but pressure. Is she right? A: Yes, in the same way that a tornado might be called an air current.

Amen. Selah. So be it.

LAUGH WITH NASTER

Most cruises have a comedian in their entertainment programs. A few weeks ago I lectured on two cruises and met one of the finest - David Naster. He's been on scores of cruises, late night TV shows, and the White House among other venues. He has entertained thousands of people with his humor.

David is somewhat short and stocky. He is Jewish, lives in Kansas, fifty-two years old and divorced. Above all, he is passionate about humor. He is one funny man. Quick of wit, he moves rapidly from one comic scenario to another.

David is different from the average comic. In addition to his humor gig, he schedules a lecture to discuss the theoretical benefits of humor. His themes are also a part of the books he has written. He discusses the work of Norman Cousins-the father of laughter as healing. In his book, "You Just Have to Laugh," he says, "Perhaps the most easily understandable work relating the effects of laughter on the human body came from Norman Cousins." David also discusses the healing effects of humor. All doctors know that immunoglobulin A is the healing agent in our bodies.

Naster says, "People with a well developed sense of humor have been proven to have increased concentrations of Ig A in their bodies." He writes like he speaks with short, pithy comments that are inspirational and motivational. Here's one: "You just have to laugh. No matter what life throws at you." Another: "Laughing makes you feel better physically." Another: "The way to make something funny is to take any subject and start exaggerating it, dissecting it from all possible angles." If you'll recall, that is exactly what Bill Cosby, Lily Tomlin and Jonathan Winters-among others-do. One more: "The ability to laugh at yourself is essential to living life with a humorous perspective.

To better understand Naster's humor, here are a couple of jokes that he uses. A woman was driving down an interstate highway in Oklahoma. She was speeding but, since every other car on the road was going faster than hers, she figured she wouldn't get a ticket. Much to her surprise, she was stopped by a highway patrolman. The policeman asked her, "Do you know why I pulled you over?" She responded quickly, "Yea, I was the only one you could catch." The policeman laughed and let her go with a warning.

United Airlines canceled a flight, so the agent at the ticket counter had to handle a long line of initiated people. Most of the passengers managed to keep some semblance of composure. One, however, had a problem. A middle aged man pushed and butted his way to the front of the line. Slapping his ticket down on the counter, he yelled, "I demand to be on the next flight and it better be in First Class!" Without raising her voice, the agent said, "I'm sorry sir, I'll be happy to help you, but these folks in line were here first. As soon as I take care of them, I'll be glad to help you."

The man yelled back, loud enough so everybody in line could hear, "Do you know "Who I am?" Without a hesitation, the ticket agent grabbed the microphone and announced the following over the terminal's public address system: "Attention, please. We have a passenger at the gate who doesn't know who he is. If anyone can help him identify himself, please come to the counter." The people in line began to laugh. The man gritted his teeth and swore, "*&%$# you!" Once again, the agent kept her cool. "I'm sorry sir," she said smiling, "But you'll have to wait in line for that, too." The man retreated as the rest of the line started applauding.

David is unique in other ways of communicating humor. He uses humor as a way of putting someone down who attacks. He calls it, "Dealing with Life's Hecklers."

He also discusses ways to turn a difficult job into a laughing situation. But, perhaps the most meaningful part of his lecture and book is the examples he gives to deal with grief or helping in tragic situations.

In a poignant account he tells of firemen who survived 9/11 who laughed at some situations in the aftermath. When asked how they could do it, they responded, "It was the only way we could keep from puking or crying."

Amen. Selah. So be it.

LAUGHING PROVIDES BENEFITS

I never cease to be amazed at the breadth of humor. From the subtle to the obvious from the intellectual to the stupid. I receive humorous anecdote that are caustic; others are totally bland. The only ones I refuse to consider for publication are the dirty and/or vulgar ones. Fortunately, as the column has aged the latter have become fewer and fewer.

I like to give credit when it is available. Too often the humorous contributions I receive are anonymous. Such is the following. I particularly like it because it is not only humorous but it has a very definite message of advice. Listen up to "Resignation." "I am hereby officially tendering my resignation as an adult. I have decided I would like to accept the responsibilities of an 8 year old again."

I want to go to McDonald's and think that it's a four star restaurant. I want to sail sticks across a fresh mud puddle and make a sidewalk with rocks. I want to think M & Ms are better than money because you eat them. I want to lie under a big oak tree and run a lemonade stand with my friend on a hot summer day. I want to return to a time when life was simple; when all you knew were colors, multiplication tables, and nursery rhymes, but that didn't bother you, because you didn't know why you didn't know and you didn't care.

All you knew was to be happy because you were

blissfully unaware of all the things that should make you worried or upset. I want to think the world is fair. That everyone is honest and good. I want to believe that anything is possible. I want to be oblivious to the complexities of life and be overly excited by the little things again.

I want to live simple again. I don't want my day to consist of computer crashes, mountains of paperwork, depressing news, how to survive more days in the month than there is money in the bank, doctor bills, gossip, illness and loss of loved ones. I want to believe in the power of smiles, hugs, a kind word, truth, justice, peace, dreams, the imagination, mankind, and making angels in the snow. So, here's my checkbook and my car keys, my credit card bills and my 401 K statements. I am officially resigning from adulthood. And if you want to discuss this further, you'll have to catch me first, 'cause…Tag! You're it.' Hope ya'll join me.

As residents of the Shady Rest Retirement and Convalescent Home for the aged, George age ninety-seven and Clara age ninety-five became infatuated with each other. At first, it was just a mere encounter at the mid-morning coffee break. Then it was dining at the same table for each of their meals. As they became better acquainted, they learned that both were surviving spouses; she had lost her husband of 50 years longer than she could remember and he had been a widower for a long, long time. They also liked the same foods and movies, and were always together. This was quite noticeable to the staff and management.

As a result, they thought it would be appropriate to suggest the two get married and live the rest of their lives in total happiness. Everyone agreed and so a vacant room was redecorated as a Bridal Suite. The wed ding was the highlight of the year. After they were in bed, he reached over and took hold of her hand. They both fell asleep. The next night he reached over and grabbed her hand. They both fell asleep. The third night he reached for her hand and she immediately withdrew and said, "Not tonight, George. I have a headache."

A little boy wanted to meet God. He knew it was a long trip to where God lived, so he packed his suitcase with Twinkies and a six-pack of Root Beer and he started his journey. When he had gone about three blocks, he met an elderly man. The man was sitting in the park just feeding some pigeons. The boy sat down next to him and opened his suitcase. He was about to take a drink from his root beer when he noticed that the man looked hungry, so he offered him a Twinkie. He gratefully accepted it and smiled at the boy. His smile was so pleasant that the boy wanted to see it again, so he offered him a root beer. Again, the man smiled at him. The boy was delighted! They sat there all afternoon eating and smiling, but they never said a word.

As it grew dark, the boy realized how tired he was and he got up to leave, but before he had gone more than a few steps, he turned around, ran back to the man, and gave him a hug. The man gave him his biggest smile ever. When the boy opened the door to his own house a short time later, his mother was surprised by the look of joy on his face. She asked him, "What did you do today that made you so happy?" He replied, "I had lunch with God." But before his mother could respond, he added, "You know what? God's got the most beautiful smile I've ever seen!"

Meanwhile, the elderly man, also radiant with joy, returned to his home. His son was stunned by the look of peace on his face and he asked, "Dad, what did you do today that made you so happy." He replied, "I ate Twinkies in the park with God." However, before his son responded, he added, "You know, he's much younger than I expected."

Amen. Selah. So be it.

LAUGHTER AND
THE RIDICULOUS

Humor takes many forms. I endorse all kinds except filthy language, suggestive types of humor. And certain kinds of ethnic humor. I particularly like ridiculous jokes and jokes that have a twist at the end. Slapstick humor really tickles my funny bone. But of all the myriad types of humor, I particularly enjoy religious and children's jokes.

Here are several sentences that appeared in church bulletins:

1. The Fasting & Prayer Conference includes meals. 2. Ladies, don't forget the rummage sale. It's a chance to get rid of those things not worth keeping around the house. Bring your husbands. 3. Don't let worry kill you off—let the Church help. 4. Miss Charlene Mason sang 'I will not pass this way again', giving obvious pleasure to the congregation. 5. For those of you who have children and don't know it, we have a nursery downstairs. 6. Next Thursday there will be tryouts for the choir. They need all the help they can get. 7. Irving Benson and Jessie Carter were married on October 24 in the church. So ends a friendship that began in their school days. 8. The evening service tonight, the sermon topic will be 'What Is Hell?' Come early and listen to our choir practice. 9. Potluck super Sunday at 5:00PM—prayer and medication to

follow. 10. The ladies of the Church have cast off clothing of every kind. They may be seen in the basement on Friday afternoon. 11. Low Self Esteem Support Group will meet Thursday at 7 PM. Please use the back door.

Joel Osteen, pastor of a mega church in Houston, Texas, always begins his sermon with a joke. A young pilot was flying with his instructor. The teacher was very impressed with his cool and composed student. They came in for a landing, hit the ground hard, bounced fifty feet in the air, can1e down, and bounced again. They eventually landed with a bang. The instructor was appalled and told his student it was the WORST landing he had ever participated in. The amazed student said, "Me? I thought you were piloting the plane."

Steve always contributes great bits of humor. Many of them with religious themes. Such as. The Sunday School teacher was describing how Lot's wife looked back and turned into a pillar of salt, when little Jason interrupted, "My Mommy looked back once while she was driving,' he announced triumphantly, "and she turned into a telephone pole!"

A Sunday school teacher was telling her class the story of the Good Samaritan. She asked the class, "If you saw a person lying on the roadside, all wounded and bleeding, what would you do?" A thoughtful little girl broke the hushed silence, "I think I'd throw up."

A Sunday school teacher asked, "Johnny, do you think

Noah did a lot of fishing when he was on the Ark?" "No," replied Johnny. "How could he with just two worms?"

A Sunday school teacher said to her children, "We have been learning how powerful kings and queens were in Bible times. But, there is a Higher Power. Can anybody tell me what it is?" One child blurted out, "Aces!"

The Priest said, "Sister, this is a silent monastery. You are welcome here as long as you like, but you may not speak until directed to do so." Sister Mary Katherine lived in the monastery for five years before the Priest said to her, "Sister Mary Katherine, you have been here for five years. You may speak two words." She said, "Hard bed." "I'm sorry to hear that," the Priest said, "we will get you a better bed." After another five years, Sister Mary Katherine was summoned by the Priest. "You may say another two words, Sister Mary Katherine." "Cold food," said Sister Mary Katherine, and the Priest assured her that the food would be better in the future. On her 151 anniversary at the monastery, the Priest again called Sister Mary Katherine into his office. "You may say two words today." "I quit," said Sister Mary Katherine. "It's probably best," said the Priest, "You've done nothing but complain since you got here."

Amen. Selah. So be it.

LAUGHTER:
PHYSICAL and MENTAL HEALTH

I never cease to be amazed at how slow many strata's of our society are to catch-up with developments in their sphere of influence. A social psychologist recently talked about this dilemma. His views are that education and medicine are fifty years behind the times and religion a hundred years.

Medicine in particular and society in general is finally catching up with the views of Norman Cousins. Thirty years ago he spoke and wrote about the benefits of humor and laughter for mental and physical health. Almost every day there are articles in magazines and newspapers and programs on radio and television advocating the benefits of both. More and more people are sending me their favorite jokes. They come from as far away as Utah, Arizona, Canada and Virginia.

A Chinese couple named Wong had a new baby. The nurse brings them over a lovely, healthy, bouncy, definitely Caucasian white baby boy. Congratulations," says the nurse to the new parents. "What will you name the baby?" The puzzled father looks at his new baby boy and says, "Well, two Wongs don't make a white. So I think we will name him Sum Ting Wong." Four young novice nuns were about to take their vows. Dressed in their white gowns, they came into the chapel with the Mother Superior and were about to undergo the ceremony to many them to Jesus, making them "brides of Christ."

Just as the ceremony was about to begin, four Hasidic Jews with yarmulkes, long sideburns and long beards came in and sat in the front row. The Mother Superior said to them, "I am honored that you would want to share this experience with us, but do you mind if I ask you why you came?" One of the Jews replied, "We're from the groom's family."

A not necessarily well prepared student sat in his life science classroom staring at a question on the final exam. The question directed: Give four advantages to breast milk. What to write? He sighed and began to scribble whatever came into his head, hoping for the best:

1. No need to boil;
2. Never goes sour;
3. Available whenever necessary. So far so good maybe. But the exam demanded a fourth answer. Again, what to write? Once more he sighed. He frowned. He scowled, and then sighed again. Suddenly he brightened. He grabbed his pen and triumphantly, he scribbled his definitive answer:
4. Available in attractive containers of varying sizes. He received an A.

Marion sent us these bushisms, attributed to President George W. Bush.

"I stand by all the misstatements that I've made."
"I am not part of the problem, I'm a Republican."
"Quite frankly, teachers are the only profession that teach our children." "The American people would not want to know of any misquotes that George Bush may or not make." "It isn't pollution that's harming the environment. It's the impurities in our air and water that are doing it." "Public speaking is very easy." Enough said.

Here's a cute but short one. A polar bear walks into a bar and says to the bartender, "I'll have a gin and tonic." The bartender says, "What's with the big pause?" The bear answers, "I don't know. My father had them, too!"

Amen. Selah. So be it.

MENTAL HEALTH
DR. HAP LECRONE

Some years ago Dr. Hap Le Crone wrote a most provocative article about humor and mental health. Among other things he said, "I have noticed that those with an active sense of humor deal more effectively with life's adversities." More and more healthcare facilities are making laughter and humor a regular part of the prescription for patient treatment.

Henry Ward Beecher, one of the great writers of pre-Civil War days, once said, "A person without a sense of humor is like a wagon without springs-jolted by every pebble in the road." Going even 'way back," Charles Darwin, the father of the Theory of Evolution, was one of the first to look at laughter from a scientific viewpoint. He declared that, "it was innate and a reflex action," to the human species.

I'm still on a blonde kick. Mainly because I keep getting e-mails from you readers about blondes. A blonde made several attempts to sell her old car. She was having a lot of problems finding a buyer because the car had 340,000 miles on it. She discussed her problem with a brunette that she worked with at a bar. The brunette suggested, "There may be a chance to sell that car easier, but it's not going to be legal." "That doesn't matter at all," replied the blonde. "All that matters is that I am able to sell this car." "Alright," replied the brunette. In a quiet voice, she told the blonde, "Here is the address of a friend of mine. He owns a car repair shop around here. Tell him I sent you, and he will turn the counter back on your car to 40,000 miles. Then it shouldn't be a problem to sell your car." The following weekend, the blonde took a trip to the mechanic on the brunette's advice. About one month after that, the brunette saw the blonde and asked, "Did you sell your car?" "No!" replied the blonde. "Why should I? It only has 40,000 miles on it."

While I'm on a roll about blondes, here's another one. She was sooooo blonde .... She thought a quarterback was a refund. She thought General Motors was in the army. She thought Meow Mix was a CD for cats. At the bottom of an application where it says "sign here," she wrote "Sagittarius." She took the ruler to bed to see how long she slept. She sent me a fax with a stamp on it. She thought Eartha Kitt was a set of garden tools. She thought TuPac Shakur was a Jewish holiday. She tripped over a cordless phone. She spent 20 minutes looking at the orange juice can because it said, "Concentrate." She told me to meet her at the corner of "WALK" and "DON'T WALK." She studied for a blood test. She sold the car for gas money When she missed the #44 bus, she took the #22 bus twice instead. When she went to the airport and saw a sign that said, "Airport Left," she turned around and went home. When she heard that 90% of all crimes occur around the home, she moved. She thinks Taco Bell is the Mexican phone company. She thought that she could not use her AM radio in the evening.

Here's a squib well worth remembering. DID YOU KNOW? At local taverns, pubs and bars, people used to drink from pint and quart-sized containers. A bar maid's job was to keep an eye on the customers and keep the drinks coming. She had to pay close attention and remember who was drinking in "pints" and who was drinking in "quarts." Hence the term "minding you P's and Q's."

The following Senior Personal Ads sound like they come from St. George, Utah. FOXY LADY: Sexy, fashion conscious bullheaded beauty, slim, 5-4 (used to be 5-6) searching for sharp looking, sharp dressing companion. Matching white shoes and belt a plus. LONG-TERM COMMITMENT: Recent widow who has just buried fourth husband looking for someone to round out a six unit plot. Dizziness, fainting, shortness of breath not a problem. SERENITY NOW: I am into solitude, long walks, sunrises, the ocean, yoga and meditation. If you are the silent type, let's get together, take our hearing aids out and enjoy quiet times. WINNING SMILE: Active grandmother with original teeth seeking a dedicated flosser to share rare steaks, com on the cob and caramel candy.

This sounds like an endorsement from a strong willed, decisive paralegal who doesn't take any sass. I love it. A man and his wife were having some problems at home and were giving each other the silent treatment. The next week, the man realized that he would need his wife to wake him at 5:00AM for an early morning business flight to Chicago. Not wanting to be the first to break the silence (and LOSE), he wrote on a piece of paper, "Please wake me at 5:00AM." The next morning the man woke up, only to discover it was 9:00 AM and that he had missed his flight. Furious, he was about to go and see why his wife hadn't awakened him when he noticed a piece of paper by the bed. The paper said, "It is 5:00AM. Wake up." MEN JUST AREN'T EQUIPPED FOR THESE SORTS OF CONTESTS.

Amen. Selah. So be it.

MINDFULLNESS

Fads of all kinds have traditionally had a limited shelf life. They become either worn out or cut out. The kind of shoes we wear; the kind of clothes that are fashionable; the cars that are in vogue or even the food we eat. Time Magazine's current cover picture is a case in point. A young lady is depicted with a look on her face as being MINDFULLNESS. Not mindlessness. The word was coined to stimulate people (you and me) to focus on what we are doing. To pay attention. For some the idea isn't new. James Baldwin, the noted novelist, suggested the same idea with different words. "The challenge of living is to be present in everything you do. From making bread to making love." In other words, to focus on what you are doing.

Go even further back to Jesus. He said for us to "consider the lilies." Or, "the birds in the air." Or, "to count the hairs on our head." In other words, to focus on them. Of course His explanation was different. If God is aware and cares for them, so He will notice and care for us.

Time magazine is suggesting the value and importance of giving full attention to what we are doing. Not paying attention can have disastrous results. For example: driving, either on the freeway or a two lane road. Accidents with other cars or driving off the road can have bad results. Keep your focus on the road. Or, taking the wrong medicine at the wrong time. Which is easy to do, if attention is absent. Perhaps the most common disaster is when one fails to give attention to a relationship: to spouse, to family or friends. The relationship disintegrates.

Some years ago I heard about an incident in the life of Andrew Carnegie. It could be an urban legend, but I doubt it. He was born on November 25, 1835 and died on August 11, 1919, at the age of eighty-four. History does him justice. As any American industrialist, he led a great expansion of the American steel industry. He was also one of the highest profile philanthropists of all times. In 1889 he wrote an article called "The Gospel of Wealth." It called for the rich to use their wealth to improve society. He practiced what he preached; Carnegie Museums, libraries, schools (university), and many other projects. He was often referred to as "rags to riches."

The story goes that at the height of his businesses, he challenged anyone to present the best idea to enhance a business. The winner would receive $20,000. The winner received the money because of a very simple idea. It dealt with decision making. We should list the ten most important things to do. Then list them in importance from one down to ten. Then start at the top, and focus all attention on it, solving any problem dealing with it. Don't move to number two, until everything that can be done on number one, has been done. That sounds to me like the theory of "mindfulness." I'm amused at Time Magazine's referring to it as a "revolution." Where have they been all these years? Never-the-less, implementing the idea into our lives can be very helpful. Especially in these times of speed-dials, dead-lines, time-payments, trillion dollar indebtedness, the absence of compromise (in any endeavor.)

Another major benefit of focusing, as in mindfulness, is the answer to the modern demand for multitasking. Time editor Radhika Jones mentioned this benefit the other day on the Morning Joe show. "Studies show that multitasking DOESN'T actually make you more productive." It takes focusing.

Several studies have proved that the mind is like a muscle. It needs use or a workout. Muscles go to pot without exercise. Focusing on mindfulness is a great way to stimulate the mind.

One further benefit is suggested in the Time article. There are health benefits in the usage of mindfulness. Primarily in the reduction of stress. Stress itself is a killer. Anything we do to alleviate stress will contribute to better health.

Amen. Selah. So be it.

MISSION IS LAUGHTER

For the last few years I've been on a "mission." It has been to encourage the infusion of humor and laughter into every phase of our lives.

"Life is difficult," says Scott Peck. And it seems to be getting more so. Anxiety about terrorism has made paranoids out of most of us. The end result is a staggering increase in clinical depression. Economic worries have not helped the situation. It's been a long time since so many families have been out-of-work. There seems to be a pervasive mood of morbidity. The need for an injection of humor is the answer. My mission is to encourage it. Unique to the "mission" is the "message." Laughter brings physical healing. Science and the laboratory have proven the value of increasing endorphins.

What about our mental attitudes? They aren't so hot either. A general mood of negativism and a feeling of unsettledness is prevalent. Laughter is the message. Then, our spiritual resources are gradually eroding. Is it apathy or tolerance? Traditional faith doesn't seem to have much room for happiness. Of course there are pockets to the contrary, but in general religion needs a dose of laughter. That's my message.

Mr. Smith was flying from San Francisco to L.A. Unexpectedly the plane stopped in Sacramento. The flight attendant explained the delay and encouraged the passengers to get off for thirty minutes. Everyone got off but a blind man. Mr. Smith had noticed him and that his Seeing Eye dog lay quietly at his feet. Smith noticed the pilot approach him and heard him say, "Keith, we'll be here for an hour. Would you like to get off and stretch your legs?" Keith said "No, but maybe the dog would like to stretch his legs."

NOW PICTURE THIS. All the people in the gate area come to a complete quiet standstill when they look up and see the pilot walk off the plane with the Seeing Eye dog. The pilot was even wearing sunglasses. People scattered. They not only tried to change planes, but they were trying to change airlines.

This story is so old, but has a different wrinkle. Grandpa Friedberg was from a small town. He made a long-delayed trip to New York and had a wonderful time. He went into a bar, sat down and was soon joined by a young lady. Suddenly the girl stood up, shouting "You scum! What do you mean propositioning me to go to your hotel room?" Grandpa was really distracted. He slipped away to another table to avoid the angry comments. Soon the girl walked up to him and said, "Gee, Mister, I hated to do that to you, but I'm doing a Master's thesis and I needed your reaction to my put-down." Grandpa decided to teach her a lesson. He got to his feet, pointed his finger at her and shouted, "One buck for half an hour? You nuts? You ain't worth that kind of money in or out of bed."

I love this squib.

My face in the mirror

Isn't wrinkled or drawn

My house isn't dirty

The cobwebs are gone

My garden looks lovely

And so does my lawn.

I think I might never

Put my glasses back on.

I am indebted to Ralph of Sierra Vista, Arizona for these words of information: The first couple to be shown in bed together on prime time TV were Fred and Wilma Flintstone. Coca-Cola was originally green. Men can read smaller print than women can, women can hear better. The youngest Pope was eleven years old. In Scotland, a new game was invented. It was entitled Gentleman Only Ladies Forbidden...and thus the word GOLF entered the English language.

Amen. Selah. So be it.

MUSLIM JOKES

I have many theories about humor and jokes. One is that jokes can be told and retold without doing them an injustice. We've heard Tony Bennett sing about San Francisco many times; without ever getting tired of it. The same goes for Sinatra or Pavarotti. My second theory is that jokes come from many different people. Some times from the least likely sources. Such is the case of Ali. He is a great "teller of jokes." He can go on and on with all kinds of humorous stories.

Here are a couple of them. A minister was going through the jungle to a village for the purpose of marrying a man and woman. On the way he meets a lion; King of the Jungle. The lion asks him where he is going and after being told, he says, "I want to get married." He is told he needs a girl-friend, so he starts looking for the lioness. He meets a hyena and asks if he has seen her. Thinking he will be eaten, he yells, "No,'" and runs away. The lion meets a bear coming out of the water and asks the same question. The bear's response is the same as the hyenas and he jumps back into the water. The lion then meets a monkey who scampers up into the trees in fear he will become breakfast. Finally, the lion meets a mouse. When he is queried about the lioness, he asks, "Why do you want to know?" Back and forth they go, "Have you seen her?" and "Why?" Finally, the lion says, "Because I want to get married to her." The mouse has a spasm of excitement "Oh, no," he says. "Please don't marry her." "Why not," says the lion. And the mouse says, "Because, before I got married, I also was a lion, King of the Jungle."

The next joke that Ali tells goes like this. It also is about a lion and a mouse. It seems that the lioness has been kidnapped. The lion is very upset and tells the elephant to bring all the animals to a certain location. When they are assembled he informs them of the kidnapping and all of them are afraid. They start crying out of fear. They are sure one of them will be the suspect and will be eaten by the lion. All of them except for the mouse. He is jubilant, laughing and jumping for joy. When asked as to why he is so happy, he joyfully responds, "He suspects me too."

One further joke from Mr. Ali that proves sexist jokes can come from Pakistan. There was an old Greek husband who had an old Greek wife and an old mule. One day the donkey kicks the wife and she died. The funeral was cause for great mourning. After the service, several of the men stopped by the husband to convey their condolences. Almost all of them would whisper something in his ear. Finally, the last man came by and asked the old Greek, "What were they saying to you?" "Nothing much," he said. "They were just asking me how much I would take for the old mule." I'm sure this story could be told with a variety of nationalities referred to besides Greeks.

Here's one from one of my favorite jokesters, Frank. Notice: "We've been notified by Building Security that there have been four suspected terrorists working at our office. Three of the four have been apprehended. Bin Sleepin', Bin Loafin', and Bin Drinkin' have been taken into custody. Security advised us that they could find no one· fitting the description of the fourth cell member,. Bin Workin', in the office. Police are confident that anyone who looks like he's Bin Workin' will be very easy to spot."

An Arab was walking through the Sahara desert, desperate for water, when he saw something, far off in the distance. Hoping to find water, she walked toward the image, only to find a little old Jewish man sitting at a card table with a bunch of neckties laid out on it. The Arab asked "Please, I'm dying of thirst, can I have some water?" The man replied, "I don't have any water but why don't you buy a tie? Here's one that goes nicely with your robes." The Arab shouted "I don't want a tie, you idiot, I need water!" "OK, don't buy a tie, but to show you what a nice guy I am, I'll tell you that over that hill there, about 4 miles, is a nice restaurant. Walk that way, they'll give you all the water you want."

The Arab thanked him and walked away toward the hill and eventually disappeared. Three hours later, the Arab came crawling back to where the man was sitting behind his card table. The Jewish guy says "I told you, about four miles over that hill. Couldn't you find it?" The Arab rasped "I found it all right. They wouldn't let me in without a tie."

Amen. Selah. So be it.

MY ATTEMPTS
TO ENLIGHTEN READERS

Through the years, in my attempts to enlighten the reading audience about the nuances, origins, paradox and psychological insights of humor, I have roamed far and wide. From Norman Cousins to Lee Berk, M.D., to Mark Twain, to the Bible, to history, to politicians, to cartoonists, to comedians to friends and neighbors-! have sought and chronicled opinions and examples.

Recently I came across a viewpoint on humor from an unexpected source. Believe it or not, the founder of Neo-Orthodox theology, Reinhold Niebuhr. While I would not endorse his theology (far from it), I am enthusiastic about his interpretation of humor. He said, "Humor is, in fact, a prelude to faith, and laughter is the beginning of prayer." Another time he argued, "The intimate relation between humor and faith is derived from the fact that both deal with the incongruities of existence." I really like this statement that he made: "Laughter is not only the vestibule of the temple of confession, but the no-man's land between cynicism and contrition."

Niebuhr was particularly adept in the use of paradox a form of humor. His writings often seem to be, contradictory. A casual reading of his theology leaves you either exhilarated or depressed. Sometimes at the same time. In any case, the above is the springboard for a few stimulants for laughter. I've used this story myself, but recently heard Joel Osteen, pastor of a mega-church, tell it on television.

The following is the kind of informative, humorous account that Dr. Niebuhr would have told. A minister was preaching about the relevance of time.

What is a billion? It is a very difficult number to grasp. One ad put it into perspective: A billion seconds ago, it was 1959. A billion minutes ago Jesus was alive and walking on the Sea of Galilee. A billion hours ago, our ancestors were living in the Stone Age-Neanderthals. But a billion dollars ago was only eight hours and 20 minutes, at the rate our government spends it.

The following is not funny, but true. The U.S. national debt in '01 was $5.7 trillion; in '08 it is $9.2 trillion. The U.S. trade deficit per year: in '01 was $380 billion; now it is $759 billion. The U.S. budget surplus/deficit in '01 was plus $236 billion; now it is minus $354 billion. These stats are from the "Hightower Lowdown."

The following comments were published in several periodicals. They are comments made by teachers on the report cards of students;

1. I would not allow this student to breed.

2. Your child has delusions of adequacy.

3. Your son is depriving a village somewhere of its

idiot.

4. This child has been working with glue too much.

5. When your daughter's IQ reaches 50, she should sell.

6. If this student were any stupider, he'd have to be watered twice a week.

A lady back in Tennessee was invited to a salad luncheon. She decided to bake a bunt cake but it "fell" in the baking. Being in a hurry, she didn't have time to bake another, so she put a roll of toilet paper in the middle and covered it with ornate icing. She hoped no one would bid on the cake. Her son was to bid high for it. Unfortunately the Mayor's wife outbid him. Following the bidding war, she announced that she had baked it and everyone could have a slice. That's called "just desserts."

An eighty year old woman was being interviewed because she had just married for the fourth time. He was a funeral director. She was then asked about her previous three husbands. What they did for a living. With a twinkle she responded. "The first was a banker; the second was a circus ringmaster; and the third a minister." When asked why she married four men with such diverse careers, she explained, "I married one for the money, two for the show, three to make ready and four to go."

Amen. Selah. So be it.

ARCTIC HUMOR

NOAH & ARK

There is a current TV commercial that depicts Noah, the ark and several pairs of animals. Noah is bitten by a mosquito. He slaps it and kills it and with dejection heads for the door. Obviously he has to get at least one more.

Recently Dave sent me a delightful analysis of, "Everything I Need to Know, I learned from Noah's Ark." Everything I need to know, I learned from Noah's Ark .... ONE: Don't miss the boat. TWO: Remember that we are all in the same boat. THREE: Plan ahead. It wasn't raining when Noah built the Ark. FOUR: Stay fit. When you're 60 years old, someone may ask you to do something really big. FIVE: Don't listen to critics; just get on with the job that needs to be done. SIX: Build your future on high ground. SEVEN: For safety's sake, travel in pairs. EIGHT: Speed isn't always an advantage. The snails were on board with the cheetahs. NINE: When you're stressed, float awhile. TEN: Remember, the Ark was built by amateurs; the Titanic by professionals.

Frank shared the following squib with me. The Smiths were shown into the dentist's office, where Mr. Smith made it clear he was in a big hurry. "No fancy stuff, doctor," he ordered. "No gas or needles or any of that stuff. Just pull the tooth and get it over with." "I wish more of my patients were as stoic as you," said the dentist admiringly. "Now, which tooth is it?" Mr. Smith turned to his wife, Sue. "Show him your tooth, Honey."

I heard this story on the radio the other day. A school teacher took her fourth graders to a military base. She asked the Captain what he was going to show them. His response includes: how to climb a rope, an obstacle course and how to shoot a gun. She was concerned. "You'll make them killers with all that equipment," she said. His answer, "Not necessarily." His answer was the ultimate put-down. "Well," he said, "You have all the equipment to be a prostitute, but you' re not."

The comics are a great source for humor. Particularly Dennis the Menace. In a recent frame Dennis and his buddy, Joey, are eating triple dip ice-cream cones. Dennis says, "I'll bet God invented ice cream to make up for broccoli and carrots."

Just about everyone has heard of Jeff Foxworthy. He's a good old boy. His penchant for exaggeration and ridicule of rednecks is also well known. Frank and Betty, local residents and regular readers, contributed several of Jeff Foxworthy's "You Might Be a Redneck If..." Your favorite suntan lotion is Crisco. Most of your in-laws are outlaws. The Jerry Springer show asks you back. You've taken a pregnancy test and a sobriety test on the same day. Your birth was announced in the Auto Trader. You window-shopped at the 99 cent store. You are one, if: Your piston rings cost more than your wedding rings. You have more previous convictions than religious convictions.

Perhaps this can be used as a quiz. You are one, if: Your

fishing license is more precious to you than your marriage license. You've sent "compliments to the chef" at McDonald's. Your dogs sleep on your bed and your wife sleeps on the sofa. Both you and your wife wore ponytails on your wedding day. Your wedding reception was a tailgate party. You think H&R Block is an auto part. You've waited in line to see a motorcycle jump twenty buses. You visited a drive-thru during your driving test. Your wedding reception features karaoke. There's an endangered species in your freezer. You could retire by recycling all the cans in the bed of your truck. You have a cousin who no one in the family ever talks about. You wake up at night shouting "bingo." The list goes on and on.

This one is true and funny. Thanks Deb for this one. An elderly woman and her little grandson, whose face was sprinkled with bright freckles, spent the day at the zoo. Lots of children were waiting in line to get their cheeks painted by a local artist who was decorating them with tiger paws. "You've got so many freckles, there's no place to paint!" A girl in the line said to the little fella. Embarrassed, the little boy dropped his head. His grandmother knelt down next to him. "I love your freckles. When I was a little girl I always wanted freckles," she said, while tracing her finger across the child's cheek. "Freckles are beautiful." The boy looked up, "Really?" "Of course," said the grandmother. "Why, just name me one thing that's prettier than freckles." The little boy thought for a moment, peered intensely into his grandma's face, and softly whispered, "Wrinkles."

I really love this one. The doctor, who had been seeing an 80-year-old woman for most of her life, finally retired. At her next checkup, the new doctor told her to bring a list of all the medicines that had been prescribed for her. As the young doctor was looking through these, his eyes grew wide as he realized she had birth control pills. "Mrs. Smith, do you realize these are BIRTH CONTROL pills?!?" "Yes, they help me sleep at night." "Mrs. Smith, I assure you there is absolutely NOTHING in these that could possibly help you sleep!" She reached out and patted the young Doctor's knee. "Yes, dear, I know that. But every morning, I grind one up and mix it in the glass of orange juice that my 16 year old granddaughter drinks .... And believe me, it helps me sleep at night!"

Amen. Selah. So be it.

NORMAN COUSINS

Remember Norman Cousins? I love to tell his story for two reasons. It was a remarkable story and I studied with him. He was a brilliant man. Editor of a national magazine and a professor at UCLA . Cousins became ill with a collagen illness. That is a breakdown of the connective tissue of the body. He was in incredible pain and was pronounced terminal by the doctors. Incidentally, his story was portrayed on television and Ed Asner played him. Accidentally hearing that he was "terminal," he checked himself out of the hospital and into a motel where he could be with his wife. A visitor came to see him and told him a funny story and he laughed. Immediately his awareness of pain decreased. The same thing happened the next day. He decided there was a connection between his laughing and the decreased pain.

Being a friend of Allen Funt, he asked him for several films from Candid Camera. His favorite was the talking mailbox. He also got several Marx Brothers movies. After several weeks of laughter, the collagen illness disappeared. Through his research at UCLA he developed his view on endorphins. When one laughs, endorphins are secreted from the brain. They have the same molecular component as morphine-a pain killer.

Laughter is the best medicine. Here are a few laughers. This laugher was sent to me by a friend. The maid wanted an increase in pay. The Madam was very upset about this and asked: "Now Maria, why do you want an increase?" Maria: Well, Madam, there are 3 reasons why I want an increase. The first is that I iron better than you. Madam: "Who said you iron better than me?" Maria: "The Master said so." Madam: "Oh." Maria: The second reason is that I am a better cook than you." Madam: "Nonsense, who said you were a better cook than me/" Maria: "The Master did." Madam: "Oh." Maria: "My third reason is that I am a better lover than you." Madam (very upset now): "Did the Master say so as well?" Maria: "No, Madam, the gardener did." SHE GOT THE PAY RAISE ...

Mothers Day is always a source of interesting stories; both serious and humorous. The following apply to both. WHY DID GOD MAKE MOTHERS? 1. She's the only one who knows where the scotch tape is. 2. Mostly to clean the house. 3. To help us out of there when we were getting born.

HOW DID GOD MAKE MOTHERS? 1. He used dirt, just like for the rest of us. 2. Magic plus super powers and a lot of stirring. 3. God made my Mom just the same like he made me. He just used bigger parts. WHAT INGREDIENTS ARE MOTHERS MADE OF? 1. God makes mothers out of clouds and angel hair and everything nice in the world and one dab of mean. 2. They had to get their start from men's bones. Then they mostly use string, I think. WHY DID GOD GIVE YOU YOUR MOTHER AND NOT SOME OTHER MOM? 1 . We're related. 2. God knew she likes me a lot more than other peoples moms like me.

An old lady was standing at the rail of the cruise ship holding her hat so that the wind wouldn't blow it away. A gentleman approached her & said, "Pardon me, madam, I do not intend to be forward but did you know that your dress is blowing up in this wind?" "Yes, I know," said the lady. "But I need my hands to hold onto my hat." "But madam," he said, "you must know that you're derriere is exposed!" The woman looked down, then back up at the man and said, "Sir, anything you see down there is eighty-five years old, but I just bought this hat!"

Amen. Selah. So be it.

OPPORTUNITIES TO LAUGH

The pressure and demands made upon someone who cares for an invalid loved one is unbelievable. There is seldom any respite from the responsibility. Anything that can bring a measure of relief should be encouraged. That's why I was particularly interested in an article on humor and care giving. Of course, caregivers should be encouraged to avail themselves of opportunities to laugh or giggle without restraint. It relieves tension and minimizes the mood of depression. Dr. Lee Berk writes in The American Journal of Medical Science, "Our studies have shown objective, measurably and significant neuroendocrine and stress hormone changes with mirthful laughter that suggest a physiological benefit."

The article declares there are significant benefits of humor socially, physiologically. psychologically and even theologically. The writer reminds us that the Bible says there is a time to mourn and a time to laugh. Each of us and particularly caretakers should "creatively look for the times they can laugh with God and laugh at themselves."

Here are a few jokes to meet the above criteria. First, the Mommy Test, sent by Chris. "I was out walking with my then four year old daughter. She picked up something off the ground and started to put it in her mouth. I asked him not to do that. "Why?" "Because it's been laying outside and it is dirty and probably has germs." At this point, she looked at me with total admiration and asked, "Wow! How do you know all this stuff?" "Uh," I was thinking quickly," …all moms know this stuff. Um it's on the Mommy Test. You have to know it, or they don't let you be a Mommy." We walked along in silence for 2 or 3 minutes, but she was evidently pondering this new information. "Oh…I get it!" she beamed. "So if you flunk, you have to be the Daddy." (When you're finished laughing, send this to a Mom who needs to hear it!)

A man went into a store and told the clerk, "I'd like some Polish sausage." The clerk looked at him and said, "Are you Polish?" The guy, clearly offended, said, "Well, yes I am. But let me ask you something. If I had asked for Italian sausage would you ask me if I was Italian? Or if I had asked for German bratwurst, would you ask me if I was German? Or if l asked for a kosher hot dog would you ask me if I was Jewish? Or if I had asked for a taco would you ask if I was Mexican? Would ya, huh? Would ya?" The clerk said "Well, no." "And if I asked for some Irish whiskey, would you ask if I was Irish?" "Well, I probably wouldn't." With deep self-righteous indignation, the guy said, "Well, all right then, why did you ask me if I'm Polish just I because I asked for Polish sausage?" The clerk replied, "Because this is Home Depot."

"Many non-living things have a gender." 1) Ziploc Bags—They are Male, because they hold everything in, but you can see right through them. 2) Tire - Male, because it goes bald and it's often over-inflated. 3) Hot Air Balloon-- Male, because, to get it to go anywhere, you have to light a fire under it, and of course, there's the hot air part. 4) Subway- Male, because it uses the same old lines to pick people up. 5) Hammer- Male, because it hasn't changed much over the last 5,000 years, but it's handy to have around.

A young college student challenged a senior citizen, saying it was impossible for their generation to understand his. "You grew up in a different world," the student said. "Today we have television, jet planes, space travel, nuclear energy, computers ..." Taking advantage of a pause in the student's litany, the geezer said, "You're right. We didn't have those things when we were young; so we invented them! What are you doing for the next generation?"

How relevant can humor be? Try not laughing at this one. ST. PETER'S WELCOME. Two doctors and an HMO manager died and lined up at the pearly gates for admission to heaven. St. Peter asked them to identify themselves. One doctor stepped forward and said, "I was a pediatric spine surgeon and helped kids overcome their deformities." St. Peter said, "You can enter." The Second doctor said, "I was a psychiatrist. I helped people rehabilitate themselves." St. Peter also invited him in. The third applicant stepped forward and said, "I was an HMO manager and helped people get cost-effective health care." St. Peter said, "You can come in too." As the HMO manager walked by, St. Peter quietly added, "But you can only stay three days ... After that you can go below."

Amen. Selah. So be it.

PAINFULLY FUNNY

An understanding of humor involves a couple of relevant thoughts. First, humor is vitally important to the female wishes and desires for their men. The female magazines always are presenting the priorities that women would like from males. Without exception, humor is among the top five characteristics. There might be money, power, physique, looks and personality, but having a sense of humor is right up there.

This came to me from "anonymous." I do not know from where it came, however, it is hilarious. Supposedly, the story was reported in a newspaper from Wichita, Kansas.

Here's the story: Fred was stationed at McConnell Air Force Base. He and his wife had a house with an upstairs apartment almost ready to rent. Everything seemed right in the world. But one night, his world fell apart. Fred was sleeping peacefully and without his pajamas. His wife thought something was wrong with the upstairs sink and sent her husband up for a look. Half asleep and without pajamas, he climbed the stars and hunkered down under the offending sink. His wife and the family cat followed a few minutes later. With the lights on and the family together, the cat decided it was time to play. She made a tentative swipe of her paw, sinking her claws into a tender portion of Fred's anatomy.

Fred's military training had taught him to react instantly.

He uttered an agonized roar and jumped straight up. The last thing he remembered was when his head smashed into the bottom of the iron sink. A severe concussion was later diagnosed. Fred's wife called the base hospital. An ambulance screamed to the scene. The still groggy Fred was carefully placed on a stretcher and picked up. At the head of the stairs, one of the attendants asked what happened, just in case the doctor wanted to know. Fred's wife told all. That was too much for the attendants. They giggled. They laughed. One lost his grip on the stretcher. Poor Fred was dumped on the stairs, breaking his leg in the process. They got him to the hospital without further mishap and repaired the damage. Many thanks again to "anonymous." Send you favorite humor to the Highland Community News.

It is amazing how popular "blonde" jokes have become. I'm receiving several each week. Bill recently told me of a the blonde who went to a club to hear a ventriloquist. He began to disparage blondes in a vicious way and she became angry. She chastised him severely; "You're insensitive, have no appreciation for women and should be ashamed of yourself." The ventriloquist tried to apologize and she interrupted with the words, "You be still. I'm talking to that little guy on your knee!" By the way, Bill lives with a family of blondes.

Another blonde story came to me from three different sources. A blonde is on an airplane in the Economy section. She moves to First Class and the stewardess tells her she can't sit there.

The blonde says, "I'm beautiful and blonde and I'm going to Montreal. I'm not moving." The co-pilot tells her the same and she tells him her response. "I'm beautiful and blonde and I'm going to Montreal." Finally the Captain is informed and that he should notify the airport police. He says, "You said she's blonde? I'm married to a blonde and I speak blonde. Let me talk to her." He goes back and whispers in her ear. She is immediately apologetic and goes back to her original seat. When asked what he had told her, he said, "I just told her that First Class didn't go to Montreal."

There are days in the month when all a man has to do is open his mouth and he takes his life in his own hands! This is a handy guide that should be as common as a driver's license in the wallet of every husband~ boyfriend, or significant other!

DANGEROUS: What's for dinner?

SAFER: Can I help you with dinner?

SAFEST: Where would you like to go for dinner?

DANGEROUS: Are you wearing that?

SAFER: Gee, you look good in brown.

SAFEST: WOW! Look at you!

DANGEROUS: What are you so worked up about?

SAFER: Could we be overreacting?

SAFEST: Here's fifty dollars.

- Most of us go to our grave with our music still inside of us.

- If Wal-Mart is lowering prices every day, how

come nothing is free yet?

- You may be only one person in the world, but you may also be the world to one person.
- Some mistakes are too much fun to only make once.
- Don't cry because it's over; smile because it happened.
- We could learn a lot from crayons: some are sharp, some are pretty, some are dull, some have weird names, and all are different colors...but they all exist very nicely in the same box.

Amen. Selah. So be it.

PATCH ADAMS

Patch Adams, MD, became famous a few years ago when Robin Williams played him in a movie about him. Dr. Patch Adam's basic premise was and is that humor and laughter are essential ingredients for good health. From youth to seniors; from incidental to terminal illness, humor is beneficial. He was born on May 28, 1945; receiving his medical degree in 1971. Adams is a professional clown and stand-up comic. Following a pediatric residency, he founded the Gesundheit Institute. In describing it, he says, "The Gesundheit Institute is a pie in the face of greed-by taking the most expensive thing in America, health care, and giving it away for free."

Thousands of patients have benefitted from the Institute. In 1997 a forty bed hospital was completed, along with a theater, exercise rooms, vegetable gardens and an orchard.

Health and humor go together. With these words as encouragement, consider the following bits of humor. From Dave: Legend has it that long ago two women came before wise King Solomon, dragging between them a young man. "This young man agreed to marry my daughter," said one. "No! He agreed to marry MY daughter," said the other. And so they began arguing until the King called for silence. "Bring me my biggest sword." said Solomon, "and I shall saw the young man in half. Each of you shall receive a half." "Sounds good to me," said the first lady. But the other woman said, "Oh, Sire, do not spill innocent blood. Let the other woman's daughter marry him."

The wise king did not hesitate a moment. "The man must marry the first woman's daughter," he proclaimed. "But she was willing to saw him in two!" exclaimed the king's court. "Indeed," said wise King Solomon. "That shows she is the TRUE mother-in-law." Then Dave gets a little religious: A Sunday School teacher began her lesson with a question, "Boys and girls, what do we know about God?" A hand shot up in the air. "He is an artist!" said the kindergarten boy. "Really? How do you Know?" the teacher asked. "You know, "Our Father, who does art in Heaven..."

A minister parked his car in a no parking zone in a large city because he was short of time and couldn't find a space with a meter. So he put a note under the windshield wiper that read: "I have circled the block ten times. If I don't park here, I'll miss my appointment. FORGIVE US OUR TRESPASSES." When he returned, he found a citation from a police officer along with this note. "I've circled this block for ten years. If I don't give you a ticket, I'll lose my job. 'LEAD US NOT INTO TEMPTATION.'

Every Saturday morning this guy goes fishing. He gets up early and eager, makes his lunch, hooks up his boat and off he goes ...all day long. Well, one Saturday morning he gets up early, dresses quietly, gets his lunch made, puts on his long johns, grabs the dog and goes to the garage to hook up his boat to the truck and down the driveway he goes. Coming out of his garage rain is pouring down; it is like a torrential downpour. There is snow mixed in with the rain, and the wind is blowing 50 mph. Minutes later, he returns to the garage. He comes back into the house and turns on the TV to the weather channel. He finds it's going to be bad weather all day long, so he puts his boat back in the garage, quietly undresses and slips back into bed. There he cuddles up to his wife's back, now with a different anticipation, and whispers, "The weather out there is terrible." To which she sleepily replies, "Can you believe my stupid husband is out fishing in that storm?"

Enjoy this one. Two beggars were sitting side by side on a street in Mexico City. One had a cross in front of him, the other one the Star of David. Many people went by, looked at both beggars, but only put money into the hat of the one sitting behind the cross. A priest came by, stopped and watched many, many people give money to the beggar behind the cross, but none to the beggar behind the Star of David and said: "Don't you understand? This is a Catholic country. People aren't going to give you money if you sit there with a Star of David in front of you, especially when you're sitting beside a beggar who has a cross. In fact, they would probably give to him just out of spite." The Star of David beggar listened to the priest and, turning to the cross beggar, said: "Moishe ... look who's trying to teach us marketing."

Finally, a very stimulating question from Debra Ramirez and Steve Micklas. It is time to elect a new world leader, and your vote counts. Here are the facts about the three leading candidates:

Candidate A: Associates with crooked politicians, and consults with astrologists. He's had two mistresses. He also chain smokes and drinks eight to ten martinis a day. Candidate B: He was kicked out of office twice, sleeps until noon, used opium in college and drinks a quart of whisky every evening. Candidate C: He is a decorated war hero. He's a vegetarian, doesn't smoke, drinks an occasional beer and hasn't had any extramarital affairs. Which of these candidates would be your choice? Candidate A is Franklin D. Roosevelt. Candidate B is Winston Churchill. Candidate C is Adolph Hitler.

Amen. Selah. So be it.

PERVERSITY

One of the favorite subjects for study by social historians is humor. Its origin, it's diversity and in particular, its ethnic identity. Their conclusion centered on three ethnic groups: Jews, blacks and the Irish. Think about it. Most of the great comedians were and are from these groups.

These groups have one thing in common. Their history is one of hardship, discrimination and adversity. A friend of mine who had experienced great hardship gave me insight into this kind of situation. He was always laughing. When I asked him how he could do it. He said, "I laugh to keep from crying."

Believe it or not, ministers are a great source for humor. I recently heard a preacher tell this one. A couple was driving down a freeway. He was speeding. When told he was going 80 MPH in a 60 mile an hour area he denied it vehemently. His wife said, "Officer, he always drives 85 MPH in this stretch." The husband yelled at her and told her to be quiet. When told he wasn't wearing a seat belt, he denied that. Again the wife said he wasn't. He yelled at her again. The same thing happened regarding the absence of a driver's license. The cop then asked the wife, "Does he always yell at you like that?" Her answer was classic. "Only when he's been drinking."

Another minister told this humorous incident recently. A renowned atheist was in a rowboat on the Loch Ness in Scotland.

The lake is supposedly inhabited by "Nessie." Suddenly the boat is raised way up in the air on the head of Nessie. The atheist cried, "God, help me! " A voice from heaven says, "I thought you didn't believe in Me." The atheist begs God to give him a break. He says, "God, I didn't believe Nessie existed either until thirty seconds ago."

I've heard the following joke several times. The first time was in church. The pastor was explaining the criteria for church membership. The following question was asked. Did you pass? During a visit to the mental asylum a visitor asked the Director what the criterion was which defined whether or not a patient should be institutionalized. "Well," said the Director, "we fill up a bathtub, then we offer a teaspoon, a teacup and a bucket to the patient and ask him or her to empty the bathtub." "Oh, I understand," said the visitor. "A normal person would use the bucket because it's bigger than the spoon or the teacup." "No," said the Director, "A normal person would pull the plug. Do you want a bed near the window?"

This story was also told in church. It is one of my favorites. Suzie came home from Sunday School very excited. "Momma," she said, "I've learned something wonderful this morning. How God made man. He took some dust, added water and formed a figure from the mud. Then He breathed on it and it became a living man." "Wonderful," said her mother. "But, Momma, I learned something even more wonderful than that."

"What was that, Honey?" said her Mom. "I learned that God put man back to sleep; took out all of his brains; and made a woman."

Children often say the most unique prayers. Mike Trent recently sent me the following humorous prayers. Three year old Reese: "Our Father, Who does art in heaven, Harold is His name. Amen." A little boy was overheard praying: "Lord, if you can't make me a better boy, don't worry about it. I'm having a real good time like I am."

After the christening of his baby brother in church, Jason sobbed all the way home in the back seat of the car. His father asked him three times what was wrong. Finally, the boy replied, "That preacher said he wanted us brought up in a Christian home, and I wanted to stay with you guys."

A mother had been teaching her three year old daughter, Caitlin, the Lord's Prayer for several evenings at bedtime. Caitlin would repeat after her the lines from the prayer. Finally, she decided to go solo. The mother listened with pride as the daughter carefully enunciated each word, right up to the end of the prayer. "Lead us not into temptation," she prayed, "but deliver us from E-mail."

One morning a man comes into the church on crutches. He stops in front of the holy water and splashed some of it on both of his legs, then throws away his crutches. An altar boy witnessed the scene and ran into the rectory to tell the priest what he'd just seen. Without batting an eye, the priest said, "Son, you've just witnessed a miracle. Tell me, where is this man?" "Flat on his behind over by the holy water, Father."

Amen. Selah. So be it.

POETRY THAT SPEAKS

Poets are notably described as dreamers. We historians often record what they have dreamed about with their metaphorical words. There seems to be no limit to their imaginations. They are predictive, but just for the physical and materialistic. Their dreams are descriptive and defining. Lovers use their words to describe their feelings. When personal words seem inadequate, a poet's literary genius can be adequate.

One insightful writer has given the poet the voice of God. He often speaks the words of the Divine, describing who we are. How we are to live. The life beyond this one; what it is like. Above all, the poet speaks to himself and to others, voicing the aspirations and desires of all mankind.

The Greeks used mythology as a poetical expression. For example the account of Narcissus. Narcissistic means "love of oneself." It is based on the Greek mythology of a youth named Narcissus, who gazed into a pool of water, saw his image not knowing it was himself and fell in love with himself. Upon his death he was turned into the narcissus flower. Today self-love is considered a personality disorder. The story is considered poetry by the Greeks. More about their poets later.

Robert Burns (1759-1796) is considered the greatest of Scottish poets. He is especially famous for composing "Auld Lang Syne," that is usually sung on New Year's Eve. Another great poem is "To A Louse ." He was inspired to write it on seeing a bug on a lady's hat while in church. He takes eight verses to describe the antics of the louse. However, it is the first two lines of the eighth verse the stimulates the mind of most readers.

"0, wad sum Power the giftie gie us to see ourselves as others see us!" The English translation is clearer. "0, would some power the gift to give us to see ourselves as others see us."

Self knowledge and insight is hard to come by. Socrates challenged all mankind to "know thy self." Shakespeare said, "To thine own self be true." Burns' words imply that others know us better than we know ourselves. The "louse" is a metaphor for imperfections, mistakes, negative impulses and even sins. We shun self revelation and human impulses, but others (spouses, parents, siblings and close friends) can tell us the truth.

All of the Psalms (150) in the Old Testament should be considered poems. The use of metaphors, allegories to a Deity, personal confessions, and affirmations of dependence upon a power beyond oneself. The 23rd poem is representative of the others. Verse 4 is the heart of the poem, "Yea, though I walk through the valley of the shadow of death; I will fear no evil, for Thou art with me."

To understand this verse, we must consider the word through and Thou. During my first visit to Israel (1st of eight); I was at the St. George Anglican Cathedral. One of the young priests asked me what I would like to see. I said, "Masada" He was rather anxious because war was about to break out. However he agreed to take me there. We took the back road through what he called, "the valley of the shadow of death." Nothing grew there. No shade at all. It makes the Mohave desert look like an oasis. The poet used it as a metaphor for death and life's problems. It provides comfort for all who read it.

Elizabeth Barrett Browning presented these memorable words; "Earth's crammed with heaven and every common bush' aflame with God. But only those who see take off their shoes." Obviously she was thinking of Moses and the burning bush. (Exodus 3:2) We get so busy we close our eyes to beauty, friendship and God's blessing. A real tragedy. The remainder of Browning's line goes like this "the rest sit around plucking black berries." What a tragedy. The most beautiful and meaningful poem in the Bible in my opinion - is I Corinthians chapter thirteen. It is often called the love chapter. It is unlike anything else the Apostle Paul wrote.

I have a copy of Dr. J Gordon Hynes dissertation (Ph.D.) that he wrote in 1936. In it he identified over 200 verses in Paul's Epistles that were direct quotations or paraphrases of the writing of Plato, Aristotle or the four great Greek poets; Aratus, Cleanthes, Menandr, Epimenides. Almost all the verses were plagiarized by Paul. The practice was often used in ancient times. The theme of the poem highlights the importance of love. No experience in life has priority over it. "Now abides faith, hope and love, but the greatest of these is love." So ends the poem.

Amen. Selah. So be it.

POPE FRANCIS

Jorge Mario Bergoglio was ordained to the priesthood on December 13, 1969. Pope John Paul II appointed him a Cardinal in 2001. He was elected to succeed Pope Benedict on the 5th ballot on March 19, 2013. In my first article about Pope Francis I gave his biography. The second article stressed a few of his beliefs. In this article I will give a few of his actions as Pope. A few days ago he appointed sixteen new Cardinals. Seven of the sixteen are from Europe or North America. Four of the seven are from the Vatican inner circle. One reporter from the Vatican stated that the Pope was obviously eliminating careerism and the idea of automatic appointments. Nine of the sixteen are from Latin America, Africa and Caribbean. Most Vatican observers feel that the Pope's choices reflect his concern for people in poverty.

On January 15th of this year the Pope took a major step toward cleaning up the scandal ridden Vatican Bank. He replaced most of the Bank's advisors with new ones. Several of the Pope's personal habits have caused a furor. Time magazine, that chose him as the man of the year had a graphic picture of him striding across the open plaza wearing black shoes. Unthinkable. The Popes traditionally wore red shoes. Not this Pope. They come from a cobbler in Buenos Aires. He has also chosen to live in the Vatican guest house instead of the Papal residence in the Apostolic Palace. He is the first Pope since Pope Pious X to do so.

Back to the Vatican Bank. Motivation for changing the Bank's Board was Pope Francis' awareness that the bank "has been connected with widespread corruption and money laundering." Recently the Pope took a less controversial move when he called for a spending freeze on expenses in the canonization of would-be saints. The reason is that very wealthy people, who supported various candidates, were spending excessive amounts to get their favorites elected more quickly.

Pope Francis has also been very vocal about world peace. Not only has he spoken publicly but has talked personally with those involved. For instance the leader of the Israelis and the Palestinians. He has also urged the leaders in Iraq, Afghanistan and Iran and the United States to pursue peace. Since he became Pope I've often wondered if he saw the movie or read the book, "The Shoes of the Fisherman" Written in 1968 by Morris West. It's about an unlikely man that becomes Pope. He often goes out at night, incognito, to help the poor. I'll never forget one l scene. He confronts a derelict and tells him about heaven. The man says, "Father, I don't need to know the way to heaven. I need to know how to live here."

Anyway, the Pope, Kiril Palovich, is concerned about world poverty. Before resigning, he divests most of the Vatican's wealth and gives it to the poor. Sure sounds like Pope Francis. Or perhaps Pope Francis is simply following the words and mission of Jesus. Perhaps the most controversial subject that the Pope has faced was and is his response to "economic justice." His 50,000 word statement is in defense of the poor and a "critique of the excesses of free market capitalism." Specifically, he challenged the trickle-down economics of President Reagan and Wall Street as "factually unproven."

Adam Smith, in his 1776 opus, "Causes of the Wealth of Nations," is considered the father of capitalism. Out of it have come such dictums as "buyers beware." This is usually in favor of the rich getting richer. In America this is particularly true with 90% of the wealth in the hands of 1% of the people.

I am impressed with the Pope's knowledge of history. For instance, he is aware that the ruthless behaviors of capitalists like Henry Ford, John D. Rockefeller and others. In my opinion they spawned the growth of Communism, Labor Unions, minimum wage laws, and workman's comp. Capitalism has also contributed to the demise of the middle class and fostered world poverty.

Congress is made up of fifty percent millionaires; and they make laws in favor of lower taxes. The rich-as Warren Buffet and Bill Gates say-pay only 14-15% taxes. Their secretaries pay 45-50 % taxes. A further problem relates to the policies of Ronald Reagan, who erased the controls on Wall St., big business, insurance companies and the drug and health companies that had been established by President F. D. Roosevelt. That organizations can do exactly what they want with our economy. Pope Francis made economic concerns having a theological and moral basis.

A recent study stated that eighty-five of the richest Americans have more money than 3.5 billion people in the world. President Obama called the Pope's statement, an "eloquent question," further saying, "How can it be that it is not a news item when an elderly homeless person dies of exposure, but it is news when the stock market loses two points?"

We refer to our nation as a Christian nation. Don't get upset when Pope Francis I emulates the teachings and actions of Jesus.

Amen. Selah. So be it.

PRIME TIME

Prime Time is the newsletter for the "Retired Employees of San Bernardino County." According to it, a recent study showed that laughter may have "some heart-healthy benefits that are almost as good as aerobic exercises." The study with twenty volunteers showed that fifteen minutes of laughter improved blood vessel functioning, which improves blood pressure.

I really enjoyed the following stories that were used to get the retirees to laugh. A little girl became restless as the preacher's sermon dragged on and on. Finally, she leaned over to her mother and whispered, "Mommy, if we give him the money now, will he let us go?" An elderly woman died last month. Having never married, she requested no male pall bearers. In her handwritten instructions for her memorial service she wrote, "They wouldn't take me out while I was alive, I don't want them to take me out when I'm dead." A police recruit was asked during the exam, "What would you do if you had to arrest your own mother?" He said, "Call for backup." A Sunday School teacher asked her class why Joseph and Mary took Jesus with them to Jerusalem. A small child replied, "They couldn't get a baby sitter."

The husband had just finished reading the book, MAN OF THE HOUSE. He stormed into the kitchen and walked directly up to his wife. Pointing a finger in her face, he said, "From now on, I want you to know that I am the man of this house, and my word is law! I want you to prepare me a gourmet meal tonight, and when I'm finished eating my meal, I expect a sumptuous dessert afterward. Then, after dinner, you are going to draw me my bath so I can relax. And when I'm finished with my bath, guess who's going to dress me and comb my hair?" His wife replies, "The funeral director would be my guess."

Anyone who has ever paid or received a child support payment will appreciate this story sent to me. Today is my baby girl's 18th birthday. I am so happy that this is my last child support payment. Month after month, year after year, all those payments! So I called my baby girl, Kathy, to come over to my house. When she got there I said, "Baby girl, I want you to take this check over to your mother's house and tell her this is the last check she will ever get from me. Then I want you to come back here and tell me about the expression on her face." So, my baby girl took the check over to her mother. I was anxious to hear what she had to say about the expression on her mother's face. She walked through the door, and I asked, "Now tell me what did your mother have to say?" She replied, "Mother said to tell you that you are not my father, and to watch the expression on your face."

Here is a short but pithy humorous thought. A highway patrolman pulled alongside a speeding car on the freeway. Glancing at the car, he was astounded to see the blonde behind the wheel was knitting. Realizing she was oblivious to his flashing light and siren, the trooper cranked down his window, turned on his bullhorn and yelled, "Pull over!" "No!" the blonde yelled back, "It's a scarf!"

Some bits of humor are only for women. He didn't like the casserole and he didn't like my cake. My biscuits were too hard. Not like his mother used to make. I didn't perk the coffee right, he didn't like the stew. I didn't mend his socks the way his mother used to do. I pondered for an answer I was looking for a clue. Then I turned around and smacked him, like his mother used to do!

Another one for women. Due to inherit a fortune when his sickly, widower father died, Robert decided he needed a woman to enjoy it with. So he went to a singles bar and he searched until he spotted a woman whose beauty took his breath away. "Right now, I'm just an ordinary man," he said, walking up to her, "but within a month or two, my father will pass and I'll inherit over 20 million dollars." The woman went home with Robert, and four days later she became his stepmother. Men will never learn.

These squibs of humor will appeal to anyone born between 1930 and 1970. Read it and laugh. First, we survived being born to mothers who smoked and/or drank while they carried us. They took aspirin, ate blue cheese dressing, tuna from a can, and didn't get tested for diabetes. Then after that trauma, our baby cribs were covered with bright colored lead-based paints. We had no childproof lids on medicine bottles, doors or cabinets and when we rode our bikes, we had no helmets, not to mention, the risks we took hitchhiking.

As children, we would ride in cars with no seat belts or air bags. Riding in the back of a pick up on a warm day was always a special treat. We drank water from the garden hose and NOT from a bottle. We shared one soft drink with four friends, from one bottle and NO ONE actually died from this. We ate cupcakes, white bread and real butter and drank soda pop with sugar in it, but we weren't overweight because WE WERE ALWAYS OUTSIDE PLAYING!

We would leave home in the morning and play all day, as long as we were back when the streetlights carne on. (Or later) No one was able to reach us all day. And we were OK.

Amen. Selah. So be it.

QUASI-RELIGIOUS HUMOR

I've recently been sent several quasi-religious bits of humor. They also have a bit of quasi -seriousness. The first comes from Ring 254, a "Brotherhood of Magicians" newsletter. Steve is the editor. It's called "The Deck of Cards." Supposedly the story takes place during World War II when a soldier gets into trouble. He goes to church but doesn't have a Bible or a Prayer Book. He spreads a deck of cards and is about to be punished for his irreverence. He then explains his purity of intentions this way. During the North African campaign, a bunch of soldier boys had been on a long hike. They arrived in a little town called Casino, and the next day being Sunday, several of the boys went to church.

After the chaplain read the prayer, the text was taken up. Those of the boys who had prayer books read them, but one boy had only a deck of cards, so he spread them out. The sergeant who commanded the boys saw the cards and said, "Soldier, put away those cards." After the service was over, the soldier was taken prisoner and brought before the Provost Marshal. The Provost Marshal said, "Sergeant, why have you brought this man here?" "For playing cards in church, sir." "And what have you to say for yourself, son?" "Much sir," the soldier replied. The mars al said, "I hope so, for if not, I shall punish you severely."

The soldier said, "You see, sir, I have been on the march for six days and I had neither Bible nor prayer book, but I hope to satisfy you, sir, with the purity of my intentions. You see sir, when I look at the ace, it reminds me there is but one God, and when I see the deuce, it reminds me that the Bible is divided into two parts, the Old and New testaments. And when I see the three, I think of the Father, the Son and the Holy Ghost.

And when I see the four, I think of the four evangelist who preached the gospel. They were Matthew, Mark, Luke and John. And when I see the five, it reminds me of the five virgins who trimmed their lamps. There were ten of them-five were wise and were saved; five were foolish and were shut out.

And when I see the six, it reminds me that in six days, God made this great heaven and earth. And when I see the seven, it reminds me that on the seventh day, God rested. When I see the eight, I think of the eight righteous persons God saved when He destroyed this Earth. These were Noah, his wife, their three sons and their wives. When I see the nine, I think of the lepers our Savior cleansed and nine of the ten didn't even thank Him. When I see the ten, I think of the 10 commandments God handed to Moses on the tablet of stone. And when I see the King, it reminds me once again there is but one King of Heaven, God Almighty. And when I see them, I think of the blessed Virgin Mary, who is Queen of Heaven. And the Jack of knave is the devil.

When I count the number of spots on the deck of cards I find 365, the number of days in a year. There are fifty-two cards, the number of weeks in a year. There are thirteen tricks, the number of weeks in a quarter. There are four suits, the number of weeks in a month. There are twelve picture cards the number of months in a year. So you see, sir, my deck of cards has served me as a Bible, almanac and prayer book." Then Ralph s ends a most relevant account. It's called "The Sneeze." They walked in tandem, each of the ninety-three students filing into the already crowded auditorium. With rich maroon gowns flowing and the traditional caps, they looked almost as grown up as they felt. Dads swallowed hard behind broad smiles, and moms freely brushed away tears. This class would not pray during the commencements. Not by choice but because of a recent court ruling prohibiting it.

The principal and several students were careful to stay within the guidelines allowed by the ruling. They gave inspirational and challenging speeches, but no one mentioned divine guidance and no one asked for blessings on the graduates or their families. The speeches were nice, but they were routine... until the final speech received a standing ovation. A solitary student walked proudly to the microphone. He stood still and silent for just a moment, and then he delivered his speech ... an astounding SNEEZE! The rest of the students rose immediately to their feet, and in unison they said .... "GOD BLESS YOU." The audience exploded into applause. The graduating class found a unique way to invoke God's blessing on their future ... with or without the court's approval. GOD BLESS AMERICA.

Amen. Selah. So be it.

RABBI and POPE

Anyone who has read this column knows that I present humorous stories sent to me by way of e-mail. Three weeks ago was unusual because I received three of the funniest stories that cracked me up.

Many years ago the Pope decreed that all Jews must convert or leave Italy. Because of the outcry the Pope set up a debate between himself and a Rabbi. If the Rabbi won, the Jews could stay. Since the Pope didn't speak Hebrew and the Rabbi didn't speak Italian, the debate was silent. The Pope raised three fingers, the Rabbi one. Next the Pope waves his fingers around his head, the Rabbi pointed to the ground. The Pope then brought out a wafer and a challis of wine. The Rabbi pulled out an apple. The Pope declared he was beaten.

When asked he, explained. "First, I raised three fingers, for the Trinity. The Rabbi countered with one, meaning one God. Second, I circled my head meaning God ruled the heavens. The Rabbi pointed down meaning the earth as well. When I held the elements of the Eucharist the Rabbi took out an apple, meaning the Fall of Adam and Eve. He won." Meanwhile, the Jewish community was gathered around the Rabbi. "How did you win the debate?" they asked. "I haven' t a clue," said the Rabbi. "First he said to me that we had three days to get out of Italy; so I gave him the finger! Then he tells me that the whole country must be cleared of Jews and I said to him we're staying right here." "And then what?" asked a woman. "Who knows?" said the Rabbi, "He took out his lunch. So I took out mine."

A chicken farmer went to a local bar, sat next to a woman, and ordered a glass of champagne. The woman says, "How about that? I just ordered a glass of champagne, too!" "What a coincidence," says the man. As they clinked glasses he asked, "What are you celebrating?" "My husband and I have been trying to have a child, and today my gynecologist told me I'm pregnant!" What a coincidence," says the man. "I'm a chicken farmer. For years all my hens were infertile, but today they' re finally laying fertilized eggs." "That's great!" says the woman. "How did your chickens become fertile?" "I switched roosters," he replied. "What a coincidence," she said.

A young monk arrives at the monastery. He is assigned to helping the other monks in copying the old canons and laws of the church by hand. He notices, however, that all of the monks are copying from copies, not from the original manuscript. So, the new monk goes to the head abbot to question this, pointing our that if someone made even a small error in the first copy, it would never be picked up! In fact, that error would be continued in all of the subsequent copies. The head monk, says, "We have been copying from the copies for centuries, but you make a good point, my son." He goes down into the dark caves underneath the monastery where the original manuscripts are held as archives in a locked vault that hasn't been opened for hundreds of years. Hours go by and nobody sees the old abbot. The young monk gets worried and goes down to look for him. He sees him banging his head against the wall and wailing. "We missed the R! We missed the R! We missed the R!" His forehead is all bloody and bruised and he is crying uncontrollably. The young monk asks the old abbot, "What's wrong, father?" With a choking voice, the old abbot replies, "The word was ... CELEBRATE!!!"

As a senior citizen was driving down the freeway, his car phone rang. Answering, he heard his wife's voice urgently warning him, "Herman, I just heard on the news that there's a car going the wrong way on 280 Interstate. Please be careful!" "It's not just one car," said Herman. "It's hundreds of them!"

It seems that people never get tired of jokes about blondes. Here are some I've received. Two tourists were driving through Texas. As they were approaching the town of Nacogdoches, they started arguing about the pronunciation of the town. They argued back and forth until they stopped for lunch. As they stood at the counter, one tourist asked the blonde employee, "Before we order, could you please settle an argument for us? Would you please pronounce where we are ... very slowly?" The blonde girl leaned over the counter and said, very slowly, "Burrrrrrr-gerrrrrr, Kinnnnnggg."

Two blondes are walking down the street. One notices a compact on the sidewalk and leans down to pick it up. She opens it, looks in the mirror and says, "Hmm, this person looks familiar." The second blonde says, "Here, let me see!" So the first blonde hands her the compact. The second one looks in the mirror and says, "You dummy, it's me!"

Amen. Selah. So be it.

Zoe Belle Loves to Play and Laugh

READING TO LEARN

I am a believer in reading. As young as possible to begin learning how. The other day 1 heard that among minorities and low income families there is one book for every three hundred kids. Among middle income families there are thirteen books for each child. Astonishing. A few years ago there was a bumper sticker that said, "If you can read this, thank a teacher." Whatever happened to it?

More Bibles are sold each year than any other book. However, it is common knowledge that it is the least read book. There are many subjects that demand the attention of students. Science, Math, History, the Arts, Economics, Health, Geography, and Government to name a few. None are as important as Literature. Stories capture the attention of all kids. Reading them opens the doors to more difficult subjects. They also teach values and moral truths.

My Dad only went to the 6th grade, but he introduced me to reading. Horatio Alger, Zane Grey and Arthur Winfield. Alger wrote stories about boys in poverty that persevered into successes. Grey wrote westerns where the heroes defeated the bad guys. Winfield wrote about three brothers that overcame the problems of youth. My Dad also gave Hulbert's story of the Bible. I avidly read about its heroes: David, Samson, Noah and Joseph. My knowledge of the Bible today is based on what I learned back then.

Libraries are in jeopardy. In many cities they are either cut back or eliminated. Libraries are a great source for books for young readers. Reading and education go hand in hand. Consider that just a few years after the Pilgrims landed at Plymouth Rock in 1620, public education became common in the colony. A law was passed that wherever there were 50 families, they must have a school. Very shortly thereafter, Harvard was established. The first of the Eastern Universities: Dartmouth, Princeton, Yale, etc. The printing of books was essential. Writing became a normal process. Reading became the essential element for the process of education.

History has recorded the serious fact that censorship has been the bain of education, from the very beginning of records. The Romans restricted certain manuscripts from being copied. During the Dark Ages, religions censored every thought that challenged their beliefs. The history of our country has also been victimized by censorship. Through the years books have been taken from libraries and ideas have been expunged from books. Books like "Catcher in the Rye" and "Lady Chatterley's Lover" were censored. The issue of evolution is currently being censored from certain schools and libraries.

Fundamentalism is not limited to religious views. It is also expressed in attitud.es toward scientific issues or academic subjects. Reading is the key that open a closes mind. Bigotry, racism, prejudice and intolerance will not long dominate a person when his mind is enlightened by reading.

Years ago I heard an adage that I still remember. "Those that CAN but do not read have no advantage over those that CANNOT read." The problem of creating an interest in reading must be dealt with. Teachers, librarians and parents are the key.

Competition comes from TV, music, video games, the Internet and fellow students. Those who motivate kids must be creative. What is of interest for boys and girls? Sports (football, basketball, baseball, for boys; figure skating, swimming for girls)' entertainment, space travel. These are all action events. Begin by TELLING stories about these activities; then have books available that tell about them. It'll work every time. Remember reading is also the best discipline.

Amen. Selah . So be it.

RETIREMENT

Retirement is the dream of many of our citizenry. Questions like, "Will I have enough resources to live comfortably? What will my health be like? How long will I live? Will I be able to leave something for my children? Will I be able to pay for my medications?" These are just a few questions most people face after they reach the age of fifty.

Retirement is a relatively new concept. Most seniors on earth retire to the care and support of their children and grandchildren. It's a cultural thing in parts of the world. For example, the Asian countries revere the elderly and they stay with the younger members of the family. The same goes for many of the Latin countries. Italy, Spain, Mexico and others. The wisdom of the elders is respected. Very often the elderly look for retirement with foreboding. But I appreciate a Spanish word for retirement-JUBILADO. Get the word that is similar in English? Jubilation. Unfortunately, retirement is not always a time for jubilation among the elderly. Limited incomes, loneliness, failing health, victims of abuse and the death of close friends all contribute to a lack of jubilation.

I grew up in a coal mining, steel mill town. The citizenry consisted of Italians, Germans, Polish, Jews and a mixture of at least a dozen other nationalities. As I recall, every family had one or more elderly parents or other relatives as part of the family.

Retirement came when a man could no longer hold a pick or use a shovel-or stand the heat of a blast furnace. Those who could not make it on their own were sent to an "old folks home." Then came August 14, 1935. That's when President Franklin Delano Roosevelt signed the Social Security Bill into law. Five years later on January 1, 1940 the first Social Security checks were sent out. It was a significant step toward retirement for thousands of people.

According to the U.S. Department of Health and Human Services, in 2009 there were 39.6 million persons sixty-five years or older in our country. They represented 12.9 percent of the U.S. population. That makes it about one person out of eight is a senior citizen, or retirement eligible. By the year 2030 it is predicted that 20 percent of our population will be sixty-five years or older.

In the first paragraph of this article I suggested several thought provoking questions. They need to be addressed. With the increased number of retirees in the coming years, there will be a greater demand for elderly care facilities. As seniors get older it is obvious that health needs become greater.

The cost of living is ever increasing and most seniors live on a fixed income. A major problem also involves a reversal of what is commonly called the "sandwich generation." This is described as those adults who take care of their parents (seniors) and their own children. That is also a serious problem. But what is seldom addressed is the fact that elderly parents often assume the care of their children or grandchildren with living quarters or financial help. This becomes difficult as medical costs become greater and the economy becomes more critical. A few suggestions seem apropos as we seniors cope with our future.

1 - Consider the possibility of a "reversed mortgage." This cuts back on overhead and provides increased income. It eases the money problems for all concerned. I personally know several seniors that have availed themselves of it.

2 - Seniors are often victimized by shysters of one kind or another. Be careful and seek advice.

3 - Develop coping strategies.

- Conserve your finances. GET OUT OF DEBT AS SOON AS POSSIBLE.
- Continue to build your base of family and friends. Replace the ones you've lost with new friends.
- No one knows how long he/she will live. MAKE A PLAN FOR THE REST OF YOUR LIFE.
- Above all: Exercise your BODY AND your MIND. Cater to both.
- The best way to have peace of mind is to attend church.

Amen. Selah. So be it.

SATIRE OF JESUS

Satire and sarcasm were a part of Jesus' techniques in communication. A couple of good examples. In ridiculing the Scribes and Pharisees, He referred to them as "Whited sepulchers" filled with "dead men's bones." That is humor with a bite.

On another occasion Jesus talks about the rich getting into heaven. In an incredibly caustic way He says something to the effect that it would be easier for a camel to go through the eye of a needle.

- People ask, when they learn that Jesus fed the 5000, whether the two fish were bass or catfish, and what bait was used to catch 'em.

- The choir robes were donated by (and embroidered with the logo from) Billy Bob's Barbecue.

- There is a special fund raiser for a new church septic tank.

- Finding and returning lost sheep isn't just a parable.

- Opening day of deer season is recognized as an official church holiday.

- The choir is known as the "OK Chorale."

- People think "rapture" is what you get when you lift something too heavy.

- The baptismal font is a #2 galvanized washtub.

- A member of the church requests to be buried in his 4-

wheel-drive truck because "It ain't never been in a hole it couldn't get out of."

- In a congregation of 500 members, there are only seven last names in the church directory.
- When the pastor says, "I'd like to ask Bubba to help take up the offering." five guys and two women stand up.
- The finance committee refuses to provide funds for the purchase of a chandelier because none of the members knows how to play one.
- The collection plates are really hub caps from a '56 Chevy.

A city boy, Kenny, moved to the country and bought a donkey from an old farmer for $100.00. The farmer agreed to deliver the donkey the next day. The next day the farmer drove up and said, "Sorry son, but I have some bad news. The donkey died." Kenny replied, "Well then, just give me my money back." The farmer said, "Can't do that. I went and spent it already." Kenny said, "OK, then just unload the donkey." The farmer asked, "What ya gonna do with him?" Kenny: I'm going to raffle him off." Farmer: "You can't raffle off a dead donkey!" Kenny: "Sure I can. Watch me. I just won't tell anybody he is dead." A month later the farmer met up with Kenny and asked, "What happened with that dead donkey?" Kenny: "I raffled him off. I sold 500 tickets at $2 a piece and made a profit of $898.00." Farmer "Didn't anyone complain?" Kenny: "Just the guy who won. So I gave him his $2 back." Kenny grew up and eventually became the chairman of

Enron.

Three boys were playing and were bragging about their fathers. The first boy said: "My dad scribbles a few words on a piece of paper and calls it a poem. He gets $50 for it." The second boy said, "That's nothing! My dad scribbles a few words on a piece of paper; he calls it a song and he gets $100 for it." The third boy then said to the first two: "I got you both beat. My dad scribbles a few words on a piece of paper, calls it a sermon and it takes eight people to collect all the money!"

Two mice live in a movie studio warehouse and are looking for food. Suddenly one hears the other chewing. "What did you find?" he asks. "I am not sure," comes the answer from the second mouse. "It looks like a piece of film celluloid from an old movie. Let me see…Ah, yes. It is from 'Gone with the Wind'." "And how is it?" asks the first mouse. "Not so great," replies the second mouse, "The book was better."

A game warden met a man with 2lobsters along the sea shore. The warden said, "I'll have to turn you in and confiscate the lobsters." The man said, "You can't do that, they are my pets. I bring them down for exercise every morning an when I call them, they come back." "Show me," the warden said. The man put them in the ocean. After a while the game warden asked, "When are you going to call the lobsters back?" The man said, "What lobsters?" We had a power outage at our house this morning and my PC, laptop, TV, DVD, iPad were all shut down. Then I discovered that my iPhone battery was flat and to top it off it was raining outside, so I couldn't play golf. I went into the kitchen to make coffee and remembered this also needed power. So I sat and talked with my wife for a few hours. She seems like a nice person.

Amen Selah. So be it.

Clergy Can Be Humorous

SENIOR HUMOR

Seniors have a distinct sense of humor. Hang out with a group of them and their laughter will be raucous. An example. A couple, both seniors went into town and stopped in Wal-Mart for a few minutes. Coming out they saw a policeman writing a parking ticket. They approached him and quietly asked him for consideration for a senior couple. He ignored them. The wife called him a Nazi cop and he wrote another ticket. The husband called him a Fascist-pig. The cop wrote a third ticket. They went on for 20 minutes harassing the cop. He kept writing tickets. The couple walked off laughing their heads off. They didn't care because they had come to town on the bus. The car wasn't theirs.

Laughter at any age is important. Especially for seniors. Nora is a one hundred-two year old senior, going on twenty. A perpetual smile, fastidious dresser, hair always neat, and sharp as a tack. How does she do it? "I eat sparingly, exercise every day, good genes and laugh several times a day."

John told me this story and cracked up laughing as he told it. A ninety-two year old man married a ninety year old woman. His kids asked him why he married such an elderly woman. Was she beautiful? "No," he said. "She's uglier than a mud fence." Was she rich? "No, she's poorer than a church mouse." Was she a good cook? "No, we eat at McDonald's every day." Then why? His answer was classic. "Because she can drive at night."

The importance of laughter and humor reached front page and TV news in the 60 's and 70's. Norman Cousins was the leader. He had been stricken with a collagen illness that affected the connective tissue of the body. He was diagnosed as terminal. Through laughter he became well. As a professor in the medical department at UCLA, he was the person to discover ENDORPHINS. This secretion of the brain is stimulated by laughter. It affects the immune system and wellness.

Laughter seems to be indigenous to seniors. They laugh, smile, giggle and tell jokes. I know many elderly or aging people. They all laugh and make fun of each other.

No one remembers Jack Benny, George Burns, Red Skelton, Lucille Ball, Bob Hope, and Jimmy Durante as young people. In their heydays, they were seniors. So, seniors, show the way to the younger generations, Laugh a little and live a lot."

Betty lived one hundred plus years. She retired as chief of nurses at Patton State Hospital at age fifty. She and her husband Charley raced horses until he died. Willy Shoemaker was one of their riders. She was an inveterate joke teller. Many of them a little risqué. Two I remember very well. John and Mary made a pact that whoever died first would try to contact the remaining spouse. John died and Mary waited anxiously for his contact. Finally it happened. Mary heard a weird voice calling her. "What is it like over there?" John's answer was enigmatic. "I wake up and have sex; take a nap and have sex; eat a bit and then more sex; another nap and more sex. Sex, sex, sex all day long." "My word, John. Is that what heaven's like?" "Who said anything about heaven, Mary? I'm a jack-rabbit in New Mexico."

Another one that Betty loved to tell. An elderly Pasadena matron drove a 1950 Packard with only 5,000 select miles. She drove into a strip mall and looked for a parking slot. Just as she was about to turn into one, a bright red corvette zipped in ahead of her. A beautiful, sassy blonde jumped out, wiggled and yelled. "That goes to show what a young, beautiful blonde can do." Those Packard's were big. The elderly matron backed up and with top speed smashed the back of the corvette. Three successive times. The corvette looked like an accordion. She popped out; adjusted her hat and said, "That shows you what your can do when you're a senior and rich." Every senior I know loves a joke.

Amen. Selah. So be it.

SERENDIPITY NEW YEAR

What's on your agenda for the New Year? Your goals, your aspirations, your dreams: Don't have any? Why not? If you do not have expectations, they will probably be realized. Even the Bible urges us to plan for the future. "Where there is no vision the people perish." (Proverbs 29: 18)

I begin each year with a new date book. The back is filled with names, phone numbers and addresses. Then I fill in the front with appointments and birthdays. Leaving plenty of room for the unexpected.

The word that applies for the latter is SERENDIPITY. It has overtones of adventure and unexpected pleasures. The word was coined in 1754 by Sir Horace Walpole, noted British author. It is based on a fairy tale that began in the land of Serendip. This country is an island off the coast of India. For many years it was called Ceylon. Today its name is Sri Lanka. The fairy tale concerns the king of Serendip and his three sons. They are sent throughout the world to learn about it. They always meet the unexpected. Thus the word serendipity. Or, discoveries by accident of things they were not seeking. Certainly there should be a word for that, because life is full of it. Ralph Waldo Emerson said, "Columbus, looking for a direct route to Asia, stubbed his toe on America." Serendipity.

Of course, many of the experiences in the New Year are

predictable. We' ll be getting older. Doctors visits; Dentists as well. Some of our friends will die. The government will probably continue to be a mess. The very essence of serendipity is indirection. Going after one thing and in the process, finding something else. A similar concept is used by magicians- misdirection. The word "by-product" is also appropriate.

What do Velcro, penicillin, x-rays, Teflon, dynamite, the Dead Sea Scrolls, quinine, smallpox vaccination, iodine, discovery of America, law of gravity, synthetic rubber, insulin, photography, sulfa drugs, glass, nylon, methane, interferon and hundreds of other things have in common? THEY WERE ALL THE RESULT OF SERENDIPITY. On and on. One example of serendipity after another. However, most of us will never be explorers or inventors. Are there other ways for us, in the New Year, to experience it? Absolutely.

The unknown days (365) are uncharted. Never traversed by us before. Our journey will be like the three men of Serendip. Like them, we will indirectly meet NEW FRIENDS. Just about every day Stella and I go to a local Jack-in- the- Box for an egg sandwich. Several months ago, a young lady came in for coffee. We started talking, found several common interests and soon we were meeting every day. Friendship developed. Serendipity.

HAPPINESS is always a by-product. It is experienced because of something else: an activity, a great dinner, winning the lottery, a family gathering, etc. The year ahead will provide many opportunities for those or similar serendipities. I have an insatiable curiosity. The subject doesn't matter. I want to learn all I can about places, people and things. More often than not, opportunities present themselves unexpectedly. Serendipity.

A year ago one of our daughters moved to Boston. She met a college roommate of mine who is now retired from the college. To cement our renewed friendship he sent me a science book written by a colleague of his. "The Language of Science and Faith." By Karl W. Giberson.

Thrilling and satisfying for my curiosity. Unexpected. A genuine serendipity. I am anticipating the New Year because of the potential of more SERENDIPITY.

Amen. Selah. So be it.

SHAGGY DOG

Shaggy Dog stories have been around for a long time. They are at the same time nebulous and distinct. While their origin is unknown, they are particularly popular in the UK. The British are known for their staid, stoical approach to humor. That would help explain the popularity of "shaggy dog" stories among them.

Webster's dictionary says, "A shaggy dog story is a long and involved story, regarded as humorous by the narrator, often told with extraneous detail and culminates in an absurd or irrelevant punch line." One of two factors are necessary to categorize a story as "shaggy." It is either excessive in detail or it is laborious in the telling. I have a friend who can turn the shortest story into "a shaggy dog" by the slow and measured way of speaking. I often say, "Al, get to the point." Supposedly the original was really about a shaggy dog. Thereafter, whenever a story was told as described above, it was referred to as a "shaggy dog." The punch line is an absolute must.

Here is a typical example: Deepest in the darkest jungles of old time Africa there were two tribes and they hated each other. One tribe lived at the foot of a massive mountain and they panned for gold in the river and mined for gold in the mountain. They were RICH! The other tribe lived in a swamp area and lived on crocodiles and fish and they were POOR! They never visited each other except to raid each other's grass huts and plunder them. Of course there were pretty poor pickings when the RICH tribe raided the POOR tribe, but it had become a time un-honored tradition and each tribe kept the tradition alive.

One day the chief of the RICH tribe had a visit from his resident snitch who said, "Hey, Chief The POOR people have heard about your solid gold throne and they are planning to come over tomorrow and steal it from you!" The RICH Chief was beside himself, he loved that gold throne and so he called in his resident Wise Man and asked him what he should do. The Resident Wise Man said, "Chief you have got to make the Gold Throne disappear! I suggest that you get your men to stick long wood poles into the roof of your Grass palace and using pulleys and your strongest men stick the throne up in the roof of your Grass Palace. The POOR people will never think to look up there!" The Chief immediately ordered this to be done.

The very next day the POOR tribe attacked and swept through the village searching everywhere. They found NOTHING! The RICH tribe were hiding in the mines in the mountains and when the POOR tribe left the RICH tribe came out and went back down to their village and began a great celebration. The Chief stood in the center of his Grass Palace and looking up at the roof started to crow, "Those POOR shmucks ain't got no idea! Right over their heads and they missed it!" Suddenly there were several tremendous large bangs and the wooden poles supporting the Gold Throne snapped and down came two ton of Gold Throne on top of the RICH Tribes Chief and killed him stone dead. The Moral of this story is...People who live in Grass Houses shouldn't stow thrones!

For those of us getting on in Years I thought I would let you in on a little secret I've found for building my arm and shoulder muscles. You might wish to adopt this regimen; three days a week works well. I start by standing outside behind the house and, with a five pound potato sack in each hand, extend my arms straight out to my sides and hold them there as long as I can.

After a few weeks I moved up to ten pound potato sacks, then fifty pound potato sacks and finally I got to where I could lift a hundred pound potato sack in each hand and hold my arms straight out for more than a full minute! Next, I started putting a FEW potatoes in the sacks, but I would caution you not to overdo it at this level.

What can you get for two dollars anymore. A bum, who obviously has seen more than his share of hard times, approaches a well-dressed gentleman on the street. "Hey, Buddy, can you spare two dollars?" The well-dressed gentleman responds, "You are not going to spend it on liquor are you?" "No, sir, I don't drink," retorts the bum. "You are not going to throw it away in some crap game, are you?" asks the gentleman. "No way, I don't gamble," answers the bum. "You wouldn't waste the money at a golf course for greens fees, would you?" asks the man. "Never," says the bum, "I don't play golf." The man asks the bum if he would like to come home with him for a home cooked meal. The bum accepts eagerly. While they are heading for the man's house, the bum's curiosity gets the better of him. "Isn't your wife going to be angry when she sees a guy like me at your table?" "Probably," says the man, "but it will be worth it. I want her to see what happens to a guy who doesn't drink, gamble or play golf." HAVE A GREAT DAY!!!!!!!

Amen. Selah. So be it.

"I'm getting so old that all my friends in heaven will think I didn't make it."

SITUATION ETHICS

I'd like for you to think about the concept of Situational Ethics. Situation Ethics is a Christian ethical theory that made a first impact in the 1960's. It was developed by John Fletcher; an Anglican/Episcopal priest. Basically it states that love is at times more important in ethical matters than other moral principles.

Paul Tillich, the great theologian, said, "Love is the ultimate law." Both men use the Greek word Agape, in the understanding of love.

Fletcher denied any absolute moral law outside of love. Other ethical laws were only guidelines to achieve love. The definition he used for AGAPE was, "The absolute, universal, unchanging and unconditional love for all people." Fletcher also equated situation ethics as the best understanding of Jesus' "love thy neighbor" as He taught in the Gospels.

SE (situation ethics) must be viewed as a consequential theory. It is concerned with the outcome of an action. Simply put, THE ENDS CAN JUSTIFY THE MEANS. Fletcher further clarified his views by declaring there were three possible approaches to ethics.

First, there is the path of legalism. It is the "thou shall and thou shall not," approach. Many Christians have used proof texts from the Bible to justify legalism. Second, is the very opposite. It is against any ethical system. It is an unprincipled approach. It is opposed to all moral and ethical boundaries. Third, is the SE viewpoint. It is based on the Golden Rule and altruism that puts others before self. Fletcher says, "SE relies on one principle that best serves love." The probing question is how SE effectively is expressed, when in conflict with biblical and traditional moral values. One example that Fletcher tells is about the bombing of Hiroshima and Nagasaki that ended World War II. Over 200,000 Japanese were completely obliterated. The bomb was described, "the most terrible weapon ever known."

Military leaders and scientists advised President Truman to order the dropping of the bombs. That act certainly saved thousands of American lives. In the light of moral values and the Bible's commandment against killing, was it the right thing to do?

What about adultery? Is it always wrong? Fletcher tells of a German woman, Mrs. Bergmeier, who was taken captive by Russians while she foraged for food for her three children. She was taken to a POW camp in the Ukraine. Her husband spent months searching for her. Mrs. Bergmeier learns that her release was only possible if she was pregnant. After much inner turmoil, she decided to allow herself to become impregnated; after verification, she was released and sent home. She was welcomed with open arms, even when they heard how she had managed it. The baby was born and he was loved as well. What about the moral law against adultery? Her decision was based on love.

Is stealing always wrong? What about the person who

steals to feed his family? Is lying always wrong? If a favorite friend hides in your home to avoid being beaten by her husband; is it wrong to lie and say she wasn't in your house?

Finally, was Jesus' command to not be angry always wrong? What about His taking a whip and driving the money changers out of the Temple? How could that be done without anger? Or maybe He did it as an act of love.

Fletcher categorically stated, "The situation determines the rightness or wrongness of an event." That is SE.

Amen. Selah. So be it.

SOMETIMES HUMOR
ISN'T POLITICALLY CORRECT

Al lives in Chilliwack, British Colombia. He's a retired school administrator and humorist. He introduced me to the writing of Douglas Todd, columnist for the Vancouver Sun. He specializes in writing articles about humor. Many of his articles include jokes contributed by his readers. I've included some of his humor in my articles. He recently wrote about his concern for religious humor-it isn't often politically correct. Racial humor is taboo. Sexual humor is out. Female gender humor is a no-no.

The rule of thumb is pretty simple. Blacks can tell jokes about blacks; gays can tell gay jokes; women can even tell jokes about other women. It's the insider thing. If you're Italian~ you can poke fun at Italians. The same goes for Polish, Irish and Jews. Catholic jokes are O.K. if you're a Catholic. Again, the same goes for Baptists or Methodists. But never, never tell a Muslim joke. Douglas Todd says, "Religion-based humor is the touchiest. Anyone who ventures into it must walk an exceedingly fine line."

There's an old adage that goes like this. "Fools rush in where angels fear to tread." Here goes. Just call me a fool. Christian joke: Presbyterians feel guilty about things they haven' t even done. Jewish joke: In the Bible, we're the Chosen people. In the locker room, we' re the last-chosen people. Muslim joke: Our family has four women who wear veils. We all share the same bus pass.

There is a group of liberal Muslims who are swapping jokes on the Internet. A favorite theme is their favorite pick-up lines. They include: "Oh my gosh, I just saw part of your hair. Now you' re obligated to marry me." Or: "Our parents engaged us when we were little-they must have forgotten to tell you."

Many thanks to Debra for the following: There were three good arguments that Jesus was Black:

1. He called everyone " brother."

2. He liked Gospel.

3. He couldn't get a fair trial.

But then there were three equally good arguments that Jesus was Jewish:

1. He went into His Father's business.

2. He lived at home until he was 33.

3. He was sure his Mother was a virgin and his mother was sure he was God.

But then there were three equally good argument that Jesus was Italian:

1. He talked with his hands.

2. He had wine with every meal.

3. He used olive oil.

But then there were three equally good arguments that Jesus was a Californian:

1 . He never cut his hair.

2. He walked around barefoot all the time.

3. He started a new religion.

But then there were three equally good arguments that Jesus was Irish:

1. He never got married.

2. He was always telling stories.

3. He loved green pastures.

But the most compelling evidence of all three proofs that Jesus was a woman:

1. He had to feed a crowd at a moment's notice when there was no food.

2. He kept trying to get a message across to a bunch of men who just didn't get it.

2. Even when he was dead, He had to get up because there was more work for Him to do.

A Baptist couple felt it important to own a Baptist pet, so they went shopping at a kennel specializing in this particular type of animal, and they found a dog they liked. When they asked the dog to fetch the Bible, he did it in a flash. When instructed to look up Psalm 23, the dog complied just as quickly, using his paws with great dexterity. They were so impressed that the couple purchased the animal and took him home.

That night the couple had friends over. They were so proud of their new Baptist dog and his skills that they wanted to show him off. They called the dog and gave him his commands. Their friends were impressed and asked whether the dog could do any of the usual tricks as well. This stopped the couple cold: They hadn't thought about the "usual" tricks. "Well," they replied, "let's try it out." Once more they called the dog to them and they commanded it to "heel!" As quick as a wink, the dog jumped up, put his paw on the man's forehead, closed his eyes in deep concentration, and bowed his head. It was then they knew they had been deceived. He was actually Pentecostal!

Amen. Selah. So be it.

PRESIDENTIAL HUMORIST

SOUTHERN HUMOR

Southerners are noted for many things: Their drawl, Southern fried chicken and a sense of humor among them. When it comes to people from Tennessee you can add fishing, hush puppies and the Grand Ole Opry. Of course, Southern Comfort has to fit in there someplace. It seems that a group of Southern belles had a southern club. Each month they would rotate fixing a southern dinner for the group.

When it came t o Betty Jo's turn, she wanted a special southern dish. She decided on southern fried steak, smothered in mushrooms. However, she could not find any of the southern kind she liked. Her husband, a good ole boy, suggested the ones by the creek. "Aren't those poisonous," she asked. His suggestion was to feed some to ole Jake, their hound-dog. So, she gathered some southern mushrooms and cooked them in bacon grease. She fed them to the dog and he was more than satisfied. So, she fixed the meal of southern fried steak, smothered in southern mushrooms to the southern ladies. At that moment, the southern maid Betty Jo had hired to help serve, announced that Jake was dead.

Holy southern pandemonium ensued. 911 was called. Para-medics arrived and pumped the stomachs of the southern belles. Finally, the ladies sitting around, exhausted. At that moment, the southern maid announced in a southern mournful tone: "I think it was awful that the car didn't stop after it hit and killed ole Jake." 'Nuff said.

Ali is an outstanding auto mechanic. He's a native of Pakistan but has lived in Highland for fifteen years. Also, he always has a joke. He told me this one the other day. A husband and wife were in their car driving down the street. She was driving. They were discussing their impending divorce. The husband says, "I want this car; I want the boat at the lake and I want the BMW at the house. And, I want the condo and the house. Do you agree to this?" As he recites these demands she is driving faster and faster. She says, "Absolutely." Then comes the punch line. "By the way, there is only one air-bag in this car and it's on the driver's side. See that tree up ahead? Here we go."

A blonde pilot decided she wanted to learn how to fly a helicopter. She went to the airport, but the only one available was a solo-helicopter. The instructor figured he could let her go alone since she was already a pilot for small planes and he could instruct her via radio. So up the blonde went. She reached 1,000 feet and everything was going smoothly. She reached 2,000 feet. The blonde and the instructor kept talking via radio. Everything was running smoothly. At 3,000 feet the helicopter suddenly came down quickly! It skimmed the top of some trees and crash landed in the woods. The instructor jumped into his jeep and rushed out to see if the blonde was okay. As he reached the edge of the woods, the blonde was walking out. "What happened?" the instructor asked. "All was going so well until you reached 3,000 feet. What happened then?" "Well," began the blonde, "I got cold. So I turned off the ceiling fan."

There was a tradesman, a painter called Wayne, who was very interested in making a penny where he could, so he often would thin down paint to make it go a wee bit further. As it happened, he got away with this for some time, but eventually the Baptist Church decided to do a big restoration job on the painting of one of their biggest buildings. Wayne put in a bid, and because his price was so low, he got the job. And so he set to erecting the trestles and setting up the planks, and buying the paint and, yes, I am sorry to say, thinning it down with turpentine. Well, Wayne was up on the scaffolding, painting away, the job nearly completed when suddenly there was a horrendous clap of thunder, and the sky opened, the rain poured down, washing the thinned paint from all over. the church and knocking Wayne clear off the scaffold to land on the lawn among the gravestones, surrounded by telltale puddles of the thinned and useless paint. Wayne was no fool. He knew this was a judgment from the Almighty, so he got on his knees and cried: "Oh God! Forgive me! What should I do?" And from the thunder, a mighty voice spoke ... (you're going to love this) "Repaint! Repaint! And thin no more!"

Amen. Selah. So be it.

STAND UP COMEDY

In the last ten years a new venue of stand-up comedy has developed. Previously most comics worked clubs or theaters. Old timers like Bob Hope, George Burns and Red Skelton played all of the above. The new generation like Robin Williams, Eddie Murphy and Chris Rock did the same. Most of them were personal friends with vulgarity. Red Foxx made a career of obscenity.

The current modality is referred to as Christian Comedy. It is clean and humorous. It is also NOT limited to churches. Many of the stand-ups perform at night clubs on Saturday night and then perform in church on Sunday. A recent newspaper article was about the Rev. Mark Fetter. He is such a comedian. He is also the pastor of the Desert Winds Community Church in Adelanto. He says, "When you turn 40, you start to see God's sense of humor because God starts repositioning your hair." Dan Rupple, president of the Southern California based Christian Comedy Association says that Christian comedy has simply exploded.

I like this humorous story. One day, two rednecks were standing and staring at a flag pole, scratching their heads. A blonde woman walked by and asked what they were doing. " We're supposed to find the height of the flagpole," said Bubba, "but we don' t have a ladder." The blonde took a wrench from her purse, loosened a few bolts, and laid the pole down. Then she took a tape measure from her pocket, took a measurement, announced,

"Eighteen feet, six inches," and walked away. Bubba shook his head and laughed, "Ain't that just like a blonde! We ask for the height, and she gives us the length!"

Jeff Foxworthy is a well known southern comic. Under the banner of "You Might be a Redneck If," he gives the following squibs. You pick your teeth from a catalog. You think "Long John Silver" is formal underwear. You can entertain yourself for more than an hour with a fly swatter. Your property has been mistaken for a recycling center. You think Liberation was the funny dressed guy who played the piano. You take a fishing pole into Sea World. You list your parole officer as a reference. Maybe you haven't heard this one. Three men are walking along the shore of a raging, wild river. They need to get to the other side.

The first prays. "Oh, God. Give me the strength to swim across." He struggles and finally makes it to the other side. The second man also prays for strength to row a boat across the river. After some time he also makes it. The third man starts to pray for wisdom and strength and immediately is turned into a woman. She looks at a map; walks a hundred yards downstream; and crosses the river on a bridge.

A teenage boy had just gotten his driving permit. He asked his father, who was a Minister, if they could discuss his use of the family car. His father took him into his study and said, "I'll make a deal with you. You bring; your grades up. Study the Bible a little, get your hair cut and then we'll talk about it." After about a month, the boy came back and again asked his father if they could discuss his use of the car. They again went into the father's study where the father said, "Son, I've been very proud of you. You have brought your grades up, you've studied the Bible diligently, but you didn't get: your hair cut." The young man waited a moment and then replied, "You know, Dad, I've been thinking about that. You know Samson had long hair, Moses had long hair, Noah had long hair, and even Jesus had long hair." The Minister said, "Yes, and everywhere they went, they walked."

The following bit of humor comes from several sources. Obviously it struck a funny bone. A guy walks into the local welfare office for his check, marches straight up to the counter and says, "Hi. You know, I just HATE drawing welfare. I'd really rather have a job." The social worker behind the counter says, "Your timing is excellent. We just got a job opening from a very wealthy old man who wants a chauffeur/bodyguard for his nymphomaniac daughter. You'll have to drive around in his Mercedes, but he'll supply all of your clothes. Because of the long hours, meals will be provided. You' 11 be expected to escort her on her overseas holiday trips. You'll have a two-bedroom apartment above the garage. The starting salary is $200,000 a year." The guy says, "You're kidding me!" The social worker says, "Yeah, well, you started it."

Amen. Selah. So be it.

STEPHEN HAWKING

Stephen Hawking of England, is one of the greatest scientists of this era or any other era. He is a world-renowned physicist. Recently he changed one of his basic views regarding black holes. He now confirms what Albert Einstein advised many years ago. That, matter can be transformed (changed) but never fully destroyed. It fits in with my theory about humor. I get jokes constantly on e-mail that-with a few changes- I heard years ago.

A case in point. Gov. Arnold committed a gaffe or pulled a joke the other day. He referred to a few politicians as "girlie men." He obviously was quoting a squib from a skit on Saturday Night Live many years ago. The skit was about the Governor.

I heard this one forty years ago with variations. A female from New York returns to her home in Ohio. She has lots of money, drives a Cadillac, obviously wealthy. Her father, who is hard of hearing, asks about the source of her wealth. She responds, "Daddy, for many years I've been a prostitute." He has a heart attack and is rushed to the hospital. When he is in recovery, a priest arrives and asks him how long he knew his daughter was a prostitute. With a sigh of relief, he says, "Thank God, I thought she said she was a Protestant." As I said. This is an old one with many variations.

These others are in the same venue. Taxing down the tarmac, a DC-I 0 abruptly stopped, turned around and returned to the gate. After an hour-long wait, it finally took off. A concerned passenger asked the flight attendant, "What exactly was the problem?" "The pilot was bothered by a noise that he heard in the engine," explained the flight attendant. "It took us a while to find a new pilot."

Blonde jokes are as old as dirt. A gal pulled into a crowded parking lot and rolled down the car windows to make sure her golden retriever had fresh air. He was stretched out on the back seat, and the blonde wanted to impress upon him that he must remain there. She walked to the curb backward, pointing her finger at the car and emphatically said, "Now you stay .... Do you hear me? ... Stay! . .. Stay!" The driver of a nearby car, perhaps noting that she was a blonde, gave her a strange look and said. "Why don't you just put it in park?"

Change a few names and this one goes back to FDR. "President Bush spoke on how we will hand power over to the Iraqi people." We're going to fix their infra-structure, their economy and give them more jobs-and if it works there we' ll try it over here."

This one is so old it's almost new. A Florida officer pulls over an eighty six-year-old woman because her hand signals were very confusing. "Lady, first you put your hand up, like you' re turning right, then you wave your hand up and down, then you turn left," said the officer. "What's all that supposed to be about?" "Well, I decided not to turn right," she explains. "Then why the up and down?" asks the baffled officer. "Oh, officer," she says, "anybody would know I was just erasing!"

Another change that provides food for humor. Many thanks to Carolyn Mathers. Here are ten items for your continuing education! 1. A dime has 118 ridges around the edge. 2. A cat h a s 32 muscles in each ear. 3. A crocodile cannot stick out its tongue. 4. A dragonfly has a life span of 24 hours. 5. A goldfish has a memory span of three seconds. 6. A "jiffy" is an actual unit of time for 11100th of a second. 7. A shark is the only fish that can blink with both eyes. 8. A snail can sleep for three years. 9. An ostrich's eye is bigger than its brain. 10. Butterflies taste with their feet.

I've heard this one is a repeat from the Readers Digest. God and a scientist were in a debate. The scientist said "I can make a man better than yours." They make a bet. God picks up a handful of dirt. The scientist starts to pick up a handful of dirt. God says, "Hold on, buddy. Make your own dirt."

Now that we're thinking about science, here's a delightful story. These are real answers given by children on science tests. Can you imagine being the teacher reviewing these? Q: Name the four seasons. A: Salt, pepper, mustard and vinegar. Q: Explain one of the processes by which water can be made safe to drink. A: Flirtation makes water safe to drink because it removes large pollutants like grit, sand, dead sheep and canoeists. Q: How is dew formed? A: The sun shines down on the leaves and makes them perspire. Q: How can you delay milk turning sour? A: Keep it in the cow.

1. ARBITRATOR: A cook that leaves Arby's to work at McDonalds.

2. AVOIDABLE: What a bullfighter tried to do.

3. BERNADETTE: The act of torching a mortgage.

4. BURGLARIZE: What a crook sees with ..

5. CONTROL: A short, ugly inmate

6. COUNTERFEITERS: Workers who put together kitchen cabinets.

7. ECLIPSE: What an English barber does for a living.

8. EYEDROPPER: A clumsy ophthalmologist.

9. HEROES: What a guy in a boat does.

10. LEFTBANK: What the robber did when his bag was full of money.

11. MISTY: How golfers create divots.

12. PARADOX: Two physicians.

13. PARASITES: What you see from the top of the Eiffel Tower.

14. PHARMACIST: A helper on the farm.

15. POLARIZE: What penguins see with…

16. PRIMATE: Removing your spouse from in front of the TV.

17.	RELIEF: What trees do in the spring.

18.	RUBBERNECK: What you do to relax your wife.

19.	SELFISH: What the owner of a seafood store does.

20.	SUDAFED: Brought litigation against a government official.

Amen. Selah. So be it.

STRESS IS A KILLER

Stress is a killer. Laughter is a healer. Stress aggravates illness but laughter contributes to healing. This awareness goes back to the days of Hippocrates. He advocated humor as one of the basic elements for good health. Along with massage and nutrition. However, the Bible preceded Hippocrates with these words. "A merry heart doeth good like a medicine." (Proverbs 17:22) Interestingly enough Hammurabi, ancient founder of civilization, advocated humor as a significant element for wellness.

A friend sent me this anonymous writing on, The Value of a Smile. "It costs nothing, but creates much good. It enriches those who receive it without impoverishing those who give it away. It happens in a flash but the memory of it can last forever. No one is so rich that he can get along without it. No one is too poor to feel rich when receiving it. It creates happiness in the home, fosters good will in business, and is the countersign of friends. It is rest to the weary, daylight to the discouraged, sunshine to the sad and nature's best antidote for trouble. Yet it cannot be bought, begged, borrowed, or stolen for it is something of no earthly good to anybody until it is given away willingly."

Studies have shown that 60 percent of stress is job related and 40 percent is family related. These graphics change drastically after retirement. Aging, the economy, health and the loss of loved ones become primary stressors. We should be grateful we don't live in Tacoma, Washington. It ranks as the most stressful city in the U.S. Closely followed by Miami, New Orleans, Las Vegas, New York and Mobile.

Evidence of stress is the rate of suicide. Causes are high unemployment, theft and the gloomy weather. This information is all the more important for those under great stress. One answer is to cultivate laughter by reading and listening to jokes. I received the following two jokes from several people. Both are old but worth laughter.

John's handyman wasn't the swiftest guy on earth. But he was cheap and so was Jim, which is why he hired the guy to paint his porch for $50.00 "You tightwad," scolded Jim's wife. "Our porch covers half of the house! He'll be there for days." Jim simply smirked. An hour later, there was a knock at the door. The handyman had finished. "How did you get done so quickly?" Jim asked. "It was a piece of cake," the handyman replied. "Oh, and it's a Ferrari, not a Porsche."

The State Trooper pulled up alongside a speeding car and was shocked to see that the little old lady behind the wheel was knitting. The officer switched on his lights and sounded his siren, but the driver was oblivious. So the trooper cranked up the bullhorn and yelled to the woman, "Pull over!" "No," the old lady shouted back "Cardigan!" All of us have experienced the following situation. In fact, I read this joke in a doctor's office. The huge backlog in the doctor's waiting room was taking its toll.

Patients were glancing at their watches and getting restless. Finally one man walked to the receptionist's station and tapped on the glass. She slid back the window, saying, "Sir, you'll have to wait your turn." "I just had a question," he remarked dryly. "Is George W. Bush still President?" Years ago I took a train in Mexico from Mexicali to Mexico City. It was very, very slow. This joke was standard among gringos. After several days on the train an obviously pregnant woman asked about the arrival. She said, "I'm pregnant and I need to know." The conductor sarcastically said, "You should have thought of that before you got on." Her reply, "Senor, I wasn't pregnant when I got aboard."

Here's one about Arnold Palmer. A humorous story about golfer Arnold Palmer. Palmer was invited to play a series of exhibition golf matches in Saudi Arabia. The king of Saudi Arabia was so impressed with "Arnie" and so appreciative of Palmers' impact on his countrymen that he wanted to give him a gift. "It really isn't necessary," Palmer insisted. "I am honored to have been invited." The king was persistent. "I would be unhappy if I could not show you my appreciation," he said. Finally, Palmer relented. He thought for a moment and said, "Well, how about a golf club? That would make a nice memento of my visit to your country." The next day Arnold Palmer received the title to a golf club- consisting of thousands of acres of real estate, a club house, beautiful trees~ etc. Sometimes a labor of love is richly rewarded!

Amen. Selah. So be it.

STUDY OF LAUGHTER

Recently at the University of Maryland a group of cardiologists made a study of laughter. They were interested in what affect laughter had on the arteries. The result was very positive. They found that a steady diet of laughter increased the artery size up to twenty-five percent.

We've known for years that, "laughter is the best medicine." Now, medical science is saying that the heart attacks and strokes can be mitigated through laughter. Here are a few stories that will aid in arterial expansion.

A Russian, an American and a blonde were discussing their contributions to space exploration. The Russian bragged about being the first into space. The American boasted about being the first to land on the moon. The blonde vigorously stated that blondes would be the first to land on the sun. The other two laughed at her and said, "Don't you know it's too hot to land on the sun?" "Of course," she said. "But we're going to land at night."

Another blonde joke. Have you heard about the blonde who won a gold medal at the recent Olympics? She was so proud of it she had it bronzed.

Hospital regulations require a wheelchair for patients being discharged. However, while working as a student nurse, I found one elderly gentleman-already dressed and sitting on the bed with a suitcase at his feet-who insisted he didn't need my help to leave the hospital. On the way down I asked him if his wife was meeting him. "I don't know," he said. "She's still upstairs in the bathroom changing out of her hospital gown."

Three women die together in an accident and go to heaven. When they get there, St. Peter says, "We only have one rule here in heaven: don't step on the ducks!" So they enter heaven, and sure enough, there are ducks all over the place. It is almost impossible not to step on a duck, and although they try their best to avoid them, the first woman accidently steps on one. Along comes St. Peter with the ugliest man she ever saw. St. Peter chains them together and says, "Your punishment for stepping on a duck is to spend eternity chained to this ugly man!"

The next day, the second woman steps accidentally on a duck and along comes St. Peter, who doesn't miss a thing. With him is another extremely ugly man. He chains them together with the same admonishment as for the first woman. The third woman has observed all this and, not wanting to be chained for all eternity to an ugly man, is very, VERY careful where she steps. She manages to go months without stepping on any ducks, but one day St. Peter comes up to her with the most handsome man she has ever laid eyes on ... very tall, long eyelashes, muscular, and thin. St. Peter chains them together without saying a word. The happy woman says, "I wonder what I did to deserve being chained to you for all of eternity?" The guy says, "I don't know about you, but I stepped on a duck!"

Attending a wedding for the first time, a little girl whispered to her mother, "Why is the bride dressed in white?" "Because white is the color of happiness, and today is the happiest day of her life." The child thought about this for a moment, then said, "So why is the groom wearing black?"

Three boys are in the schoolyard bragging about their fathers. The first boy says, "My Dad scribbles a few words on a piece of paper, he calls it a poem, they give him $50." The second boy says, "That's nothing. My Dad scribbles a few words on a piece of paper, he calls it a song,. They give him $100." The third boy says, "I got you both beat. My Dad scribbles a few words on a piece of paper, he calls it a sermon. And it takes eight people to collect all the money!"

A Sunday School teacher asked her class why Joseph and Mary took Jesus with them to Jerusalem. A small child replied: "They couldn't get a baby sitter."

A Sunday School teacher was discussing the Ten Commandments with her five and six year olds. After explaining the commandment to "honor your father and thy mother," she asked "Is there a commandment that teaches us how to treat our brothers and sisters?" Without missing a beat one little boy answered, "Thou shall not kill."

This story is somewhat hairy with age, but is worth telling: After spending time with Eve, Adam was walking in the Garden wit God. Adam told God how much the woman meant to him and how blessed he felt to have her. Adam began to ask questions about her. Adam: Lord, Eve is beautiful. Why did you make her so beautiful? God: So you would always want to look at her. Adam: Lord, her skin is so soft. Why did you make her skin so soft? God: So you would always want to be near her. Adam: That's wonderful Lord, and I don't want to seem ungrateful, but why did you make her so stupid? God: So she would love you.

Amen. Selah. So be it.

THANKSGIVING DAY

Thanksgiving Day is a very unique holiday. It has a strong historical heritage as well as a religious one. While there is some question as to which early settlement started the first one, most traditions point to the Pilgrims.

The year was 1620. A company of one hundred-two made up of Saints and Strangers-set sail from Plymouth England. Two months later they landed at Cape Cod. The weather was bitter and many of the original group died. Rations were sparse. It is recorded that for several months they existed on only a few kernels of corn per day. The next Fall, after a bountiful harvest, the first Thanksgiving feast was celebrated. The feast lasted for three days. Pilgrims, Indians and fowl (probably wild turkeys) were present. That's common knowledge.

But did you know? "Within ten years of landing at Plymouth Rock- back-breaking years of cultivating the soil and coping with the severe New England weather- those sturdy ancestors had established the town of Boston. Five years later they began the famous Boston Publication School. A year later Harvard College was in existence. In 1640 the first American book was published.

By 1647, twenty-seven years after landing on alien soil there was a law passed requiring an elementary school in every town of fifty families. After a mere quarter of a century of Pilgrim government in Massachusetts that colony had an educational system that was not to be matched by the mother country for another two hundred years. That was the Pilgrim spirit. We should strive to maintain that spirit in our everyday lives and a new nation."

Abraham Lincoln was the first President to establish the 4th Thursday as Thanksgiving Day. Every President since then has announced the Day. By the way, it was finally sanctioned by Congress as a legal holiday on the fourth Thursday in November in 1941. There are four basic elements in most Thanksgiving celebrations. The first is FAMILY. The nuclear family as well as the extended family--FRIENDS. Family members often travel many miles to be together; making it the most traveled holiday.

A favorite topic of conversation is regaling each other of memories of previous Thanksgivings. A favorite custom these days is to celebrate the Day on the Sunday before. This is done because so many grown kids have their own get-togethers. We do, and about 40 join together on the earlier celebration. FOOD is the second essential. Turkey and ham, mashed potatoes, gravy, corn, pumpkin pie and favorite dishes are always on the table. Then there are cranberries, stuffing and noodles. A major addition to many dinners is ethnic and geographic contributions. Mexican, Italian, German along with Southern and New England dishes.

The Third element is FAITH. Asking God's blessing on the food and family is an essential. Scripture, like the one-hundredth Psalm is expressive of thanksgiving. Those of Catholic, Anglican and Episcopal persuasions under the word "Eucharist. ... ' It is always used in the phrase "Holy Eucharist." The meaning is Greek and means "thanksgiving." Karl Barth, noted Protestant theologian has stated, "The only appropriate conurbation That we can make to God is thanksgiving."

Family, food, faith, these three; but the last one is purely secular. FOOTBALL. What would Thanksgiving be like without at least four football games? Relaxing, being stuffed, along with the turkey, is the order of the day. And the second helping of dessert. Whatever you do, be safe. Stella and I wish you a Happy and Blessed Thanksgiving.

Amen. Selah. So be it.

THE TEN COMMANDMENT
OF HUMOR

Do you know why there are Ten Commandments? Well, God went to the Irish and told them He had a commandment. "What is that?" they said. The answer was, "You shall not kill."

The Irish opposed that because of their temper that often led to murder. God than went to the Italians with the same proposition. God told them, "You shall not commit adultery." With their propensity for passion, they turned this down. God then went to the Jews. Their question was, "How much are they?", when God gave His proposition. God says they are free and the Jews said, "We'll take ten of them." It's an old, old story but when the Bible says, "There is nothing new under heaven that also includes jokes.

Twenty-five years ago I started speaking and writing about the power of humor. Since that time at least one way of change has occurred. Almost every support group and service club now makes jokes a regular part of their meetings. In fact, a few weeks ago I was a judge at a joke-telling contest at a local Kiwanis Club.

One day God was looking down at Earth and saw all of the rascally behavior that was going on. He decided to check it out. So he called one of His angels and sent the angel to Earth for a time. When he returned, he told God, "Yes, it is bad on Earth; 95%

are misbehaving and 5% are not. God thought for a moment and said "Maybe I need to send a second angel to get another opinion." So God called another angel and sent him to Earth for a time too. When the angel returned he went to God and said, "Yes, the Earth is in decline; 95% are misbehaving and 5% are being good." God was not pleased. He then decided to E-mail the 5% that were good because he wanted to encourage them, give them a little something to help them keep going. Do you know what that E-mail said? No? Hmmmm...I didn't get one either.

I was performing a complete physical, including the visual acuity test. I placed the patient twenty feet from the chart and began, "Cover your right eye with your hand." He read the 20/20 line perfectly. "Now your left." Again, a flawless read. Now both," I requested. There was silence. He couldn't read the large E on the top line. I turned and discovered that he had done exactly what I had asked; he was standing there with both his eyes covered. I was laughing too hard to finish the exam.

I really love this one that was endorsed by several humorists. Two blondes are in heaven. One blonde says to another, "How did you die?" "I froze to death, stuck in a freezer," says the second blonde. "That's awful," says the first blonde. "How does it feel to freeze to death?" "It 's very uncomfortable at first," says the second blonde. "You get the shakes, and you get pains in all your fingers and toes. But eventually, it' s a very calm way to go. You get numb and you kind of drift off, as if you' re sleeping.

So, how about you, how did you die?" "I had a heart attack," says the first blonde. "You see I knew my husband was cheating on me, so one day I showed up at home unexpectedly. I ran up to the bedroom, and found him alone watching TV. I ran to the basement, but no one was hiding there either. I ran to the second floor, but no one was hiding there either. I ran as fast as I could to the attic, and just as I got there, I had a massive heart attack and died." The second blonde shakes her head. "What a pity .. .if you had only looked in the freezer, we'd both still be alive."

I promise you, this joke will keep you laughing for days. Jacob age eighty-five, and Rebecca age seventy-nine are all excited about their decision to get married. They go for a stroll to discuss the wedding and on the way go past a drugstore. Jacob suggests that: they go in. He addresses the man behind the counter: "Are you the owner?" The pharmacist answers "Yes." Jacob: "Do you sell heart medication?" Pharmacist: "Of course we do." Jacob: "How about medicine for circulation?" Pharmacist: "All kinds." Jacob: "Medicine for rheumatism?" Pharmacist: "All kinds." Jacob: "Medicine for rheumatism?" Pharmacist: "Definitely." Jacob: "How about Viagra?" Pharmacist: "Of course." Jacob: "Medicine for memory?" Pharmacist; "Yes, a large variety." Jacob: "What about vitamins and sleeping pills?" Pharmacist: "Absolutely." Jacob: "Perfect! We'd like to register here for our wedding gifts."

Amen. Selah. So be it.

THE TOUCH OF
THE MASTER'S HAND

The auctioneer felt the battered and scarred violin was hardly worth his time . But holding it up he said, "What am I bid? A dollar, or two, going for three?" But from the back of the room came an old gray-haired man and picked up the bow, wiped the dust off and tightened the loose strings. He played a melody, pure and sweet as caroling angels sing. The music ceased and in a quiet voice the auctioneer said, "What am I bid; a thousand, two or three? Going and gone." The people cheered, but some of them cried, "We don't understand what changed its worth?" Swift was the answer, "The touch of the Master's hand."

And many a person with life out of tune, and battered and scarred is auctioned cheap to the thoughtless crowd, much like the old violin. They travel on. They fall once, twice and they are almost gone. But the Master comes and the foolish crowd never quite understands the worth of a person and the change that's brought by the touch of the Master's hand.

The original composition was written by Myra Welsh. The concept of life-changing experiences is not new. From as far back as mankind can remember, Shamans have promoted ways for humans to change their deviant behavior. Thereby re-directing their lives. Advance a few thousand years and there are Mithras,

Aztecs and Mayas; as well as Incas. They sacrificed slaves, virgins and various animals to stimulate life changes in others. In the Yucatan area of Mexico there are scores of "cenotes"- deep pits - that were used as sacrificial receptacles.

And, of course, there is Christianity. Changing lives has been the theme, the message of the Gospel. From Nicodemus- being born again-the Apostle Paul -the just shall live by faith –to the millions of followers; the truth of the Master's hand is relevant. Notables like Martin Luther, John Wesley, Dwight L. Moody, Billy Sunday, Billy Graham, Martin Luther King, Joel Osteen, and Rick Warren all bear witness to faith in Christ as changing their lives.

Perhaps the most succinct and explanation of a religious experience was given by William James, the greatest of all American born psychologists. He wrote, "To be converted, to be regenerated, to receive grace, to experience religion, to gain an assurance, are so many phrases which denote the process, gradual or sudden, by which a self-hitherto divided, and consciously wrong and inferior and unhappy person, becomes unified and consciously right, superior and happy." James further sees this as a moral change and implies a divine intervention.

There isn't any doubt that secular and religious history agree on two basic thoughts. First, was the powerful growth of the three major religions in the last 3000 years: Hebrew, Christianity and Muslim. All felt impelled to invade society as the will of

Jehovah, Allah and Jesus. The three, in subsequent times, dominated the then known world. The purpose? TO EFFECT CHANGE.

This was accomplished by two means: by conversion with their beliefs and by their military dominance. These two strains were strong from their inception. They are strong in their beliefs and in their militant attitudes. The second view is obvious. Metaphorically speaking, the Master's hand was a sword. The Jews conquered Canaan by military might. They felt Jehovah wanted all heathen residents to be killed. Men, women and children. Some 10 million inhabitants were eliminated according to the Old Testament.

Written by King David, one translation of Psalm 137:9 reads, "Take the children by their heels and beat their heads against the wall." The Christians and Muslims slaughtered millions of each other during the Crusades. All in the name of Jesus and Allah. Then came the Inquisitions. Catholics against Protestants, Muslims, and Jews-killing millions. And then Protestants against Catholics, Jews and Muslims killing millions.

What about today. Each religion has their rabid terrorists. Muslim Shari Law adherents; Christians with their Klu Klux Klan and Jews with their Jewish Activists. All in the name of Jehovah, Allah and Jesus. The God of Peace, Love, Tolerance and Forgiveness extends His hand to all of them and they ignore it.

Amen. Selah. So be it.

TRAGEDY OF HUMOR

The tragedy and grief that occurred at the Trade Center on 9-11-01 was pervasive. It touched every person in the country. Two years have diminished the intensity of it-but not much. Our lives will never be the same. Our world will never be the same. Along with those lost at the Pentagon and the crash at the small town in Pennsylvania, a great void has been left in our lives. Yet, on the television show, The View, a statement was made that captured my attention. After discussing various ramifications of the tragedy, one of the ladies said, "We need to laugh." The implicating was clear to me. Laughter was an essential ingredient for RECOVERY. I had forgotten its importance for healing.

Years ago a nurse had told me that the first sign of a patient's getting better was when they started smiling and laughing at a bit of humor. This would also apply to grief recovery.

Dave sent me this old but goody. The new pastor was visiting in the homes of his parishioners. At one house it seemed obvious that someone was at home, but no answer came to his repeated knocks at the door. He took out a card, wrote "Revelation 3 :20" on the back and stuck it in the door. When the offering was processed the following Sunday, he found that his card had been returned. Added to it was this cryptic message, "Genesis 3:1 0." Reaching for his Bible to check out the citation, he broke up in gales of laughter. Revelation 3:20 begins "Behold, I stand at the door and knock." Genesis 3: 1 0 reads, "I heard you voice in the garden and I was afraid for I was naked."

Seniors are always good for a joke. An elderly Florida lady did her shopping, and upon returning to her car, found four males in the act of leaving with her vehicle. She dropped her shopping bags and drew her handgun, proceeding to scream at the top of her voice, "I have a gun, and I know how to use it! Get out of the car!"

The four men didn't wait for a second invitation. They got out and ran like mad. The lady, somewhat shaken, then proceeded to load her shopping bags into the back of the car and get into the driver's seat. She was so shaken that she could not get her key into the ignition. She tried and tried, and then it dawned on her why.

A few minutes later she found her own car parked four or five spaces farther down. She loaded her bags into the car and then drove to the police station. The sergeant to whom she told the story doubled over on the floor with laughter. He pointed to the other end of the counter, where four pale men were reporting a carjacking by a mad, elderly woman described as white, less than five feet tall, glasses, curly white hair, and carrying a large handgun. Imagination is essential for appreciation of a good story. Let yours go.

This fellow had owned a large farm for several years. He had a large pond in the back forty, had it fixed up nice, picnic tables, horse shoe courts, basketball court, etc. The pond was fixed for swimming when it was built. One evening the old farmer decided to go down to the pond as he hadn't been there for a while and look it over. As he neared the pond, he heard voices shouting and laughing with glee. As he came closer he saw it was a bunch of young women skinny dipping in his pond. He made the women aware of his presence and they all went to the deep end of the :pond. One of the women shouted to him, "We're not coming out until you leave!" The old man replied, "I didn't come down here to watch you ladies swim or get out of the pond, I only came to feed my alligators!" Talk about speed.

An elderly gent was invited to his old friends' home for dinner one evening. He was impressed by the way his buddy preceded every request to his wife with endearing terms-Honey, My Love, Darling, Sweetheart, Pumpkin, etc. The couple had been married almost 70 years and clearly, they were still very much in love. While the wife was in the kitchen, the man leaned over and said to his host, "I think it's wonderful that, after all these years, you still call your wife those loving pet names." The old man hung his head. "I have to tell you the truth," he said, "I forgot her name about 10 years ago." A man was telling his neighbor, "I just bought a new hearing aid. It cost me four thousand dollars, but it's state of the art." "Really," answered the neighbor. "What kind is it?" "Twelve thirty," was his answer.

Morris, an eighty-two year-old man went to the Doctor to get a physical. A few days later the doctor saw Morris walking down the street with a gorgeous young lady on his arm. A couple of days later the doctor spoke to the man and said, "You're really doing great, aren't you?" Morris replied, "Just doing what you said, Doctor. 'Get a hot mamma and be cheerful.'" The Doctor said, "I didn't say that. I said you got a heart murmur. Be careful."

A blonde walked up to the front desk of the library and said, "I borrowed a book last week, but it was the most boring I've ever read. There was no story whatsoever, and there were far too many characters!" The librarian replied, "Oh, you must be the person who took our phone book."

Amen. Selah. So be it.

UNEXPECTED HUMOR

I like the unexpectedness of humor. When the punch line comes out of nowhere. The other night I awakened in the middle of the night and heard a talk show host tell this story. It cracked me up.

A school teacher, addressing her class, said, "I'm a liberal Democrat. Those of you that are with me raise your hand." All the kids-wanting to please her-raised their hands except one. He explained the reason, that he was a conservative Republican. He believed in less government control and a strong military. Then he said he was a conservative Republican because his parents were and even his grandparents. Frustrated, the teacher then said, "What if your parents were morons. What would you be? The student responded with ease; "Then I would be a liberal Democrat." I love it; I love it.

You have to know something about football to appreciate the following. I laughed so hard, I choked. Two captains from each team were called to the center of the field to determine who would kick-off and which team would receive. The referee turned to the two of them and said, "Call it in the air, heads or tails. The lumbering, 350 lb. Lineman yelled out, "Heads or tails." That's one for the record books.

This guy sees a sign in front of a house "talking dog for sale." He rings the bell and the owner tells him the dog is in the back yard. The guy goes into the back yard and sees a mutt sitting there. "You talk?" he asks. "Yep," the mutt replies. "So, what's your story?" The Mutt looks up and says "Well, I discovered this gift pretty young and I wanted to help the government, so I told the CIA about my gift, and in no time they had me going from country to country, sitting in rooms with spies and world leaders, cause no one figured a dog would be eavesdropping. I was one of their most valuable spies eight years running. The jetting around really tired me out, and I knew I wasn't getting any younger and I wanted to settle down. So I signed up for a job at the airport to do some undercover security work, mostly wandering near suspicious characters and listening in. I uncovered some incredible dealings there and was awarded a batch of medals. Had a wife, a mess of puppies, and now I'm just retired." The guy is amazed. He goes back in and asks the owner what he wants for the dog. The owner says "Ten dollars." The guy says he'll buy him but asks the owner, "This dog is amazing. Why on earth are you selling him?" The owner replies, "He's such a blasted liar."

This is an old one but bears repeating. Dear Marty, I have been unable to sleep since I broke off your engagement to my daughter. Will you forgive and forget? I was much too sensitive about your Mohawk, tattoo and pierced nose. I now realize motorcycles aren't really that dangerous, and I really should not have reacted that way to the fact that you have never held a job. I am sure, too, that some other very nice people live under the bridge in the park. Sure my daughter is only 18 and wants to marry you instead of going to Harvard on a full scholarship. After all, you can't learn everything about life from books. I sometimes forget how backward I can be. I was wrong. I was a fool. I have now come to my senses and you have my full blessing to marry my daughter. Sincerely, your future father-in-law. P.S. Congratulations on winning the lottery. Love, Always.

Oh, the wisdom of kids. "If l sold my house and my car, had a big garage sale and gave all my money to the church, would I get into Heaven?" I asked the children in my Sunday School class. "No!" the children all answered. "If I cleaned the church every day, mowed the yard, and kept everything neat and tidy, would I get into Heaven?" Again the answer was, "No!" Well, I continued, "then how can I get into Heaven?" A five-year-old boy shouted out, "You gotta be dead."

If this story doesn't scare you, you're beyond hope. I quote. "Driving to the office this morning on the Interstate, I looked over to my left and there was a woman in a brand new Mustang doing 75 miles per hour with her face up next to her rear view mirror putting on her eyeliner! I looked away for a couple seconds and when I looked back she was halfway over in my lane, still working on that makeup!!! It scared me so bad, I dropped my electric shaver, which knocked the donut out of my other hand. In all the confusion of trying to straighten out the car using my knees against the steering wheel, it knocked the donut out of my other hand. In all the confusion of trying to straighten out the car using my knees against the steering wheel, it knocked my cell phone away from my ear which fell into the coffee between my legs, splashed and burned me, ruined the phone and DISCONNECTED AN IMPORTANT CALL!!!!!!!!" Those women drivers."

Amen. Selah. Amen.

IT'S BEEN A PLEASURE LAUGHING WITH YOU!

UNEXPECTED INSPIRATION

Inspiration comes to us at unexpected times. I have been afflicted by it on various and sundry times.

A most unusual occasion happened a few years ago. One afternoon while I was watching TV, our daughter Pamela called me from Sausalito, a suburb of San Francisco: She had been attending a potential membership class in an Episcopal Church. Pamela was somewhat confused about various doctrinal beliefs and called me with a pressing question. "Dad, what do we believe?" She had heard me preach hundreds of sermons. Had gone through catechism class, been baptized and joined the church. Now she was asking me, "Dad, what do we believe?" To say the least, I was stunned. But my inspiration kicked in and I responded spontaneously. Life Is Worth Living; People Are Worth Loving; God Is Worth Trusting and Jesus Is Worth Following. The years have passed by; but I've thought of my answers often. I believe them as much today as I did when Pamela first asked me, "Dad, what do we believe?"

Life Is Worth Living. Fannie Hurst wrote these immortal words. "Life, I salute you. Whether I have one hour or one day left. To have lived you up to now, to have known and to know people. The going is strong, but life, I salute you, for the riches and wonders of you." Life at best is short. Be it for one more year or a hundred more. Years ago I ran across these words by David Starr

Jordan: "Be a life short or long; its completeness depends on what it was lived for."

There are two significant thoughts that contribute to making life worth living. James Baldwin challenged his readers to be present in everything they did. "From getting up in the morning to going to bed at night."

Being present is important but so is one's attitude in the " time." In his eulogy for his brother (Robert) Edward Kennedy said of him: "He loved life and lived it INTENSELY."

People Are Worth Loving. Why? Because God made each human as a unique person. The Jews have a saying that in every birth, "it is a partnership. A father, a mother and the Spirit of God." Some are tall, others short; some fat, others skinny. But humans have a brain with the potential of choice and creativity. Skin color has nothing to do with it. Love, caring, appreciation, admiration are human traits that can be given and received. The Bible states that God created us in His image; and a little lower than the angels. Significantly the Bible also states that God loves everyone. That certainly makes all of us worth loving.

My third affirmation is that God Is Worth Trusting. This statement 1s so fundamental that "In God We Trust" is engraved on coinage and our currency. The words were first recorded by Francis Scott Key in 1814 when he wrote the: Star-Spangled Banner. In 1861, the Secretary of the Treasury Department, Mr. Chase made the decision to have the motto inscribed on coinage. It first appeared in 1864. "On July 11, 1955 President Dwight D. Eisenhower signed Public Law 140 making it mandatory that all coinage and paper currency display the motto."

Finally, I believe that Following Jesus Is Worthwhile. He has been depicted as the most important Person in all of history. He changed the course of human destiny. Christianity is based on His life, His death and His resurrection. And yet His personal profile is an enigma. I recently drew up a profile of Jesus' human characteristics that challenges us to follow Him and seek to be like Him. The only source we have to make a decision is the Bible. From it we read that He hungered, was thirsty, was surprised, had limited knowledge, wept at the death of a friend, was angry, became indignant, and was confused. And, yet, He said that, "My Father and I are "ONE." The best we know about God is reflected in the life of Jesus. He certainly is worthy of our following Him.

My four beliefs: Life is worth living; People are worth loving; God is worth trusting and Jesus is worth following.

Amen. Selah. So be it.

VICE-PRESIDENT CHENEY

Vice-President Dick Cheney is not noted for his humor. However, at a recent news people roast in Washington, D.C., he was humorous. He began with these words. "The other day I developed a breathing problem. I detected a tightening in my chest and turbulence in my stomach. In response to my condition, my wife said, 'Dick, that's called laughter.'"

My friend Ali local automotive specialist, devout Muslim and former Pakistani, always has a humorous story. Here is his latest. Very few know that ten years before his capture, Saddam Hussein developed heart trouble and needed a heart transplant. Word was sent out to the people for the need of a donor. They responded with enthusiasm On the designated day, 100,000 people gathered to volunteer. With so many, a method was devised to pick the donor. A feather would be dropped and the person it landed on would become the donor. Here's the punch line. As the feather floated down, the people screaming, they would yell "me, me," and then they BLOW UPWARD.

I really laughed at this one from Steve. A college class was instructed to write a short story in as few words as possible. The story must contain the following components: 1) Religion, 2) Sexuality, and 3) Mystery. There was only one A+ paper in the entire class. The story contained only nine words. "Good God! I'm pregnant. I wonder who did it."

Following my lecture on a recent cruise ship the Norwegian Star I was told this story. A blonde was tired of being called "a dumb blonde." So, she had her hair changed to red. With her new found confidence, she stopped at a pasture where a shepherd was watching a flock of sheep. She told him that she would bet she could tell him how many sheep he had. "I'll give fifty dollars if I'm wrong," she said. "If I'm right I take a sheep." He answered in the affirmative. She then told him there were 178 sheep. He confessed to that number and then said, "You' re really a blonde aren't you?" "Yes, I am but how did you know?" "It's simple, lady. Just give me back my dog that you took."

Here's a laugher. A girl was visiting her blonde friend, who had acquired two new dogs. When asked what their names were, the blonde responded by saying, "Their names are Rolex and Timex." Her friend says, "Whoever heard of someone naming dogs that. Those are watches." "Helloooo," answered the blonde. "They're watch dogs."

Norm is a former resident who now lives in Las Vegas. He sent me this one. Finally, a blonde is winning a contest: A lawyer and a blonde woman happen to be sitting next to each other on a flight from LA to New York. The lawyer leans over to the blonde and asks if she would like to (play a fun game. The blonde is tired and just wants to take a nap. So she politely declines and turns over to the window to catch a few winks. The lawyer persists, saying that the game is really easy and a lot of fun. He explains how the game works. "I ask you a question, and if you don't know the answer, you pay me, and vice-versa." Again the blonde politely declines and tries to get some sleep.

The lawyer figures that since his opponent is a blonde he will easily win the match, so he makes another offer. "Okay, how about this. If you don't know the answer you pay me only $5, but If I don't know the answer, I will pay you $500." This catches the blonde's attention and figuring that there will be no end to this torment unless she plays, she agrees to play the game. The lawyer asks the first question. "What's the distance from the earth to the moon?" The blonde doesn't say a word, reaches into her purse, pulls out a five-dollar bill, and hands it to the lawyer.

Now, it's the blonde's turn. She asks the lawyer "What goes up a hill with three legs, and comes down with four?" The lawyer looks at her with a puzzled look. He takes out his laptop computer and searches all his references. He taps into the Air-phone with his modem and searches the Net and even the Library of Congress. Frustrated he sends E-mails to all his coworkers and all of his friends. All to no avail. After over an hour of searching for the answer he finally gives up.

He wakes the blonde and hands her $500. The blonde politely takes the $500 and turns away to go back to sleep. The lawyer, who cannot imagine what the answer is, is going nuts trying to figure it out. He is more than a little frustrated. He wakes the blonde and asks, "So? What does go up a hill with three legs and come down with four?" The blonde reaches into her purse, hands the lawyer $5, and goes back to sleep.

Amen. Selah. So be it.

WANNABE AN ANTHROPOLOGIST

As a wannabe anthropologist with historical academic credentials, I am constantly researching ancient evidences for humor. The earliest evidence for homo sapiens goes back to about 200,000 years. Believe it or not, there seems to be a connection between spiritual awareness and humor from man's earliest cognition.

Sumerian and Egyptian cultures have recorded histories going back 8000 year. Humorous anecdotes are found in both. There is prolific evidence in the ancient Greek culture. "One liners were delivered tens of thousands of years before Homer." So says Professor Owen Ewald of Seattle Pacific University. The aboriginals of Australia go back 35,000 years According to Dr. Joseph Polimeni, they were amused and laughed at things like the clap of thunder.

Rabbis stated categorically that the Old Testament is filled with humor. Example? The story of Jonah. Humor was used to deliver a potent message. Monks in the 8th century used frequent riddles as teaching tools. "Who was not born but died? (Adam).

The above mentioned Joseph Polimeni observed in the journal "Evolutionary Psychology, "To my knowledge, no anthropologist has ever suggested he or she had visited a humorless society."

In the spirit of Jewish irony, read this quote delivered in

the Roman Senate 2063 years ago by Cicero (55 B.C.). "The budget should be balanced, the Treasury should be refilled, public debt should be reduced, the arrogance of officialdom should be tempered and controlled, and the assistance to foreign lands should be curtailed lest Rome become bankrupt. People must again learn to work, instead of living on public assistance." Now we know why Rome fell. It didn't live within its means.

Mike sent this one. "Mark, a loving husband, was in trouble. He forgot his wedding anniversary and his wife was really ticked off at him. She told him, "Tomorrow morning I expect to find a gift in the driveway that goes from 0 to 200 in under 6 seconds, AND IT BETTER BE THERE." The next morning Mark got up really early before work. When his wife woke up a couple of hours later, she looked out the window, and sure enough, there was a small gift wrapped box sitting in the middle of the driveway. Confused the wife put on her robe, ran out to the driveway and took the box into the house. She opened it and found a brand new bathroom scale.

Mark is not yet well enough to have visitors. Dan was a single guy living at home with his father and working in the family business. When he found out he was going to inherit a fortune when his sickly father died, he decided he needed a wife with which to share his fortune. One evening at an investment meeting he spotted the most beautiful woman he had ever seen. Her natural beauty took his breath away. "I may look like just an ordinary man," he said to her, "but in just a few years, my father will die, and I'll inherit 2.0 million dollars." Impressed, the woman obtained his business card and three days later, she became his stepmother.

Lena called the airlines information desk and inquired, "How long does it take to fly from Minneapolis to Fargo?" "Just a minute," said the busy clerk. "Well," said Lena, "If it has to go that fast, I think I'll just take the bus."

A miner was taking gold from Arizona to New Mexico. He hired a shot gun rider to avoid bandits and Indians. He sees dust behind them in the distance. The gunman informs him they are being followed. "How big are they?" he asks. The gunman indicates with his fingers they are one inch tall. Six hours later, he reports there are definitely men on horses following them. "How big are they?" asks the miner. The gunman indicates with his fingers they are 2 inches tall. They continue to watch as the figures get bigger and bigger. After several hours the miner asks how big they are. The gunman indicates with his arms wide open that they are this big and that they are right on them. "Shoot. Shoot" yells the miner. "I can't" replies the gunman. "Why not?" asks the miner. "Because I've known them since they were this big," replies the gunman holding up his fingers to show one inch.

Amen. Selah. So be it.

WILL OF GOD

I make no apologies for this article. I am relying completely on a small book, written in 1944 by one of my "literary mentors," Dr. Leslie Weather head. It was the height of World War II. He pastored a large church in London, England. Hitler's planes destroyed the church and killed many in his parish. Was it the will of God?

I cherish the insight that he brings to the issue of " the will of God." The phrase is very ambiguous, to say the least. Is a tornado that leaves devastation and death behind, God's will? The same question can be applied to war, hurricanes, malignancies, heart attacks, divorce, chronic pain, sorrow, jobless and depression.

Successes and victories elicit the same question. Is the will of God responsible for victories as well as tragedies? Weatherhead clarifies the issue by dividing God's will into three parts:

1. The Intentional Will of God
2. The Circumstantial Will of God
3. The Ultimate Will of God.

As an eighty-six year old man I am afflicted with Neuropathy, Diabetes and Glaucoma plus a couple of other ailments. Expression of the will of God? Hardly! The Intentional will of God? No more than the Cross was God's will for Jesus.

"God's will for all of us is perfect health." But it ain't going to happen. My Literary Mentor says, "He (Jesus) came with the intention that mankind should follow Him, not kill him." That was God's ideal purpose. In other words it was discipleship that was the intentional will of God.

A Scriptural reference is apropos. "It is NOT the will of your Father which is in heaven, that one of these little ones should perish." Matthew 18:14. This reference is in regards to one's sheep. God is like the shepherd that rejoices over one being recovered. He doesn't want anyone to hurt, be bruised, sick or abused. His intentional will is for wellness. As the Bible says, we are heirs of God and joint heirs with Jesus.

The second interpretation of the will of God, Weather head calls "CIRCUMSTANIAL" These situations are the result of actions of evil men. Either because of the lack of research or failure to anticipate catastrophes. Obviously they include many of the events mentioned previously. The word "perish" is too drastic in English. The metaphoric meaning should be identified with the shepherd's care of his flock. The sheep are often afraid of wild animals, they are often bruised and need the healing oil on their heads. They fall and cannot get up. They are vulnerable. The sheep represent you and me.

All these conditions can be related to Weather head's view of "circumstances." The imperfections of we humans demands what the will of God is for us; as in the case of Helen Keller or Bill

Abersold, me. How will I deal with my circumstances? Do I become a victim and feel sorry for myself? Or do we make the best of our circumstances?

It is inconceivable that the intentional will of God was for Jesus to be crucified and die on the cross. It was the evil of Pilate that turned the perfect will of God into different circumstances. In other words, God's will was thwarted by the actions of evil men. God's will is then the uniqueness of His creation to .. make good dominate evil. Victor Frank l referred to the "indomitable power of the human spirit." That is an expression of the "circumstantial will of God."

As rational people we must challenge the behavior of people who insist that disease is the will of God. All of us live in the realm of the Circumstantial will of God. The circumstantial will of God begins in this battle between humans and nature. Wilen l was a teenager, polio ravaged many a family. But the Salk vaccine and other remedies have pretty well controlled it. If the money spent on wars and the machinery of war was directed toward research, there would be fewer serious illnesses. But the major insight of the circumstantial will of God is the potential that each of us has when we are confronted by failures, sickness, grief, disappointment or depression. Jesus turned the Cross into redemption for us all. The poet John Greenleaf Whittier has said, "I only know l cannot drift beyond His love and care ."

Carlyle Marney tells of a girl who was born without arms

and legs. When asked by the thoughtless person if she had ever wished she had never been born, she said, "I guess I would not have missed the chance to be alive for anything in the world. When compared to not having lived at all, to never have seen, tasted, smelled, heard, know the delight of reading and thinking, I am overwhelmingly grateful to God for the opportunity to live that has been mine." It is the circumstantial will of God that ushers us to the ULTIMATE will of God.

Marney's story of the young lady is an example of the circumstantial will of God. Her reward? The ULTIMATE will of God, "Well done, thou good and faithful servant; enter into the Kingdom of God."

Amen. Selah . So be it.

WILL ROGERS

William Penn Adair Rogers was born on November 4, 1879. Affectionately known as Will Rogers and the Indian Cowboy, he was a Cherokee Indian. "He became the most popular and best loved American of his time." He was an expert rider and rope twirler performing on the stage and in many movies. He wrote 2800 articles and had his own radio show. Married to Betty Blake in November 1908, They had one son. An avid supporter of aviation, he died in a plane crash with Wyley Post near Barrow, Alaska. His memorial is in Claremore, Oklahoma.

Will Rogers is still remembered for his pithy, pungent one-liners that made Americans laugh. One famous line that everyone knows was, "I never met a man I didn't like." My favorite line: "I don't belong to an organized political party. I'm a Democrat." Here are a few of his lines:

"We are here just for a spell and then pass on...So get a few laughs and do the best you can. Live your life so that whenever you lose, you are ahead." "I don't make jokes, I just watch the Government and report the facts ... " "We'll show the world we are prosperous, even if we have to go broke to do it." "Never blame a legislative body for not doing something. When they do nothing, that don't hurt anybody. When they do something is when they become dangerous." "Things in our country run in spite of government. Not by aid of it!" "If we got one-tenth of what was promised to us in these acceptance speeches there wouldn't be any inducement to go to heaven."

Steve sent me these squibs from Rogers'

- Never slap a man who's chewing tobacco.
- Never kick a cow chip on a hot day.
- There are 2 theories to arguing with a woman ...neither works.
- Always drink upstream from the herd.
- The quickest way to double your money is to fold it and put it back in your pocket.
- Good judgment comes from experience, and a lot of that comes from bad judgment.
- Eventually you will reach a point when you stop lying about your age and start bragging about it.
- The older we get, the fewer things seem worth waiting in line for.
- You know you are getting old when everything either dries up or leaks.
- One of the many things no one tells you about aging is that it is such a nice change from being young.
- One must wait until evening to see how splendid the day has been.
- Being young is beautiful, but being old is comfortable.
- If you don't learn to laugh at trouble, you won't have

anything to laugh at when you are.

Have you ever thought of some of the crazy laws on the books? In Rumford, Maine, it's against the law to bite your landlord. It's against the law in Atlanta, Georgia, to tie a giraffe to a telephone pole or street lamp. It's against the law in Chicago to eat in a place that is on fire. It's illegal to catch fish while on horseback in Washington, D.C. It's illegal to take a lion to the theater in Maryland.

Brawley, California, passed a resolution banning snow within the city limits. In Tennessee, it's illegal to drive a car while you're asleep. It's illegal in Hartford, Connecticut, to kiss your wife on a Sunday. It's against the law in Kentucky to remarry the same man four times. It's illegal in Fairbanks, Alaska, for two moose to have sex on city sidewalks.

Joel Osteen, famous TV preacher tells this story. Three students are taking a test to become psychologists. They are given three words and are to give the opposite word. The first one is given the word "sadness." His answer is "happiness." The second is given the word "depression. His answer is Joy." The third is a blonde. She is given the word "woe." She thinks about it and says "giddy-up."

Amen. Selah. So be it.

WORDS FOR LOVE

Recently Larry Stamper, a friend of mine, sent me a provocative story that is probably an "urban legend." It seems that after 21 years of marriage the writer's wife suggested he take another woman out to dinner and a movie. To his surprise the other woman was his mother. She immediately wanted to know "why." He finally persuaded her that he just wanted to spend some quality time with her. She dressed up for her night out. And the evening was great.

Even though he had to read the menu for her; her eyes were bad. The roles were reversed. She had commented that when he was a boy, she had read the menu for him. The conversation was easy and pleasant, catching up on each other's life. They talked so long they missed the movie. On arriving back at her house, she said, "I'll go out with you again, only if you let me invite you." He agreed. He later assured his wife that his dinner date was great.

A few days later his mother died of a massive heart attack. Sometime later, he received an envelope with a copy of a restaurant receipt from the same place they had dined, with an attached note. It said, "I paid this bill in advance. I wasn't sure I could be there. I paid for two dinners - one for you and the other for your wife. You will never know what our night out meant for me. Love you, son." At that moment he understood the importance of saying in time: "love you" and to give our loved ones the time they deserve. Nothing in life is more important than our families. Give them the time they deserve. Thoughtfulness should not be put off 'till some other time. The implication of this urban legend is pretty obvious. Life is a fragile commodity. At best it is very short. Unpredictable.

Rod McKuen, nationally famous poet stated: "There is no harm in not being loved; only in not loving."

The Greek language is unusual. It has three words that are used for different kinds of love. They are eros, phileo and agape. We get our word "erotic" from the Greek eros. It has physical desire and pleasure in its meaning. It is intimate and sexual in its understanding. Phileo is the love between friends, brothers/sisters and family members. An excellent example is the city of Philadelphia- the city of "brotherly love." It is made up of phileo (love) and adelphos (brother).

The word that has the deepest meaning and the most spiritual significance is AGAPE. It is God's love for humanity; a mother's love for her children; a husband and wife's love for each other. Examples: "For God so AGAPE the world." "Thou shall AGAPE the Lord thy God...and AGAPE thy neighbor as yourself." And in the strongest of usages; "and now abide faith, hope and AGAPE. These three. But the greatest of these is AGAPE."

Thalidomide was supposedly a miracle drug in the 60's for pregnant women. However, it proved to be disastrous. Many children were deformed at their birth: no eye sight, partial Limbs, and organ dysfunction. One mother's son was born without ears. It affected him emotionally. One day word came to him that two transplants had been given for him.

The surgery was successful and he went on to become a brilliant scholar and taught at Harvard. On the occasion of her death, while looking at her in the casket, he casually brushed back her hair and to his amazement both of her ears were gone. He had never known. Such is a mother's AGAPE.

Amen. Selah. So be it.

YOUR LAUGH METER

I am indeed privileged. Since a new source of humor is always on my wish list,. I've become acquainted with a new one. As a sit-down comic I speak to a lot of senior groups and heard these. Telling jokes seems to trigger jokes from other people. There are always those who want to tell their jokes.

A friend shared the following medical definition associations with me. Use your imagination. Barium. It is what is done when someone dies. Dilate. That is when a person lives a long time. Node. That is when a southerner knew someone. Genital. That happens to be a non-Jewish person. Seizure. Believe it or not, that refers to a Roman Emperor.

It is amazing how many jokes keep appearing or are told again and again. However, I think they are good the second or third time around.

A rather attractive middle-aged lady was in a spiritual setting and had a revelation from God. God told her that she would live forty-five more years. That stimulated her to seek out a plastic surgeon and she had a complete makeover: nose job, breast implants, tummy tuck and a butt lift. Everything imaginable. As she was leaving her home, after a period of recuperation, she was killed in an automobile accident. Standing before God, she reminded Him that she was to live 45 more years. How come? God had a simple explanation, "I didn't recognize you."

A couple went on vacation to a fishing resort up north. The husband liked to fish at the crack of dawn. She liked to read. One morning the husband returned after several hours of fishing and decided to take a short nap. Although she wasn't familiar with the lake, the wife decided to take the boat. She rowed out a short distance, anchored and returned to reading her book. Along came the sheriff in his boat. He pulled up alongside her and said "Good Morning, Ma'am. What are you doing?" "Reading my book," she replied. "You're in a restricted fishing area," he informed her. "But officer, I'm not fishing. Can't you see that?" "Yes, but you have all the equipment. I'll have to take you in and write you up." "If you do that, I'll have to charge you with rape," snapped the irate woman. "But, I haven't even touched you," groused the sheriff. "Yes, that's true," she replied, "but you have all the equipment." MORAL: Never argue with a woman who knows how to read. It's likely she can also think!

Now a change of pace, reverting to one of my favorite subjects-blondes. OVERWEIGHT BLONDE: A blonde is overweight, so her doctor puts her on a diet. "I want you to eat regularly for two days, then skip a day, and repeat this procedure for two weeks. The next time I see you, you'll have lost at least five pounds .. " When the blonde returns, she's lost nearly 20 pounds. "Why, that's amazing!" the doctor says. "Did you follow my instructions?" The blonde nods. "I'll tell you, though, I thought I was going to drop dead that third day." "From hunger, you mean?" asked the doctor. "No, from all that skipping."

RIVER WALK: There's this blonde out for a walk. She comes to a river and sees another blonde on the opposite bank. "Yoo-hoo" she shouts, "how can I get to the other side?" The second blonde looks up the river then down the river then shouts back, "You are on the other side."

KNITTING: A highway patrolman pulled alongside a speeding car on the freeway. Glancing at the car, he was astounded to see that the blonde behind the wheel was knitting! Realizing that she was oblivious to his flashing lights and siren, the trooper cranked down his window, turned on his bullhorn and yelled, "PULLOVER!" "No," the blonde yelled back, "IT 'S A SCARF!"

BLONDE ON THE SUN: A Russian, an American, and a Blonde were talking one day. The Russian said, "We were the first in space!" The American said, "We were the first on the moon!" The Blonde said, "So what, we're going to be the first on the sun!" The Russian an d the American looked at each other and shook their heads. "You can't land on the sun, you idiot! You'll bum up!" said the Russian. To which the Blonde replied, "We're not stupid, you know. We're going at night!"

SPEEDING TICKET: A police officer stops a blonde for speeding and asks her very nicely if he could see her license. She replied in a huff, "I wish you guys would get your act together. Just yesterday you take away my license and then today you expect me to show it to you!" *Amen. Selah. So be it.*

www.ingramcontent.com/pod-product-compliance
Lightning Source LLC
Chambersburg PA
CBHW060240100426
42742CB00011B/1591